PLAYING OVER-TIME

A Celebration of Oldtimers' HOCKEY

TED BARRIS

All the best! [signature] Nov '98

Macmillan Canada
Toronto

Canadian Cataloguing in Publication Data

Barris, Ted
  Playing overtime : a celebration of oldtimers' hockey

Includes index.
ISBN 0–7715–7361–8

1. Hockey.   2. Hockey players.   I. Title.

GV847.B37 1995   796.96'2   C95–931500–4

1 2 3 4 5 FP 99 98 97 96 95

Cover design by Ken Rodmell

Cover photo by John Reeves

Macmillan Canada would like to thank Wayne Lilley and Al Zikovitz, members of the Write-offs, and John Eby who appear in the jacket photo.

Macmillan Canada wishes to thank the Canada Council, the Ontario Ministry of Culture and Communications and the Ontario Arts Council for supporting its publishing program.

Macmillan Canada
A Division of Canada Publishing Corporation
Toronto, Ontario, Canada

Printed in Canada

Contents

For all those
who endure the aches,
defy the years
and continue to play our game

Foreword

Once upon a time there was no such thing as the Canadian Oldtimers' Hockey Association. This meant that when a player's stamina began to take earlier and earlier lunch breaks and the shots didn't zing like they used to, all those guys across our often icy land who had had great fun in the game since childhood were hung out to dry. Tens of thousands—be they famous stars or unknown corner-lotters in Canada's national game—still remained as fans, students of the game and enthusiasts, but simply didn't have the chance to play much any more.

This entertaining book, a product of Ted Barris's characteristically tireless research, is about the fact that every corner of this land has its hockey devotees whose legs might be going, but whose enjoyment of the game is still intact. Given the chance to keep on playing at any age (and never mind who wins the Stanley Cup), players lined up in their thousands to play in age groups right up to 80-year-olds once oldtimers' hockey was organized. The recreational benefits, including travel to dozens of tournaments near and far, now stretches coast to coast and abroad, with lots of laughs along the way.

Of all the team games that North Americans play and watch, why does hockey lead the recreational field for the over-the-hill gang? Author Ted Barris assembles a lot of the answers, some slightly chauvinistic, but there you are. One player opined, "There isn't a game in the world like it. I feel sorry for Americans who've only played baseball. They grow old and can't do it any more. Canadian kids grow up into old men like us and can continue to play our game."

Scott Young

Acknowledgements

"Barris's Goal a Big One as Light Blues Ice Senior Title"

That's what the headline in the sports section of my local newspaper read one Saturday last spring. It was the wind-up of the senior men's recreational hockey league season in my community. The league has been operating for eighteen years. And our team—the Light Blues—won the championship. The fact that I scored the winning goal was a delicious accident. No matter. Winning a title—any title—in my favourite sport is still a thrill.

I thought my hockey career had ended in 1965, the year I turned sixteen. Not because of a debilitating injury. Not for lack of interest. But because the local Lions Club house league officials told me there wasn't anywhere left for me to play. The system back then said that, unless I was an all-star or a junior prospect, after age sixteen there was no league, no arena, no organization where I could play the game I love. Goodbye. End of story.

Disappointed but resigned to my fate, I chucked my CCM tube skates, stick and pads into the basement, forever.

Fifteen years later, I was working as a freelance writer in Edmonton. I suddenly found myself close to hockey again, watching the fledgling Oilers take flight in the NHL. Through a wonderful series of coincidences, I ended up reporting on the Oilers' home games that season. Perhaps it was their now legendary exuberance on the ice. Or maybe it was Gretzky's scoring touch. But one day, a bunch of media friends and I felt inspired; instead of going out for lunch, we decided to rent some ice at a local arena and play a little shinny.

I fell in love with hockey all over again. I played that fall and winter. We all brought out the pads and gloves that had been tucked away for years. The next season we formed a team. The year after, we began competing in recreational hockey tournaments. Every year since then, I've suited up at least once, and often two and three times every week year round to play the game they took away from me in 1965.

That's one of the reasons for this book—to celebrate the reclaiming and rediscovery of our national game by ordinary players like me. A second is to trace the emergence of old-timers in this its official twentieth anniversary year. A third is to acknowledge the extraordinary influence oldtimers has over its participants—men, women, pick-up groups, tourna-ment teams, city leagues or small town after-midnighters.

Playing Overtime is their book.

Many have helped me make this book of celebration possi-ble. Some are friends and family, including Kay and Alex who have always cheered me on both at the arena and the key-board. Others are the players, coaches, referees and organiz-ers I've met and listened to over the years. But most are those who just shake their heads in awe that so many of us have suc-ceeded in taking back our game.

Among them I owe special thanks to those who put me in touch with unique oldtimer stories: Mike Malott, Bob Spence, Al Harvey, Keith Morrison, Mike Buchanan, Iain MacLean, Joe Cey, Kurt Wintermute, Bob Kendall, Peter Handley, John Challis, Cam Kinapen, Rosaleen Dickson, Ric Davey, Bill Triolo, Nick Ricci, Fred Walker, Dennis Boyle, Garth Vaughan, Junior Moore, Jim MacDonald, Dave Mac-Donald and Bob McQuay. For their enthusiasm about this project, I thank Sean Rossiter, D'Arcy Jenish, Rick Cluff and Brian McFarlane. In that regard, my thanks also go to the Toronto Antiques hockey team who took a flyer on a rookie and helped me get to Santa Rosa, California; for their help at the Snoopy Tournament I am indebted to Cecilia and the late Murray Shortt.

For his assistance in putting early oldtimers' history and images into perspective and for his comprehensive collection of editions of the *Canadian Oldtimers' Hockey News* I am grateful to Dave Tatham. I thank Dick Cordick and Pat Curran of the COHA for giving me access to their association's records and journals. And for his Latin translation, thanks to Professor Ross Kilpatrick.

I offer particular thanks for the patience and time given me by those who transcribed hundreds of hours of interviews—Marlene Lumley, Braunda Bodger, Mary Jane Varro, Sam Wales, Philippa Campsie, Jenny Kanis, Jim Nidd, Linda Kerr and Kate Barris. Praise too for my editor Susan Girvan (of the wicked pencil) who coached *Overtime* in by the end of regulation time.

And thanks especially to my teammates—the guys I played shinny with at the Kenilworth Arena, the Rink Rats, the Hawks of Wednesday nights and the Light Blues who put my name in the headlines this year. This one's for you.

Ted Barris, 1995

ONE

Hockey Night in Uxbridge

"O Canada" has been sung. Hockey fans from the central Ontario town of Uxbridge have settled onto the spectator benches at the local arena. The players are coasting to centre ice. Two hockey legends are about to face off.

One is Paul Henderson, hero of the 1972 Soviet-Canada hockey series. The other is the 1960s star left-winger for the Toronto Maple Leafs, Eddie Shack, remembered fondly for his unscheduled mad dashes up the ice and for his fearlessness in taking on anyone check for check, punch for punch.

What's out of the ordinary, considering his notoriously frequent visits to the penalty box (he's still twenty-third on the all-time NHL list with 1,437 penalty minutes), is that Shack isn't dressed in short pants and the Leafs' traditional blue and white jersey but in a striped referee's sweater. He's the ref who's preparing to drop the puck at an oldtimers' hockey game.

Tonight it's Paul Henderson and the Toronto NHL Orion Oldtimers versus the Uxbridge Blackhawk Oldtimers.

"Are you ready?" shouts Shack. He's not talking to either Paul Henderson or Brian St. John, the centre taking the opening face-off for the Blackhawks. Instead Eddie has his arms raised and his head cocked, waiting for an answer from the bleachers.

"Yeaaaaah!" the spectators yell back.

Nearly 600 people are here, a capacity crowd who range from kids barely beyond the skate-on-your-ankles stage to adults eager to see if the former NHLers are wearing their age

1

any better than they are. The mayor is present; she once played girls' hockey and pokes fun at the non-contact game the oldtimers play as "no-touch hockey." A young boy in the crowd has never heard of most of these ex-Leafs, but he took the advice of his coach to come see them play. Another boy, wearing his minor league hockey sweater, had to coax his dad to come. And a middle-aged spectator didn't have to be coaxed at all; he's come "for the entertainment and the nostalgia of seeing Henderson and the others…who don't look much older than me!"

"Are you ready?" Shack repeats.

The reply is even louder and includes hoots and applause.

Certain that he now has everybody's attention, Shack finally drops the puck to begin the game. But as the visiting Orions and the hometown Blackhawks begin to scrimmage, Shack ignores the play completely. With his trademark Black Bart cowboy hat and handlebar mustache flapping in the breeze, he takes off away from the play, accelerates into his characteristic bowlegged skating stride and leads the crowd in his favourite chant.

"Clear the track. Here comes Shack!" he shouts again and again, each time increasing his breakneck speed around the ice, entreating the fans to join him in the chant. Then he motions the crowd to get a wave going. They respond. They're cheering, chanting and doing the wave when Eddie the Entertainer decides to put himself back in the game.

"Hold it! Hold it!" Shack shouts between whistle blasts.

The game is barely three minutes old when Shack awards a penalty shot to the Blackhawks. Shack has played "seventeen years of oldtimers' hockey. Travelling on buses. Putting up with injuries. Once we played fourteen days straight, from coast to coast. That's tough. Playing every day for two weeks and cocktails after—it kills you.

"That's why I like refereeing," smiles Shack. "They can't talk back to you. You can tell them what to do. And if a guy yaps at you, he's gone."

Borrowing a page from the Harlem Globetrotters, Shack again steals the limelight by warming up Orion Oldtimers' goalie, Peter McDuffe, before letting the Blackhawks take their penalty shot. And when the Blackhawk chosen to take the penalty shot fails to beat McDuffe, Eddie applauds him anyway.

"Nice try," Shack says, playing to the hometown crowd. "Better luck next time."

Following the penalty shot, Brian St. John again lines up at centre ice against some of his Maple Leaf heroes—wingers Norm Ullman and Ron Ellis and centre Paul Henderson.

"It's the first time I've done this," says St. John, admitting to a few jitters facing all these former NHLers. He has played plenty of rep, semi-pro and oldtimers' hockey over the years, but this time, "I'm standing there at centre ice, facing off with Paul Henderson, the hero of the 1972 Russia-Canada series....It took me back.

"I was actually in Vancouver in 1972 for an exhibition game with the Leafs," recalls St. John, who was then playing with Tulsa, a Leafs' farm team. "I remember being at a Vancouver hotel watching [the series] on satellite...watching Henderson score the winning goal." Henderson was 29, St. John, 24.

After his brief fling with Tulsa in the Central Hockey League, St. John made a career change; he went to medical school and later came home to Uxbridge to join his father's general practice. After his heroics in Moscow, Henderson went back to the Leafs' roster, chalked up several thirty-plus-goal seasons and retired in 1980 to pursue work in a Christian mission.

Tonight in Uxbridge, twenty years later, the only thing St. John and Henderson really have in common is the title "old-timers"—by definition, any recreational hockey player over the age of 35.

Oldtimers' hockey is pretty straightforward. The rules favour offence and, under most circumstances, no body checking or contact is allowed. A defender can poke-check the puck free or manoeuvre a forward away from a clear shot at the goaltender and nullify a rush, provided he doesn't get penalized for interference. No slapshots are allowed. And there's very little stick work along the boards or jostling for the puck in the corners of the rink. The gist of the game is skating, passing and shooting.

And the Uxbridge spectators see plenty.

Early in the game, the Henderson-Ellis-Ullman line put on a demonstration. All three come from an era when fast footwork and deft stickhandling were the only way to move the puck from the defensive to the offensive zone. Taking a pass from former New York Islanders' defenceman Bob Lorimer behind the net, Ron Ellis gathers speed with a series of long, powerful strides up the right-wing boards. Using the quick pass to outflank the Uxbridge forwards, Ellis finds Henderson as he moves through the centre ice area. Henderson stickhandles across the Blackhawk blueline past a couple of defenders, flips the puck to Ullman, who is storming straight to the net, and he snaps the puck home.

It's not flashy. But it's what got them into the six-team NHL when only one in a thousand actually made it to the pros. Together, Ellis, Henderson and Ullman scored more than a thousand regular season goals and totalled almost 2,400 points during their careers in the NHL. And many of these were scored when all three were in Maple Leaf uniforms.

"We played together six years on the Leafs," says Ron Ellis. "So we know each other pretty well."

For seventeen years Ron Ellis was a pro. For seventeen years he was a Maple Leaf. He retired twice—in 1975 and for good in 1981—and for two years didn't put on a pair of skates to play recreational hockey. But when the Toronto Oldtimers called him, he couldn't resist the attraction of seeing and playing with old friends.

"We can do the things that come automatically," says Ellis. "We can still put the puck in the net. Put on a show for the fans. We go into communities not to embarrass anyone...just to entertain. We make sure it's a fun game for the guys we're playing against and the people who come out to see us."

Eventually, the Uxbridge Blackhawks score, to the delight of the hometown fans. But a minute later, the Orion Oldtimers take the Blackhawks' momentum away by stopping the play for some more antics and a bit of a breather. It's an accepted part of an oldtimers' match when a celebrity team comes to town.

"We want to trade our goalie," former New York Ranger Dean Prentice tells referee Shack.

"You want to trade your goalie," Shack echoes, and he looks to the Orion bench for a response.

"Trade him," comes the reply.

"Get rid of him," shouts another Orion.

With that, Shack ushers goalie Peter McDuffe up the ice to change places with Blackhawks' goaltender Wayne Cordingley. He accepts this clowning around readily. There's a pause in the action as each side warms up its new goalie. Then play resumes. And almost immediately, Dean Prentice and his linemates move the puck up the ice and in on McDuffe in the Blackhawks' net. Finishing the ruse, McDuffe leaves the net unattended and the Orions score an easy goal to give them back the lead.

"Uxbridge has a good skating, strong passing oldtimers' team," admits Billy Harris. "They force us to work extremely hard to keep ahead of them. It's a tough workout....But I feel fortunate that I'm still physically able to play the game."

From the moment CHUM broadcaster Ed Fitkin took young Billy Harris inside the Leafs' dressing room in 1946 until 1965, his last year on the Maple Leaf roster, Billy Harris's life on the ice was a love affair with the blue and white. Along the way he was rewarded with three Stanley Cups and numerous lasting friendships. Nearly sixty, Harris still finds satisfaction from the game he's played all his life.

"One of the rewards of playing oldtimers," says Harris, "is that everywhere we play in Canada we're raising money for different charities."

Tonight in Uxbridge is no different. After expenses—ice time, post-game refreshments and the cost of bringing in the ex-NHLers—the rest of the gate proceeds will go to the Uxbridge Youth Hockey Association. And while Harris and the rest of the Toronto Oldtimers can feel good about raising funds for local minor hockey, for the Blackhawks, this is business as usual.

The Uxbridge Blackhawk Oldtimers are a community team. From the beginning, their raison d'être has been fund-raising for the town and its people. Each year team members run an oldtimers' hockey tournament, a ball tournament, a golf tournament and the weekly Monday night bingo at the arena. In twenty years of community service, the Blackhawks have raised money for the hospital, the swim club, and minor league soccer and baseball; they've helped retile the ceiling at the Legion hall and outfit minor hockey players with new socks and sweaters. The Blackhawks have raised $6,000 a year, although according to the team's convenor, Len Nicholl, "We don't raise money for the Blackhawks. We raise it for the town."

The Blackhawks' roots are deep. The original outfit was begun in 1958 and consisted of players in their early twenties who competed in an Ontario Intermediate C league. They were supported by local businesses and the gate proceeds from the town's original arena—a barn-like building on Franklin Street—where spectators would be "hanging from the rafters" during most home games. But after four or five seasons the novelty wore off and the team was dissolved.

By the mid-1970s, something new was happening in hockey. Adult men—some of them former professional players, but most of them not—were rediscovering their national game. Shinny players, men who played pick-up hockey on Sunday nights when nobody else wanted the ice, and those who had once played hockey for a living were digging out their old sticks and skates and pads to play the game just for the fun of it. Somebody had nicknamed it "oldtimers'" hockey and they were even staging oldtimers' hockey tournaments.

"I was sitting in an office," remembers Blackhawk Oldtimers' coach Jack Ballinger. With him was Gene More, one of the original Intermediate C Blackhawks from the early 1960s. More was flipping through the pages of the then one-year-old *Canadian Oldtimers' Hockey News*. In a column headlined "Personally Speaking," the executive director of the Canadian Oldtimers' Hockey Association, John Gouett, outlined plans for the COHA 1977 tournament program.

Ballinger recalls, " 'You know, we could join this thing,' said Gene. 'It'd be a good idea, don't you think, Jack? Maybe we could get the Blackhawks back together. Let's make some phone calls,' he said, and by September we had eight of the original Blackhawks. Some had played a bit since the sixties; but most of them had been off their skates a good ten years."

By Friday, January 21, 1977, the Uxbridge Blackhawks—like the phoenix—had re-emerged and arrived in Niagara Falls for the Central Canada International. A hundred teams had entered and, when the weekend tournament ended, remembers Ballinger, "We'd won. We won the over-35 [age bracket] in F Division. We played the RCMP in the semi-final. And it was rough. No body contact. No slapshots. But it was actually a rough, tough game.

"We went into the dressing room between periods. We were down 1–0. And we had two men in the penalty box. I said to Bob Cherry, 'You're the captain of this team. We gotta get back even.' And I remember going back out there, playing short-handed. And I remember Cherry taking the puck right from the face-off and scoring to make it 1–1. We went on to win that game and the final. And Dave Tatham, the editor of the *Oldtimers' Hockey News*, was there. He came into the dressing room to interview us after the game."

The following month, the *News* published a feature story on the Blackhawks ("Old Team Back on Blades"), including a photograph of a smiling captain Bob Cherry hoisting the F Division trophy high over his head.

After Niagara Falls the Blackhawks' organization became an institution in Uxbridge. Monday night was bingo. Thursdays were practices or exhibition games. And more tournaments. But the one who has kept the whole enterprise functioning smoothly is the guy who describes himself as "the water bottle carrier, the team door opener and the bench warmer." Len Nicholl skated as a kid in Belfast, Northern Ireland, but even after emigrating to Canada he never played hockey. Still, he's a vital cog in the Blackhawks' machine, setting game dates, phoning players, writing up the game sheets and even passing out the gum before a game.

"I didn't play," says Nicholl, "but I wanted to belong."

In the winter of 1981, Len Nicholl entered a Toronto hospital suffering from peripheral vascular disease. He had to have his left leg amputated. That same week, the Blackhawks left by bus for an oldtimers' tournament in North Bay. On Tuesday Nicholl had his surgery. By Thursday he was plotting to get out of his hospital bed and up to North Bay for the tourney. He had no cash but figured he could use a credit card to pay for the cab to Pearson International Airport and the airfare to North Bay. He knew the team would find room for him on the bus home. He had even persuaded the nursing staff he could make it. And Nicholl would have done it, except that a blizzard on Friday night snowed everybody in.

It's assumed that the NHL oldtimers will win tonight's game in Uxbridge. The fans expect it. The Orions expect it. And the Blackhawks expect it. However, the inevitable lopsided score doesn't mean that individual oldtimers—both the ex-pros and the lifetime amateurs—can't enjoy success along the way. There's room for that in oldtimers' hockey.

For lumbering defenceman Ernie Pase, success doesn't mean scoring goals. It means saving face in front of the home-town crowd. At one point in the game Pase looked up to see one of his heroes, Norm Ullman, coming toward him on a two-on-one break. Ernie prayed they wouldn't make him look foolish.

"Ullman tried to pass the puck across," recalls Pase, "and I anticipated the pass. I think it's the only time I stopped a play all night. But oh, it's great to stop a star. I mean everybody's got an ego here."

"The thing about playing NHL oldtimers," says Len Nicholl, "is that you can never win the hockey game. You should never win the hockey game. It's their show. As soon as you begin to win, they come up with a gimmick to tie the score."

In the first period the gimmicks were the penalty shot and the goalie trade. In the second period the Toronto Orion Old-timers toss an extra puck or two on the ice just to confuse the opposition and to amuse the crowd. And in the third period the ex-NHLers pull another vaudevillian trick out of their bag.

After a seemingly innocent collision at the Toronto blue-line, former Leaf centre Jack Valiquette tumbles to the ice. As he rolls around on the ice, apparently in considerable pain, his concerned teammates gather round. Bob Lorimer brings a towel, Bill Derlago a bucket of water. But Derlago "accidentally" splashes one of his teammates and a tussle ensues.

"You asked for it," shouts big Leaf winger Wayne Carleton as he retreats to the bench for another bucket of water.

"Oh, yeah?" retorts Derlago, facing Carleton with his own bucket at the ready.

The two skate back and forth through the centre ice area, each threatening to soak the other, while all the other players stand well out of the way. In one last desperate lunge at Carleton, Derlago launches the bucket's contents just as Carleton passes the Blackhawks' bench. Of course, he ducks and the water drenches the entire Blackhawks team instead.

"You know it's coming," says Len Nicholl. "They've been doing it for years. You just have to learn to duck."

And no matter how many times spectators have seen the water bucket gag—courtesy of the Barnum & Bailey Circus, the Harlem Globetrotters or the NHL Oldtimers—it still gets a terrific laugh. It even makes June Prentice laugh. And she's seen it hundreds of times. But then she's biased. She's a self-confessed rink rat. She's been hanging around arenas like this one ever since her childhood days in northern Ontario. In fact, that's where she met her husband, Dean Prentice.

"Dean and I grew up together in Schumacher," says June. "We just lived in the arena. My only thoughts were to be on the ice as a figure skater and Dean's goal was to get into the NHL. We became boyfriend and girlfriend, then married. Dean broke into the New York Rangers' lineup in 1952, played until 1974 and was 42 when he retired. Now it's hockey schools and oldtimers."

In ten seasons with the Rangers, Prentice enjoyed the thrill of scoring nearly 200 goals (including a four-goal game) and being several times an all-star. And yet, despite twenty-two successful years playing pro, Prentice still calls his return to the game as an oldtimer, especially after the age of sixty, "a highlight." Perhaps it's because of the pleasure he continues to derive from the skills of the game itself.

"Kids today," Prentice says, "they love to skate with the puck. They're good skaters. They're good stickhandlers. But

they don't make the plays. That's what we learned back in the
fifties and sixties. Move the puck around. We can move the
puck around, get into the holes and make the pretty
plays....And when we play the kids today, they're all mesmer-
ized by what's going on around them."

That's probably why Prentice keeps coming out with the
Toronto Oldtimers. Of all the goals in his career, he scored
not one as a Leaf. Now with the Leaf alumni he pots a couple
a game. But the real reason he plays oldtimers' hockey is for
the laughs, the dressing room kibitzing and the joy of the
game. And in the stands, it's equally enjoyable for June Prentice, although, "The big difference is that when Dean played
in the NHL, the trainers washed his underwear, shirts and
socks after the game....I've been doing it now for the last
twenty years. Ah, the price of leaving the pros and becoming
an amateur again!"

As memorable as this Toronto–Uxbridge oldtimers' game is
for its slapstick, it is equally memorable for some of its rushes,
displays of puck-handling, precision passing, pinpoint shooting and dazzling saves on both sides. For Blackhawks' netminder Wayne Cordingley, who's been playing goal since he
was five years old, tonight is the first time he has ever faced
the prospect of Dean Prentice muscling through his goal
crease. It's the first time he's had to contend with the passing
combination of Ellis to Henderson to Ullman. And while
Cordingley has seen Billy Harris on skates at close range
before, he has never faced him in a one-on-one breakaway.

"Some of these guys were playing hockey before I was
born," admits the stocky Cordingley. "But I have been out on
the ice with Billy Harris before...at his hockey school when I
was a kid. There's quite a difference today, quite a change. I
was a little faster then...and so was he. He's no spring
chicken...but he still got a hat trick tonight."

Harris's three goals, two each from Henderson and Ellis,
and a whole game sheet full of goals and assists by the
remaining Toronto Orion Oldtimers decide the game for the
ex-pros in the third period. There was never really any doubt.
The game ends the way it should. The visiting Toronto Oldtimers win and the two teams, in a long-standing oldtimers'

tradition, line up to shake hands one by one along the full length of the ice.

It's been a good night all around.

The local youth hockey association has banked a few more dollars toward what will one day be a second ice pad at the Uxbridge arena. The Blackhawks have staged another successful community event. Spectators go away believing that their hockey heroes still have what it takes. And the former Leaf stars have enjoyed another mini-reunion.

Their pleasure doesn't come from the score sheet. It's "the good feeling of playing with Dean Prentice and Ullman again," smiles Billy Harris. "Before the game and between periods, I look around the dressing room and here are guys I played with or coached at one time throughout my career. It's a good feeling. I also feel pretty fortunate I'm still physically able to play the game."

Winning isn't the name of the game for Norm Ullman either. If it were, he would have given up the game long before this. The journeyman centre scored 490 NHL career goals (on par with Gordie Howe, Jean Béliveau and Alex Delvecchio), but he never played on a Stanley Cup winner.

"It's the fun," says Ullman. "It's the camaraderie. It's the exercise....It's something we've done all our lives. And you never forget how to play. It's just that sometimes your old legs won't get you there in time to do it."

Pleasure for the local Blackhawks Oldtimers also doesn't come from winning, at least not in this kind of game. For them, as for most oldtimers' teams, it's the atmosphere of the dressing room. Despite its cramped quarters and simple conveniences—it looks more like an oversized prison cell than a team meeting place—the dressing room becomes a sanctuary when it fills with oldtimer hockey players.

Generally off-limits to spectators, oldtimers' wives, and the players' children, the team dressing room is usually governed by whatever habits and rituals the team has developed over their years of being together. And it's always alive with loud conversation, more talk than on the ice and the distribution of the post-game beer. Some players strip off their equipment quickly, others are too weary to remove anything but a helmet and sweater for perhaps half an hour, but all rehash the game.

Good plays and bad, goals for and against, and unfair refereeing (because fair reffing just doesn't exist) are described from every vantage point. And the foul-smelling air of a steamy, congested room is soon full of could have's, should have's and next time's. In this rarefied atmosphere, everyone and everything is fair game. Nothing—not a goaltender's brilliant save, nor a forward's breathtaking goal, nor a defenceman's heroic block—escapes the incessant wisecracking of the jokers and the one-line artists in the group. Being brutally ridiculed is not only accepted, it's expected.

Len Nicholl reviews the stats on the game sheet. Tongue-in-cheek, he laments the Blackhawks' less than impressive goal production. In particular, he enjoys poking fun at the high-flying Dr. Brian St. John.

"What happened, Saint?" Nicholl asks.

"Haven't got my signing bonus yet," deadpans St. John, "so I'm holding back."

"I think it's 'cause he's on the helicopter line," pipes up Bill Scott, another centre. "You know. No wings."

Meanwhile, Ernie Pase has peeled off his sweater and is feeling pretty good about his one stop on Norm Ullman.

"Amazing what happens when you close your eyes, eh, Ern," somebody jibes.

"Yeah," says another, looking at goalie Wayne Cordingley, "just ask Cord."

"What do you mean?" Cordingley responds, "I went to Billy Harris's hockey school, way back when."

"Maybe you ought to enroll again and get it right."

It's all water off a duck's back. As temperamental as some goalies are, Cordingley won't go away angry. Weathering the shots in the dressing room or on the ice is just a matter of course with the Blackhawks. Nor is Cordingley about to be kicked off the team. "In fact," says convenor Len Nicholl, "nobody ever gets cut from this team. You quit. And until such time as you quit, there's no replacement. And we don't even have a recruiting program."

Few oldtimers' hockey teams are so organized that they

would do anything so premeditated as recruit. Most teams barely manage to get through the winter (or the summer) with all team members arriving at games on time. At each game, someone is always minus an elbow pad or the cup for a jock strap. When somebody forgets a team sweater, the goalie (who doesn't need to wear the same colour uniform as much as a forward or defenceman) usually forfeits his jersey for the game. And as long as the player responsible for bringing the post-game beer comes through, an oldtimers' game—win or lose—is considered a success.

One by one the Toronto Orion Oldtimers undress, shower, share a few more laughs, pack up their gear and slip out a back door of the Uxbridge arena.

Harris, Ellis, Ullman and Lorimer are on autograph duty tonight. Bill Derlago (a more recent Leaf alumnus) is there too. He grew up in a small Manitoba town and used to go to Winnipeg to cheer on the Jets; he was a young autograph hound himself not so long ago, so it takes him a little longer to sign the last program and stick before tasting that cold beer in the dressing room.

"The first year I came on the team," says Derlago, "I was playing with Andy Bathgate, Eddie Shack and Norm Ullman. I used to watch these guys play and hear about them. To play with them is quite a thrill for me. I'm one of the youngest on the team so in the dressing room I sit and don't say too much. It's like being a rookie again."

A rookie oldtimer. It's almost an oxymoron—but not quite. The truth is, as a phenomenon, oldtimers' hockey is younger than Bill Derlago.

TWO

The Birth of Oldtimers

It's an unlikely place for the inauguration of a hockey tradition, but Bracebridge, Ontario, can lay claim to it. In the winter of 1952, more than two decades before anyone had formally used the term "oldtimers" for the recreational hockey that adults play, Bracebridge was alive with talk that some oldtime NHL stars were coming to town.

That was the year that the Chicago Blackhawks' Bill Mosienko shattered a long-standing record by scoring three goals in 21 seconds. That was the year Detroit's Gordie Howe, in his sixth NHL season, won the scoring race with forty-seven goals and thirty-nine assists, earning him a princely $1,000 bonus. And that was the year Terry Sawchuk and his Red Wings registered four shutouts in an eight game sweep of the Stanley Cup playoffs—the first such lopsided winning streak in NHL history.

However, none of the 1951–52 NHL greats were anywhere near Bracebridge on January 25, 1952. Instead, it was former greats who were on the bill at the arena that night: NHL stars from the 1930s and '40s such as the Leafs' Busher Jackson, Red Heron, Harry McQuestion, Jimmy Fowler, Rhys Thomson, Red Horner and Billy Taylor, along with the Conacher brothers and Bucko McDonald. Also from that era were former Montreal Maroons' forwards Lorne Duguid and Andy Bellemer, Boston Bruins' forwards Dit Clapper and Irwin "Yank" Boyd and a goaltender known as "the half-pint sensation" for the old New York Americans, Roy Worters.

14

At the invitation of the Bala branch of the Royal Canadian Legion and the Bala Lions Club, two squads of former NHL all-stars had agreed to lace on the blades for a benefit game in Bracebridge that night. The referee was local goalie and sometimes referee, Fred Decaire.

"Roy Worters was my hero," remembers Decaire. Fred had grown up and played his minor hockey as a goalie in Bala. "I had had all kinds of speed when I played goal back in public school. And I got as far as a tryout with the Junior B Owen Sound Greys in 1947." Decaire should have advanced into the pro leagues. He had good hands catching shots, and this in the days before the trapper glove was invented. But he suffered from recurring injuries. His catching hand would swell so badly he'd have to stick it in a bucket of ice water after each game. And, worse, he suffered from periodic blackouts. Consequently, "I was often catching pucks in the teeth."

That's when Fred Decaire took up refereeing. He was hanging around at the Bala Arena one night when a girls' hockey game needed a ref. "Never having read a rule book, I volunteered," he says, and because "my skates were always at the rink," Decaire qualified. Before long he was officiating Intermediate B games for the Muskoka Lakes League (including four games a week in places such as Port Carling, Gravenhurst and Bracebridge) "for $5 a game, $5 for my mileage—and a lot of abuse."

Remuneration wasn't a whole lot better when Decaire got the call to referee the 1952 ex-NHLers game in Bracebridge. He was invited to ref simply "for the thrill of it." The Legion and Lions Club members were also counting on the generosity of some ex-pros who had cottages in the area; surprisingly, they had agreed to play. The local newspapers downplayed the event's potential; they described it as "Has-Beens Put Up Big Benefit." However, after only a few weeks of radio promotion on Toronto's CFRB by broadcaster Gordon Sinclair (who had a cottage on Acton Island in the Muskokas), it was clear that interest was high. When advance ticket sales closed in on 300, the organizers realized they would have to move the game to a larger venue—the 2,000-seat arena in Bracebridge.

On Friday, January 25, 1952, spectators from across
Muskoka gathered at the Bracebridge rink. Among those in
attendance were members of the Smythe and Primeau families, along with the legendary Leaf winger and Bracebridge
native, Irvine "Ace" Bailey. To kick off the evening there was a
brief hockey contest between two bantam teams from Bala
and Port Carling and an artistic exhibition of figure skating by
a duet from Port Carling. The Bracebridge Citizens' Band
provided the skaters' music. And then came the main event,
refereed by Fred Decaire in his snow-white Ontario Hockey
Association referee's sweater.

"I was fussier about my appearance than most," remembers
Decaire. "Under my sweater, I wore a white shirt and black tie.
And I had to have the crease just so in my pants. I had to look
my best....And that rule book was in my head. I could just
about quote you any page if you wanted." But this game of
"has-beens" and heroes was not going to go by the book at all.

Decaire was told just before he stepped onto the ice to call
the game like any other; however, "this wasn't any ordinary
game. I was supposed to make sure I called lots of penalties
on Andy Bellemer....Nail him two or three times, they told
me. And I was told at some point there would be a big fight
between Bucko McDonald and Lionel Conacher. Now, these
are big men. And I envisioned all kinds of things happening."

One thing he hadn't expected was television. Television was
introduced to Canada in 1952 but thanks to a bunch of former NHL stars gathering for this charity game TV came to
Bracebridge early. During the day a crew from an American
station had set up lighting along the boards and put a camera
in the stands. During the game "it was like being in a spotlight
all night," remembers Decaire. "They would swing the lights
to follow you. So when you'd come around, you'd suddenly
be looking right at all these huge lights. And you couldn't see
anything. That, and the flash bulbs from all the photographers' cameras, drove me crazy."

And when he wasn't blinded by the TV lights, Decaire was
upstaged by the celebrities. Following the script, Decaire did
manage to penalize the forty-seven-year-old Andy Bellemer at
least once for high sticking. Of course, Bellemer disputed it.

But when Decaire finally put him in the penalty box, Belle-mer just signed a few autographs for some spectators and then headed right back onto the ice. Lionel and Charlie Conacher (then in their late forties) generated a lot of excitement by playing opposite each other. Billy Taylor (at thirty-two) hadn't lost his touch stickhandling. Roy Worters (fifty-one) goaltended like the days of old. And radio man Gordon Sinclair did player introductions and then coached both benches at the same time.

At one point late in the game, it appeared that Fred Decaire was getting into the act. The referee suddenly found himself in one end of the rink, too deep to follow an offensive play developing in the other direction. He realized his mistake, wheeled around to retrace his steps and crashed into defenceman Red Horner. Horner's head caught Decaire in the pit of the stomach, knocking the air right out of him. He couldn't even inhale enough air to blow his whistle to stop the play. His linesman finally did. But the crowd roared with laughter, thinking Decaire's tumble was just another choreographed stunt.

"Then there was the fight," laughs Decaire. "Normally it would be a linesman breaking up a fight, not me. But as soon as I saw it start, I knew I was supposed to go in and break it up. It was "Big Train" Lionel Conacher and Bucko McDon-ald. And they were really sluggin'. They weren't mad at each other, but they were smacking at each other with plenty of body punches.

"I didn't know what to do. These were big boys. So the only thing I could think of doing was put my hands over their eyes, so they couldn't see. Well, Lionel reached around, grabbed me by the chin, picked me up and set me out of the road and continued slugging....So I gave him a game misconduct for manhandling me—and the crowd just went bananas."

Toward the end of the game, the oldtime NHLers were taking intentional penalties and not hurrying back onto the ice. They kibitzed even more to help the clock run out. And Decaire admits he was letting some pretty obvious offside plays go so that, mercifully, this marathon would end. When it did, the Red Squad had beaten the White Squad 8–5.

Following the game, the players were mobbed by fans, photographers, the television crew, and newspaper reporters from Toronto and the local press. And as bothered by the flash bulbs as he had been during the game, Decaire will always remember being asked for his autograph alongside his heroes—the Conachers, Bucko McDonald and Roy "Shrimp" Worters. But that was the first and last oldtimers' hockey game Fred Decaire ever worked.

"And it was probably years," he says, "before I recall hearing about another game with oldtimers again."

It took Canada's 1967 centennial celebration to move oldtimers' hockey one step further. Under the federal minister responsible for the centennial, Judy LaMarsh, the government of Lester Pearson spent millions of dollars to ensure that Canada's hundredth birthday was memorable. Among the thousands of grants given to build libraries, art galleries, theatres and sports complexes, and to finance plays, musicals, operas, ballets and other public spectacles, one grant was issued to a team of hockey players from Penetang, Ontario. Most were in their thirties. Their idea was to travel around Ontario in 1967, see the countryside, celebrate the country's centennial and get in as many hockey games with as many teams as the winter and their aging legs would allow.

"With the $300 grant from the government," says John Gouett, the team's organizer "we bought sweaters. We called ourselves the Penetang Centennials and played exhibition games with other teams in places like Fenelon Falls and Haliburton. Then we'd invite them back to play in our arena. It was our centennial project."

The whole hockey tour was really John Gouett's doing, and it was very much in keeping with his personality and temperament. As a kid in Long Branch, just west of Toronto, John organized a year-round ball hockey league; they played each fall until it was too cold and each summer until it was too hot or until the tennis players kicked them off the tennis courts, whichever came first.

When hockey was on television but most homes didn't have one, Gouett convinced the owner of a local appliance store to leave a TV set on in the window and to hang a loudspeaker outside the store. John and his friends would set chairs on the sidewalk in front of the store and watch the games "whether it was ten degrees below zero or not." When his dad got tickets to Leaf games, John would sit in the greens wearing his Montreal Canadiens' hockey jersey, just to drive the Leaf fans crazy.

"When I was sixteen, I tried out for an intermediate team in the Toronto Hockey League," remembers Gouett. "I couldn't make the team. So, I organized my own team....I went around Long Branch and got $25 from each merchant. That paid for the sweaters, socks and pants for each player. We called ourselves the Long Branch Merchants and played exhibition games around Ontario or in the THL. And because I organized the team, I was able to play. I loved playing right wing. My favourite player was Rocket Richard, [who] played right wing but shot left....Seemed to be on the wrong wing coming down the ice, but could cut in on the goalie better."

Like most Canadian youngsters, when he realized he would neither be another Rocket Richard nor play for his beloved Canadiens, John Gouett went about the business of getting an education and a job. By 1967 he was teaching and studying (what else?) recreation leadership at the University of Guelph. That's where he got the notion to help celebrate Canada's centennial on the ice. And that $300 grant sure went a long way. As well as games against other adult hockey teams he found in small-town Ontario, Gouett's Penetang Centennials played exhibition games against some ex-Maple Leafs, including Cal Gardner, Tod Sloan, Bob Goldham, and a team made up of celebrities at CKVR TV in Barrie, Ontario.

But Gouett's idea of adults playing the game they had enjoyed as ball hockey players on tennis courts, as wannabe's watching *Hockey Night in Canada* and as patriots celebrating Canada's hundredth birthday wasn't entirely original.

In the winter of 1964, a group of doctors, lawyers and civil servants interested in playing pick-up hockey had begun renting the arena at Saint Mary's University in Halifax regularly on Saturday afternoons. In 1966 a bunch of UBC business graduates had started playing shinny on Wednesday nights in Vancouver.

Also in the mid-1960s, a group of inveterate hockey enthusiasts began gathering at the arena in Pointe Claire, Quebec, on Sunday nights. Nobody seemed interested in renting the ice after seven o'clock in the evening, so this ad hoc group of over-thirty-five-year-olds, calling themselves the Pointe Claire Oldtimers Hockey Club, started a six-team league of friendly competition from 7 to 10 p.m. In fact, according to his hockey buddies, it was Pointe Claire defenceman and club organizer Bill Wilkinson, who decided not to call it "hockey for seniors" and who first coined the phrase "oldtimers' hockey." In addition to their Sunday night hockey, in 1970 Wilkinson and the Pointe Claire club inaugurated their own International Oldtimers' Invitational Tournament. Each year teams from Quebec, Ontario and the northern United States travelled to the Pointe Claire arena (which was conveniently situated right next to Dorval Airport in Montreal) to compete in a weekend tournament and, as usual, to use up that ice time that nobody else wanted.

On February 2, 1974, John Gouett turned thirty-five. In many ways it was a turning point in his life. In addition to it being Groundhog Day (which meant only six more weeks of oldtimers' hockey that winter), Gouett decided it was time for a change. He had been a school teacher in Ennismore, just north of Peterborough, Ontario, for a number of years and was tiring of it. That winter he attended the Pointe Claire tournament and that experience, as well as his own intuition about the growing popularity of the oldtimers' game, propelled him into action. Gouett sensed that the time and conditions were right to introduce a national oldtimers' tournament and a national governing body to spearhead such an enterprise.

"In March, 1974, I organized the St. Michael's Oldtimers," remembers Gouett. "I put together a bunch of guys from my old days at St. Mike's and we went out west on a barnstorming tour. During the spring break we played eight games in ten days. And while we were out there we asked everybody what they thought of oldtimer hockey and if they would come to a national tournament if I organized one."

The oldtimers' whirlwind tour included stops in Hobbema, Westlock, Grande Prairie, Spirit River and Peace River in Alberta as well as Dawson Creek, Fort Nelson and Fort St. John in British Columbia. Each night, the St. Mike's Old-timers played a local oldtimers' club, was given $500 to cover expenses (the rest of the gate went to a local charity) and then rolled on to the next town and the next arena to play and talk up the idea of a national oldtimers' hockey tournament. Much of the tour's success depended on the local contacts made by Gouett's teammate and longtime friend, Gerry Aherne.

"I'd got hold of my friends up in the Peace River country," says Aherne, "and I presented them with this idea of bringing the St. Mike's Oldtimers through. We played in front of standing-room-only crowds.

"The pace was brutal. Sometimes we travelled 500 miles a day. We'd arrive in town. Play the big game. They'd have a big dinner for us after. We'd party until three or four o'clock in the morning. Then at eight o'clock, we'd put a case of beer in the car and away we'd go in our convoy of rented cars."

Not only was Aherne backing up Gouett's idea, he was also backing up the team in net. Gerry "Tubby" Aherne had been a goalie ever since his childhood friends stuck him in net on the ice behind the Long Branch beer store. Like Gouett, Aherne honed his skills playing ball hockey, and joined the St. Mike's bantam team when he was twelve. Under the tutelage of Father David Bauer at St. Mike's and Turk Broda of the Toronto Marlies, Aherne moved up through the ranks of the Maple Leaf organization. Among the "highlights" of his career with the Leafs was defending the net opposite Johnny Bower in practice, taking a Bert Olmstead slapshot on the nose and becoming the stand-by goalkeeper for teams coming into Maple Leaf Gardens to play the Leafs.

"Back in the six-team days, NHL teams only carried one goalkeeper," explains Aherne. "And when they came to Toronto, if their goalie got hurt in the game, I'd have to go in. So I might end up playing goal for the opposition.

"Harry Lumley was goalie with the Boston Bruins then. He got food poisoning while they were in town to play the Leafs. That morning I was out of town and they had a stand-by for me, a guy from St. Mike's. When I got to the Gardens and up to the press box, the guard says, 'Why aren't you on the ice?'

"I said, 'What're you talking about?'

"He said, 'Harry Lumley's sick. Got food poisoning.'

"I looked out on the ice and there's that guy from St. Mike's. So I went to Punch Imlach to find out what the hell was going on. And he said he'd called this other guy by mistake. I think Punch was trying to pull a fast one on the Bruins. So I went to the Bruins' dressing room and told [coach] Milt Schmidt I was the stand-by goaltender. Boston was fighting for a playoff spot at the time. So Schmidt went over to Punch and says, 'What're you trying to pull here?'

"Well, the game was about to start, so Milt told me to come down after the first period and see how they were doing then. After the first period Boston was losing 2–0. But he said, 'Come back after the second and if we're really in bad shape we'll dress you.' But the score was respectable at the end of the second period, so I didn't bother going down.

"You figure it's going to be your only chance to get into an NHL game. And it ended up it was my only chance....That night I walked out of the Gardens and walked all the way home to Long Branch. I was really dejected."

After his big NHL disappointment, Gerry Aherne bounced around the semi-pro ranks of the International Hockey League and the Eastern Hockey League for a while, and even tried out with the Ottawa Nationals when the World Hockey Association was formed. But his goaltending career drew the most attention when he played intermediate hockey in Alberta's North Peace League in the early 1960s. So popular was "Tubby" Aherne from his days with the Fairview Elks and the Spirit River Rangers that when he and the St. Mike's Oldtimers toured Peace River country in the winter of 1974, signs and posters everywhere marked "The Return of Gerry Aherne."

However, after thousands of kilometres travelled, hours of hockey played and many cases of beer consumed, neither Aherne nor Gouett was any closer to knowing where old-timers' hockey, or their careers promoting it, stood. But they were confident they had taken the right first step. That June, John Gouett quit his teaching job. And while Gerry Aherne wasn't about to stop selling life insurance for a living, he wholeheartedly backed Gouett in his intention to form the Canadian Oldtimers' Hockey Association, establish a national office and stage the country's first-ever national oldtimers' hockey tournament.

The idea was a sound one. Across the country, in small towns and large cities, pockets of men born during or after the Second World War were now approaching middle age. They had played street hockey, pond hockey, some organized hockey and a few even semi-pro hockey. But by twenty or twenty-one they had quit or been forced to quit because, unless they were destined for the NHL or amateur coaching, the game had no place for them to go. Marriage, jobs and families became the priority while sticks, skates and ancient hockey equipment were discarded and forgotten. But the coming of oldtimers' hockey "opened up a brand new world for these guys," says Aherne. "Suddenly their boyhood game, the game they'd grown up with, was theirs to play again. And it didn't matter how good or bad you were...whether you played all the time as a kid or for the first time as a thirty-five-year-old, there was a competitive division in oldtimers for you."

Nevertheless, the brand-new association and its planned inaugural tournament were still a huge gamble. None knew that better than Gouett's wife. Like her husband, Patricia Gouett was a teacher. Realizing how committed John was to this dream of a national association and tournament, Pat agreed to be the primary breadwinner in the family. She also agreed to assign their house and all their personal assets to guarantee the bank's $15,000 line of credit to the new Canadian Oldtimers' Hockey Association. As a non-profit association the COHA (with Gouett, Aherne and lawyer Paul Laurent as its founding directors) managed to secure a $4,500 grant from Recreation Canada. That summer, Gouett and Aherne booked ice time at various rinks in Peterborough for February, 1975. They began arranging for accommodation through a local travel agent. They organized a mailing list and sent out scores of brochures inviting teams from every corner of the country to the First Annual National Oldtimers' Hockey Tournament in Peterborough.

Nothing happened.

In October, 1974, John Gouett began selling again. He talked his way into a free one-way ticket to Vancouver from Canadian Pacific Airlines, and one from Air Canada to the east coast. Throughout the fall, he barnstormed across the four western provinces and through the Maritimes, only this time without the fanfare, charity games or the players to catch people's attention. Gouett simply "hit a lot of the local rinks or talked to recreational directors. I went to smaller communities. I talked to hockey players. I tried to make as many contacts as I could. And in a matter of four months I had talked fifty-six teams into coming to Peterborough. In fact, every province was represented."

At eight o'clock in the morning, on Friday, February 21, 1975, five referees dropped pucks at centre ice in five different arenas in the Peterborough area, inaugurating the first national oldtimers' tournament ever staged in Canada. Fifty-six teams had arrived to play in four divisions (A, B, C and D) based on age and players' hockey backgrounds.

At the arena in Ennismore the highly favoured Toronto Italian Oldtimers met an only recently assembled Saint John Old Timers in the first B Division match-up of the tournament.

"We were lucky to even get to the ice that morning," says goaltender Don Elliott. The previous fall when John Gouett had come through Saint John, New Brunswick, on his freebie Air Canada ticket, he'd run into a house painter named Gord Myles. At the time, Myles managed the only oldtimers' club in the city and, to make the trip to Peterborough, he figured they needed to raise $5,000. They tried everything from bingos to raffles. They also staged a few exhibition games, but the only competition they could find was a team of ex-NHLers, and the Saint John 77's (of the New Brunswick Junior A League) who pounded them 10–2. A month before the Peterborough tournament, Myles's oldtimers had only $2,000. Then a Maritimes airline strike forced the team to travel by train to Montreal and by bus to Peterborough.

"We finally arrived after two and a half days on the road," recalls Elliott. "We checked into the Holiday Inn. Then we were out all night partying and having fun....And we had to be up early the next morning. Ours was one of the first games of the tournament."

When the Saint John Old Timers arrived at the Ennismore arena Friday morning, the Toronto Italians were already warming up on the ice. They had somebody taking care of sticks. They had a doctor at the bench. They had co-ordinated uniforms. It was all pretty intimidating. However, Saint John had planned on having the one advantage of a goalie tandem; Billy James was sharing the netminding duties with Don Elliott. The two had made a pact: if one goalie drank too much the night before a game, the other would play the next day. However, because of first night festivities, neither James nor Elliott was in any shape to play. At game time—8 a.m.—James lost the coin toss and took his place in the Saint John net. On the bench, Elliott sat suited up but still very much hung over.

Halfway through the second period, Elliott figured he wouldn't have to play at all. Billy James had successfully held the Italians off the score sheet and Saint John was leading 1–0. Then coach Doug MacPhee turned to Elliott and said, "If Billy's got to play half the game, you've got to play the other half."

"I'll never forget it," says Elliott. "The sweat's just pouring off me and I went in to play."

Don Elliott is not a finesse hockey player. As a kid in the east end of Saint John, he learned the basic rule of any game—make sure you know how to fight. On the outdoor ice at the Allison Grounds he generally played against boys bigger and stronger than he was and, until somebody told him to go in net, he got pushed around regularly. He learned goaltending without a mask, without a jock strap and without shin pads, but by "honing skills through fear—fear of getting hit in the head or in the privates or in the shins—I developed a quick set of hands and knew how to duck."

Despite being right-handed, Elliott felt better in goal catching with his right hand and stickhandling with his left. So, to develop his catching hand, his father often took him to a dead end alley. He would tie Don's left hand behind his back and they would face each other. Then Don's dad would throw a tennis ball behind his son and Don would have to turn quickly and get into position to catch the ball as it caromed off the walls back toward him. Aside from that little bit of training, Don Elliott learned goaltending by doing it. And he did a lot of it—from street hockey at the age of five, to school hockey, to junior, senior, intermediate and full-contact industrial league hockey when he was in his forties. But somehow it never seemed as rough or desperate as that third period against the Toronto Italian Oldtimers in 1975.

"I think we played the entire last period with somebody in the penalty box," Elliott remembers despite his foggy state of mind at the time. "We were hacking and slashing and punching. It got down to the last two or three minutes of the game and every time they tried to take a shot, one of our guys would tackle them. So we played the last three minutes with three guys on the ice. I don't think I stopped one shot, because none of them got through. And we won 1–0!"

Elliott and his Saint John teammates won their first three games that way but were eliminated in the playoffs. The Toronto Italians went on to win the entire B Division. But winning (while apparently paramount on the ice) didn't consume either the players or the tournament. "Minutes after the game," recalls Elliott, "the opposing teams would meet back at the hotel, talk, drink beer, tell stories....It was all good, clean fun and went off like clockwork."

No one was more impressed with the results of this grand experiment than its key organizers. Aherne and Gouett had to pinch themselves. Local hotels were happy; they were filled to capacity. Tournament registrar Patricia Gouett was happy; over 1,200 players had attended. And the tournament schedule, which Aherne and Gouett had laboured over for weeks—matching teams of equal calibre and keeping five arenas on time for three days and nights—worked nearly perfectly. Gouett had trophies made for all four divisional championship teams but didn't stop there. He made sure few teams went away empty-handed by organizing inter-divisional games, consolation games and even an east-west game, featuring a team from Campbell River, British Columbia, against oldtimers from Corner Brook, Newfoundland. The winner took home the Challenge Cup.

On the ice, tournament referee-in-chief Jim Orr kept the games safe, friendly and on time. With nothing to work from but amateur rules and regulations, Orr had written the seventy-five-pages of rules for the COHA Hockey Manual, covering the rink, the teams, equipment, penalties and officials.

"At registration," explained Orr, "everyone talks about the tremendous opportunity to get back into organized hockey, with an emphasis on no body contact and good sportsmanship. However, once players hit the ice...the old habits start to come back—the stick between the opponent's legs, the jab behind the knee, just a little shove to put an opponent off balance."

Consequently, the two most vital and often most difficult rules to enforce were no body contact (although Orr recognized it was impossible to play hockey without some contact) and no slapshots (although snapshots, in which the player brings the stick back about a bladelength to hit the puck with a combined snap and wrist shot, were allowed). Jim Orr felt the objective was to keep the "fun, enjoyment, exercise and fellowship" at the heart of the game.

Spectators flocked to the five arenas. Along with several hometown heroes to cheer for, such as 1950s' Peterborough Petes' stalwarts George Montague and Larry Babcock, there were plenty of bona fide former hockey stars to see again. The Grande Prairie Oldtimers, with an average age of forty-five, featured Garry "Duke" Edmundson who had played on the 1950–51 Stanley Cup champion Montreal Canadiens. A Stanley Cup alumnus with the Detroit Red Wings, Marcel Pronovost, arrived with the Toronto St. Michael's Oldtimers, while longtime Chicago Blackhawks' right-winger Chico Maki (then thirty-five) appeared with the Simcoe Oldtimers. And the Yorkton Oldtime Terriers (from Saskatchewan) had no less than six former pros, including 1940s' veteran Metro Prystai who had played on a line with Gordie Howe and Ted Lindsay.

The First Annual National Oldtimers' Hockey Tournament left plenty of unforgettable impressions.

There was the Canadian Forces Base team from Nova Scotia that had pooled cash donations from ships and messes in

Halifax/Dartmouth and equipment from bases at Halifax and
Shearwater to make the trip to Peterborough. There was the
RCMP team from Ontario and two aboriginal teams from
Alberta. There was the lasting image of a giant Pacific salmon
gracing centre ice as the Campbell River Oldtimers presented
Peterborough mayor Joe Behan with a tournament memento at
the Memorial Centre. And there was a magical moment as the
sixty-four-year-old captain of the Sudbury Oldtimers, George
Hastie, embraced both the trophy and his longtime friend and
coach Larry Rubic after winning the final in the D Division.

There were no trophies for the players from Wolfe Island that
weekend. But they didn't seem to mind. The Wolfe Island Old
Timers, like the Saint John Old Timers, were just glad to be
there. In fact, just like the Saint John group, the Wolfe Island
team owed its creation to Gouett's trans-Canada promotional
tour in that fall of 1974. At the time, thirty-eight-year-old Sid
Fawcett was commuting on weekends between his home on
Wolfe Island (near Kingston on the St. Lawrence) and his job
with a car leasing firm in St. Catharines; on one trip he picked
up the *Toronto Star* and read about the Gouett/Aherne effort
to organize the COHA and the tournament.

"I never played organized hockey until oldtimers came
along," admits Fawcett. "I was a pond and barnyard hockey
player. Not talented. Tried out for a midget team once and
didn't make it. In fact, I got more on-ice experience in winter
by skating from Wolfe Island to Kingston. That was just part
of growing up on the St. Lawrence. But I never really got
involved in playing organized hockey till John Gouett and
Gerry Aherne."

That's when Sid Fawcett really got the bug. He sent off the
$250 fee to enter the tournament without having even assem-
bled a team.

Through that fall and early winter of 1974–75, Fawcett got
in touch with Joe Hawkins, an engineer on the Wolfe Island
ferry; Sherman Niles, also with the ferry service; Bill Kyle and
Everet Hogan, two local farmers; Bill Larocque, the manager
of the Kraft cheese factory on Wolfe Island; Morley Hunt, a
friend in the construction business; Bruce and Winfield

Woodman (Bruce had once played for the Eastern Hockey League's Clinton Comets and Winfield was Sid's neighbour); Eddie Deans, who worked at Queen's University; Bob and Vince MacDonald, a couple of commercial painters; Bud Anson, a civil servant with the Ministry of Transportation; and a goalie from Gananoque named Norm Parrish. The fourteen new teammates rented some ice and formed the Wolfe Island Old Timers hockey club.

The team's sole purpose was to play "for the fun of it."

However, they got off to a slow start. Between November and February, exhibition games were hard to come by. Old-timers' teams were few and far between. But the team staged a few dances, landed a $200 donation from Harry Jemmitt, a Kingston insurance agent, and managed to assemble matching sweaters for the fourteen players. Ironically, their first fullfledged game was an exhibition match against the old-timers in Ennismore. "So we rented a bus," Fawcett recalls, "packed a few cases of beer, took our wives, partied all the way up there, had a great 8–8 game with Ennismore and partied all the way home. It was our first official road trip."

At the tournament, however, after winning games against oldtimers' teams from Aurora, East Gwillimbury and Toronto-Lakeshore, the Wolfe Island Old Timers lost to Corner Brook and saw their exhibition opponents—the Ennismore Old Timers—win the entire C Division.

"Never mind. In this, our first-ever tournament," Fawcett insists, "we won our first three games. I don't know how we did it. I even scored one into our own net. I think I was trying to clear the puck from the goal crease and I drove it into our own net. But even Wayne Gretzky has done that!

"What was important about that tournament, though, was the way it was organized; everybody had a chance to win. It was great. Here we were, just a bunch of barnyard hockey players. But we belonged to a team. And as soon as the last game of the day was over, we'd party. We'd bring our wives and children, take over a restaurant in Peterborough, have a few bottles of wine and a great feed and the high jinks would go on all night."

As successful as the players found the tournament, not everything went absolutely smoothly behind the scenes. Among the
myriad problems John Gouett had to resolve was an omission
in the rule book about how to settle tie games in the divisional
playoffs. At one point he had to eject former NHL tough guy
John Ferguson for fighting. Then he had to disqualify an
entire team from Alberta for stacking the roster with six former professionals who were playing entire games while the
original team members sat on the bench. Gouett and Aherne
had promised themselves that no team would finish a game at
any of the arenas without a case of cold beer waiting for them,
but to fulfill that promise Gouett had to drive a truck around
to all the arenas at three o'clock in the morning to replenish
supplies. And in the middle of it all Gouett had to smile for
the movie cameras; a film crew from Montreal had arrived to
document the tournament from the on-ice play to crowd and
bench scenes to dressing room banter; the working title of the
film was *For the Fun of It*. And John Gouett survived it all.

"John is a wonderful dreamer," claims Dave Tatham, the
man who did more to document that moment in hockey history than anyone. "John endured a lot of ups and downs in the
beginning of oldtimers. Somebody said, before he met John,
that he visualized Gouett as a big, scarred hockey player. Then
he met him and realized he looks more like a Wally Cox or a
Barney Fife character—a short, quiet man....Despite all the
problems in the early days of the COHA, John was always
cheerful and doing okay."

Dave Tatham almost qualified to play at that first-ever oldtimers' hockey tournament being nearly thirty-five at the
time. And he had also played the right kind of hockey—road
hockey as a kid, and recreational hockey with adult friends
on Friday nights. But from the age of fourteen Dave Tatham
had had torsion duistonia, a neurological disorder that left
the muscles in his neck and down his right side nearly always
contracted.

Still, his disability never interfered with his love affair with
hockey. As a boy, one of his biggest thrills was sitting in Maple
Leaf Gardens and admiring Leafs' face-off expert Ted
Kennedy in the final season of his career. Dave distinctly

recalls hearing the loyal Leaf fan up in the greys shouting, "Come oooon, Teeder!" In fact, Tatham was also at the first game after Kennedy retired when everybody wondered what this Teeder Kennedy fan would do. During the third period it happened. The voice boomed through a momentary silence, "Come oooon..." And he stopped. Then he simply yelled, "Let's go, Leafs!" Teeder was truly gone.

Images like these pushed Dave Tatham into sports writing. He worked in Florida for a while at the *Palm Beach Post Times*, later in the Bahamas and then back in Toronto. By 1972 he was writing freelance material for the *Peterborough Examiner*. When he heard about John Gouett's scheme to bring hundreds of adult recreational hockey players to Peterborough for a national tournament, he pitched the story to Toronto's *Globe and Mail*. They accepted.

"I love sports. I'm a true fan...a hockey junkie," admits Tatham. "And in the beginning I sat there in the stands keeping stats—goals, assists, shots on goal, penalties, power plays.

"But that stuff's dry as dust. Boring. Besides, I realized the actual games were really only for the players. There weren't that many fans. So the noise was gone. The puck didn't smash off the glass from a slapshot. Players weren't slamming each other into the boards. The NHL intensity wasn't there."

Instead of gathering statistics, Tatham decided to gather stories. He planted himself at the end of team benches, sat among the rink rats, wandered into dressing rooms and eavesdropped on the lies told over quantities of beer and post-game cigarettes. Along with some results from the tournament Tatham filed feature stories to the *Globe* on retired RCAF captain Randy Ellis and his wife Helen who were attending the event; former Boston Bruin and lacrosse hero Jack Bionda (who "was so out of shape, he was practically skating on his tongue"); and Don Shutt, the uncle of Canadiens' left-winger Steve Shutt, who joined the Huntsville Hucksters Oldtimers for the tournament. And he documented the trials of Gouett and Aherne trying to make the whole scheme work.

"There'd been teams of guys playing hockey independent of each other all over the country," said Tatham. "But what

they needed was somebody to put it all together...somebody
to give them a focus...create an association and a tournament. You know...'Build it and they will come.' And that's
about what happened. That's what Gouett and Aherne did."

The Peterborough experiment did many things. It was a
catalyst for oldtimers' teams and individual players to get
together, lace on the skates and play the game of their boyhood. It rekindled a lot of old friendships and generated new
ones. It demonstrated the viability of an oldtimers' hockey
association and the potential marketability of annual tournaments. Unfortunately for the original investors—Pat and John
Gouett, and Gerry Aherne—the first tournament made no
money. It didn't even break even. When the bills were paid
and the receipts counted, the First Annual National Oldtimers' Hockey Tournament had put its parent association,
the COHA, into the red by about $10,000.

However, by the summer of 1975, Gouett and Aherne
were already making plans for the second annual tournament
in Lethbridge, Alberta, as well as an international tournament abroad. Travel agencies were suddenly interested.
Hockey equipment manufacturers and beer companies were
now aware of the COHA. And Dave Tatham found himself
with a pile of great oldtimers' stories and no place to print
them. He called Gouett and out of that conversation came
the promise of start-up money, advertising, a string of corre-
spondents across Canada and the creation of *Canadian Oldtimers' Hockey News*.

The first edition, published in October, 1975, went out to
the growing number of member teams and players in the
COHA. It carried a banner announcement of the paper's
publication, a front page story about those hot Toronto Italian
Oldtimers winning the first-ever International Senior
Olympics in (of all places) Santa Rosa, California. There were
photos from the first oldtimers' tournament, letters of grati-
tude from participants and an ad selling copies of the now
completed film, *For the Fun of It*. A cartoon showed pucks
whizzing past a goaltender with Coke-bottle glasses. A poem
described oldtimers as "youngtimers, who've just begun to
recapture the spirit of living." And in COHA executive direc-

tor John Gouett's column, he described the momentum of the oldtimers' movement:

"Thousands of hockey players across Canada will be involved in COHA sponsored tournaments in 1976. Hockey players in the age range of 35 to 65 years will actively participate under the new modified recreational hockey rules....

"But it is not just the changing of the playing rules that has attracted these men....It is their love of the game of hockey."

THREE

"Use the Magic"

Debate about oldtimers' hockey at the semi-annual meeting of the Canadian Amateur Hockey Association in Toronto, in December, 1975, was lively. John Gouett, the executive director of the newly formed Canadian Oldtimers' Hockey Association, presented a brief asking the CAHA to accept the COHA as a fullfledged member of the body that governs recreational hockey in Canada.

"Oldtimers' hockey will have nothing but a detrimental effect on the game," warned one CAHA delegate. "There won't be a minute of ice time left for the kids."

"Oldtimers' hockey will destroy minor hockey," claimed another.

It took Gouett another five years to convince the CAHA that oldtimers' hockey would do no such thing. That oldtimers' hockey would promote amateur play at all levels, among all ages and for both men and women. That its members would provide future coaches for minor hockey. And that oldtimer hockey players would support financially strapped arenas by renting ice at times when minor hockey players would never want it. John Gouett was a staunch advocate. And he wouldn't be denied.

Even though the First National Oldtimers' Hockey Tournament had left its parent organization, the COHA, in debt, Gouett and Gerry Aherne continued to promote the concept. Under the banner "Participation, Fellowship and Friendly Competition," Gouett set up a COHA office in Peterborough. He secured an annual operating grant of $50,000 from Recreation Canada and used that money to hire ten employees for the day-to-day operation of the office. And he hired Dave Tatham to continue publishing the *Canadian Old-timers' Hockey News*, the official voice of the COHA.

Together the office, the executive and the paper carried out the COHA's primary function—recruiting players and teams for the association, and sanctioning national and regional old-timers' tournaments. The 1976 program included the Can-Am International Tournament in Niagara Falls, Ontario, in January, the Second National Tournament in Lethbridge, Alberta, in February and, to nearly everyone's amazement, an International European Tournament in Holland in March.

"Somebody just brought it up," explains Gerry Aherne. "Wouldn't it be nice to have a tournament overseas some-where? And we began looking at Holland because Canadians were seen so favourably in Holland during the Second World War."

Since the war, the Dutch have considered Canadians their "liberators," but this second invasion of Holland by thirty-two Canadian teams of oldtimers, one American team and nine European teams required almost as much planning and preparation. So John Gouett packed his bags and began barn-storming again; he made seven trips to Holland between the summer of 1975 and the tournament's first face-off on March 13, 1976.

Gouett met with Freddy Schweers of the Dutch Ice Hockey Federation to build a tournament committee overseas. With the Peterborough experience behind him, Gouett helped Dutch officials schedule more than a hundred games at their four arenas in Amsterdam, The Hague, Utrecht and Tilburg. On one trip Gouett even recruited ex-Maple Leaf Dick Duff to help organize a pre-tournament exhibition game between Team Canada oldtimers and Team Holland oldtimers. And on another trip, he introduced European officials to Jim Orr, COHA referee-in-chief, to bring them up to speed on Cana-dian oldtimers' rules and the nature of oldtimers' play.

The tournament was a success. The Canadians loved play-ing oldtimers' hockey in Europe. So did the American team, the West Covina Eagles from Los Angeles. And, while the European teams were few in number and limited in experience, they also seemed to take to this new phenomenon. For many North American oldtimers, it was their first opportunity to travel to Europe and to play on the larger European ice surfaces. They were bound and determined to enjoy themselves, win or lose.

"I had never been to Europe," said *Canadian Oldtimers' Hockey News* reporter Dave Tatham. "But it was incredible. Seven jet planes arrive in Amsterdam with about 1,500 people aboard. And all that hockey gear tumbling in.

"I remember the guy at the airport saying, 'You don't shoot guns anymore. You shoot pucks this time.' And the fans...it was like a love affair. They just couldn't do enough.

"We landed as wacky, tacky tourists, with our wild colours and our cow bells. We hit the arenas with a real commotion, yelling and chanting. And after a major win, our teams would shoot champagne all over like it was the Stanley Cup....We were the crazy Canadians."

The final scores, the game outcomes were almost secondary. The oldtimers' families traded pins furiously. One fan of the Sudbury Oldtimers, Oliver Korpela, whose Lancaster bomber had been shot down over Holland during the Second World War, was reunited with the members of the Dutch underground who had hidden him for seven months. A Newfoundland team took over a bar, performed on accordion, banjo and guitar, and drank the place dry—seven nights in a row. And while the language was initially a barrier, most Canadians managed to communicate quite successfully, except for the player who, after a few drinks, took out his guilders to pay the bill at an Amsterdam bar and asked, "How many gliders and sliders for that?"

On the ice, perhaps the most memorable match-up featured two A Division rivals—the Mount Royal X's and the North Bay Sealtest Oldtimers. The X's had been regulars on the oldtimers' circuit since Lew Greenberg entered the team in the Pointe Claire tournaments of the late 1960s. Among Greenberg's hand-picked players on the Dutch trip were ex-pros such as former Montreal Canadiens' defenceman Junior

Langlois and one-time St. Louis Blues' defenceman Ray Fortin. The X's arrived in Holland fresh from a tournament victory in Niagara Falls earlier that winter.

North Bay's roster included ex-Boston Bruins' right-winger Leo Labine, known "more as a needler than a scorer," Moe Mantha from the Montreal farm system, AHL forty-goal scorer Boris Elik of the Cleveland Barons and a couple of brothers of famous players—Gerry Horton (brother of the late Maple Leaf, Tim) and Tony Odrowski (brother of Gerry, a Red Wing). Despite the superior number of name players, North Bay was crushed by Mount Royal 8–1 in the round robin portion of the tournament.

"North Bay and the X's met again in the final of the A Division," remembers Dave Tatham. "Well, Mount Royal jumps into an early 2–0 lead. They had won nineteen consecutive games in tournaments that year.

"Surgeon Jack Stackhouse was in the North Bay net and he performed miracles after that....Anyway, the final score was 4–2 for North Bay. Of course, the team goes crazy....But the big story was that somebody called home from Amsterdam with the news. And they piped it right through to the North Bay arena where a junior game was going on. They announced that North Bay were World Champions in the A Division...and the whole place went nuts."

The COHA had done it again. Despite the odds, this young organization, operating at a deficit and by the grace of a small staff, had managed another logistical coup, this time on the international stage. Oldtimers' hockey was no longer parochial; it was widespread, popular and even a spectator sport. This first Dutch tournament would prove to be a precedent. COHA-sanctioned international tournaments would soon take place in such locations as Switzerland, Denmark, Japan and Scotland. In fact, with this tournament, Gouett and Aherne had opened the door to perhaps the one money-making dimension of the entire concept—arranging international travel packages for oldtimers with disposable income. Otherwise, the venture still suffered from its initial problem. Oldtimers' hockey was not financially viable. Not yet, anyway.

Even though the financial health of the umbrella COHA was questionable through 1975–76, its first year of operation, the heart of the movement grew stronger.

In the birthplace of national oldtimers' hockey, the Peterborough Petes Oldtimers met a team of NHL oldtimers that included Cal Gardner, Harry "Whipper" Watson, Danny Lewicki, Andy Bathgate, Hughie Bolton, Jack Hamilton and broadcaster Brian McFarlane; the NHL beat the Petes 10–6. The brand-new Ontario Oldtimers' Association organized its first annual invitational in November with thirty-two teams competing. In December, the Aurora Church Dodgers arranged for two teams of Swedish oldtimers to tour and play exhibition games across southern Ontario. That winter the newly formed B.C. Oldtimers' Association staged its first annual Pacific Oldtimers' Hockey Tournament in Campbell River on Vancouver Island. More than 1,200 players attended the CanAm Tournament in Niagara Falls, and Wintario, the Ontario lottery, kicked in $4,000 to help Ontario oldtimers travel to the Second National Tournament in Lethbridge in February.

Reporter Dave Tatham was on the move constantly, covering new teams, new tournaments and the growth of the game across the country. The increasing number of pages in each issue of the *Canadian Oldtimers' Hockey News* revealed a recreational explosion.

"Groups of guys who had been playing on Thursday nights or Sunday afternoons suddenly started coming together. …Gouett and Aherne went out and beat the bushes to build this thing. In fact," recalls Tatham, "I think two or three weeks before the Second National Tournament in Lethbridge, there wasn't an Alberta oldtimer team in the lineup. They went out and found [one].

"Same thing in 1977 at the Third National held in Saint John. John discovered there were hardly any teams from New Brunswick so Gerry and another guy were parachuted in there on special assignment. They rented cars, fanned out and hit the arenas. They'd find the older recreational players. Strategy was, be salesmen, be creative.

"So they'd go to a small town and ask, 'You guys going to the National Tournament in Saint John?'

"If they said, 'No. Don't think so,' then the line was, 'Well, the guys down in that really small town Such-and-such, they're going.'

"And they'd reply, 'Well, if they're going, we're going.'

"That's how the teams came together. They were just patchwork teams that suddenly got organized. And, of course, after being exposed to just one tournament, suddenly these disorganized teams would pop up in matching jackets with team buttons to hand out at the next tournament."

By 1980, the Canadian Oldtimers' Hockey Association was about 300 teams strong. Its tournament schedule had grown from three annual competitions to five regional cup tournaments (Atlantic, Quebec, Great Lakes, Prairie and Pacific) a National Cup, several North American and European challenges and even a World Cup match. Dave Tatham was grinding out nine sixteen-page issues of the *Oldtimers' News* each year, including editions through the summer, with almost as many tournament scores and ads as articles about the players and the game. Some younger teams—even those under age twenty-five—wanted to know if they could use COHA rules to establish their own leagues.

But by 1980, Gerry Aherne and John Gouett were burnt out. Five years of barnstorming, assigning personal assets and orchestrating Canadian and European tournaments had taken their toll, not to mention a financial bite. The COHA was operating on a $164,000 deficit. Worse, the federal Department of Health and Welfare, through its Recreation Canada branch, had cut off the COHA's annual stipend of $50,000 for running the Peterborough office.

Fortunately, John Gouett's connections in amateur hockey gave the COHA a chance at a new lease on life. On May 8, 1979, Iona Campagnolo, the Minister of State for Fitness and Amateur Sport, released a report known as "The Canadian Hockey Review." It was an exhaustive study of the "malaise permeating the entire Canadian hockey system," and it included nearly forty recommendations concerning the rules, officiating, coaching, and the structures and organizations governing amateur hockey. One committee had examined violence in hockey. John Gouett had sat on that committee along with former NHL player and L.A. Kings coach Larry Regan. After Regan finished his term as executive director of the report committee, instead of going back into retirement, he agreed to take over as executive director of the COHA.

At forty-nine, Regan had all the right credentials for the job. He had on-ice experience—with the Bruins and the Leafs in the late 1950s. He had worked behind the bench as coach of the AHL Pittsburgh Hornets and as the coach and general manager of the L.A. Kings, and he had spent three seasons coaching in Austria. Moreover, he had a profile in Ottawa having grown up in the capital and having steered the federal government's report on amateur hockey.

The Ottawa connection proved invaluable immediately. Regan convinced the COHA to move its head office to Ottawa; through his connections to the federal government, he got the COHA free office space and the use of telephones at Fitness Canada during the transition. But that was essentially housekeeping. What oldtimers' hockey really needed was a revenue base and a higher profile. It needed to be marketed.

Regan began knocking on doors—the corporate doors of potential sponsors—at Cooper Canada, Air Canada, Imperial Oil and the distillers and brewers. "The big thing that sold them," he says, "was that we were representing households. Everyone thirty-five and over was head of a household with buying power....And oldtimers' hockey was cheaper than belonging to a golf or tennis club so it was a bigger market.... We played up the social aspect of the game....Whether they were playing in tournaments or pick-up on the weekends, oldtimers had discretionary income."

Potential sponsors were quick to realize the possibilities in new hockey equipment purchases, travel packages and beer sales among oldtimers' hockey players. Regan's new marketing thrust seemed to work for both sides of the equation. Before long the COHA's membership was expanding. It grew from 300 teams in 1980 to 3,000 in 1990. The COHA's corporate sponsorship increased proportionally; in time, Regan and the Ottawa-based COHA boosted Labatt's sponsorship from $50,000 to $450,000 per year. By 1988, the Canadian Oldtimers' Hockey Association had moved to the Ottawa suburb of Gloucester and into offices in a new complex housing other federally supported amateur sport associations.

By that time, the COHA was able to offer member teams invitations to regional, national and international tournaments; economical medical and dental insurance; low-cost travel to the tournaments; standard rules and regulations on the ice; referee clinics; and free subscriptions to the old-timers' newspaper. And yet, despite the corporate and government support, the growth of the COHA continued to rely on the "barnstorming" techniques that Gouett and Aherne had pioneered.

"We had to get the word out that it was in oldtimers' best interests to belong," says Dick Cordick, who became the COHA's referee-in-chief in 1981. "We had to get them to believe that if you establish rules, establish discipline, encourage sponsorships and build a fraternity, you make a real hockey movement happen.

"That's all ideas. That's how I sold life insurance. I wasn't selling apples and oranges. I was selling an idea."

Dick Cordick's résumé contains much more than simply selling life insurance, and hockey was never far from its centre. Born and raised during the Depression in Perth, Ontario, Dick was weaned on the Maple Leafs, Bee Hive Corn Syrup hockey pictures and the junior hockey of the Perth Blue Wings at the arena on Friday nights. While he sold insurance and later joined the RCAF in 1948, he also played a little industrial hockey not far from CFB Borden near Barrie, Ontario, until his wife suggested he stop to let the cuts and bruises heal. That's when he took up refereeing—church hockey, minor hockey, Legion hockey, OHA junior hockey, and even working the lines for the WHA.

Actually, refereeing could also be a rough and tumble occupation. One night during a junior game in Hull, "before they'd finished 'O Canada,'" Cordick recalls, "I had three fights going." As a referee for both amateur and professional hockey, Cordick learned that no matter what calibre the game was, when someone dropped the puck and someone kept score, there would always be competition. Consequently, there would always be players who found it difficult to adapt to oldtimers' hockey "where when you knock somebody down, you're supposed to stop and help him up."

Getting that message out fell to Dick Cordick and COHA program co-ordinator Peter Giroux. During a two-week period in 1981, they went into oldtimers' dressing rooms and rented halls in fifteen different cities from Toronto to Dawson Creek to attract players and teams to the COHA "where hockey is fun." Along the way, they beat the bushes for undiscovered pockets of oldtimers, chatted up the benefits of COHA membership and promoted upcoming tournaments.

But Cordick had an ulterior motive for being along on this "grass-roots" trip. There was a growing concern among some oldtimers that the officiating left a lot to be desired. In fact, grumbling about inept refereeing at the second annual Great Lakes Cup in London, Ontario, had prompted the COHA to reassign some refs and remove others during the tournament.

"Because it's recreational hockey," says Cordick, "the officials have to be part of the fun of the game and [be able] to communicate with the oldtimers, but at the same time enforce the rules." So, as he and Giroux crisscrossed the country, Cordick was taking stock of the refereeing. The results of his research prompted a series of clinics for referees at which attendance was mandatory.

At least one stop along the way must have done Dick Cordick's heart good. In Saskatchewan, "where they drive a hundred miles just to say hello to you," Cordick found oldtimers' groups thriving. Saskatoon in particular was a hotbed of activity. From as early as 1976–77, teams such as the River Heights Mixers, the Eastview Flyers, the Saskatoon Berries, the Nu Centrals and the Saskatoon Wesleys had been fixtures at Saskatoon arenas. Officiating was in good shape too. By the late-1970s there was even a Saskatoon Oldtimers' Referees Association, and its referee-in-chief was another hockey stalwart.

Gord Wintermute, at least in his youth, was not obvious referee material. Even he admits to being a rough player when he played senior hockey in Winnipeg and Junior B hockey in Transcona, Manitoba; he often dropped the gloves, squared off and scrapped on the ice. But once he had completed his apprenticeship as a machinist with the CNR in Manitoba in the 1950s, Gord settled down in Saskatoon to work and raise a family. In the sixties he got involved in minor hockey, coaching his own two sons, Robin and Kurtis.

"I even took the whistle and ref's jersey along sometimes to help minor hockey out on the outdoor rinks," says Wintermute. "It's a time I'll never forget. Putting my skates on in a snowbank because the rink manager didn't open up the change shack. Standing out there when it was thirty below in a forty-mile-an-hour wind. You wonder if your head is in the right place or not."

Wintermute still hadn't learned to say no by the time adult recreational and oldtimers' hockey came on stream in Saskatoon. Once teams found out he was available, Wintermute's telephone would often ring day or night, and the voice on the line would simply say, "Gord, we've got ice at eleven o'clock tonight. Would you come out and blow the whistle for us?" And more often than not he would.

But "blow the whistle" was the only thing oldtimers' refs did in the beginning. They had few rules, regulations or guidelines for officiating an oldtimers' game, and no way to deal with disciplinary matters. So referees like Gord Wintermute just improvised until one year, "I persuaded the COHA to fly [then] referee-in-chief Jim Orr out here....I don't know why the COHA did it. They were broke at the time....Anyway, I picked him up at the airport, he gave the clinic and flew back that night.

"I'd brought in fifteen guys I thought would make good refs...guys who were old enough to be oldtimers but still able to skate. Some of them had never refereed before. I think it was the first ref clinic, certainly the first COHA ref clinic, ever held."

Eventually, every working oldtimers' official in Saskatoon had to attend an annual "level three" seminar, be tested on rule and regulation changes and pay an insurance fee before being able to step on the ice to referee a game. By the time oldtimers' hockey in Saskatoon had become an official association, there were disciplinary guidelines to deal with on-ice player misconduct and a board of suspensions. Before long, referee-in-chief Wintermute was assigning referees to nearly 2,000 games a season.

But despite all of Wintermute's refereeing from behind a desk, he still jumped at the chance to grab his whistle and ref's jersey and actually officiate oldtimers' games. His own personal philosophy of refereeing was simple: "Treat disrespect with respect." Inevitably players and fans would disagree with a call. Inevitably refs and oldtimers would argue. But no matter the circumstance, Wintermute never stooped to verbal confrontations with the players or fans because "nothing pisses off a hockey player more than when you won't get down to his level of disrespect."

Of all the season's highlights, Gord Wintermute took most pleasure in working Hans Nickel's annual Nu Central Oldtimers Hockey Tournament, one of the oldest and largest regional oldtimers' competitions in North America. Each January since 1977, Nickel had attracted more than two hundred teams for a six-day tournament in Saskatoon and a half-dozen surrounding communities. Here was the essence of oldtimers' hockey—spirited competition in small town arenas where even in indoor rinks the mercury could drop to near-Arctic levels.

"Pay wasn't great," Wintermute recalls, "but we did it for the fun of it....I remember doing the tournament one year. It was the third day. I remember going to Waldheim, where it was so cold and windy, we could feel the wind inside the arena. The ice was cracking it was so cold. But as usual everybody was having a great time.

"It was near the end of the tournament and I was reffing a game with two Saskatoon teams in it so I knew I could have a little fun with them. I had arranged for the canteen girl to cook me up a special biscuit; it was coloured, shaped and sized to look just like a puck.

"Of course, this was a final game, so everybody's really serious. They play 'O Canada.' Everybody's standing, the whole bit....Now, in those days nobody wore helmets. So I came out on the ice with a lady's blond wig, a pair of dark sunglasses, a little makeup and this biscuit.

"I get the two centremen to the face-off circle and I drop

this puck...and of course it goes fifteen ways to Sunday. I mean it was a perfect hit. It just shattered. And here were ten guys on the ice, all keyed up, suddenly chasing ten different pieces of this biscuit. And everybody figured he had the puck!"

Referee Gord Wintermute was eventually inducted into the COHA-sponsored International Oldtimers' Sports Hall of Fame where he joined his longtime friend Hans Nickel, inducted as an oldtimers' builder in 1983. But despite the honour and distinction of the award, Wintermute continues to respond to those late evening calls to "come out and blow the whistle." He grabs his skates and referee's jersey.

"When'll you be home?" his wife asks.

"It'll probably be close to midnight," he says. And Gord Wintermute heads for the arena. It's a reflex he'll never shake.

As the COHA came to life and grew, so did hundreds of grass-roots oldtimers' teams all over the country. One of them was born in a rink shack in Saskatoon's north end. As school teacher Rich Meier remembers it, in the fall of 1977, some-body called a Saturday afternoon meeting at the change shack adjacent to River Heights Elementary School. About forty men ranging in age from their late twenties to their mid-forties gathered to talk about starting up an oldtimers' hockey team.

Some had come to the meeting to help organize. Others were simply curious. But each had once played hockey and the thought of picking up the game again was too tantalizing to pass up. Rich Meier was typical. Born and raised in Saska-toon, he and his older brother, Rod, had played lots of hockey as kids. They loved it. But by the time he reached high school, Rich had stopped skating or playing competitively. From thir-teen to nearly thirty he had put hockey aside—until that Sat-urday afternoon in River Heights.

"The rink shack was packed," says Meier. "And it was kind of comical. There was a lot of posturing going on. First-timers who just wanted to be on a team. And those who wanted to get involved in organizing it....All of a sudden somebody comes in and, because he owns his own goalie pads, he's going to be the goalie of this new team. Didn't matter how good he was.

"So basically the meeting turned out: 'Give us your name, your phone number and don't call us, we'll call you,' kind of thing....No one really took ownership for organizing or coaching the team. We were no different from anybody else at the time. All we wanted to do was drop the puck and have a game."

The first puck was dropped that winter at Saskatoon's Lions Arena, one of the smallest rinks in the city. It was so small that the four and a half forward lines, four sets of defence and two goalies had to take turns changing into their equipment in the arena's dressing room. And not only was it crowded in the dressing room, but each player's ice time was limited. Soon Rich Meier and some others decided to form a team of their own.

A number of Rich Meier's friends, neighbours and working acquaintances, people who either lived or worked in the north end of the city, were among those who decided to break away. Two of Meier's neighbours, Bill Bahr, who ran a clothing store, and Dennis Krochak, who owned an environmental management firm, joined him. So did a steel worker named Arvid Nillson; Ray Perrey, the sales manager of a truck sales company; Jack Merrick, whose job with a supply firm often had him travelling to the Yukon and the Northwest Territories; Skip Wright, who owned a steel erecting firm; Morris Zuk, chief controller of a sheet metal manufacturer; and Gerry Metz, who managed a concrete ready-mix company.

Metz's ready-mix concrete company sponsored the team with a set of sweaters, and the River Heights Mixers oldtimers' hockey club was born.

During the winter of 1977 and each winter after, the Mixers played among themselves every Sunday at the Archibald Arena in River Heights. Before long they were also playing other newly formed oldtimers' teams, such as the Nu Centrals, the Saskatoon Berries, the Eastview Flyers and the Saskatoon Wesleys. The Mixers became part of the Saskatoon Central Men's Hockey Association.

Playing in the Saskatoon league never diminished the pleasure and enjoyment the Mixers derived from their regular Sunday games. Quickly, this cross section of professionals, store owners, managers, labourers and salesmen meshed into a close-knit group of friends who gathered every week to play the game they loved.

In the dressing room, the Mixers' idiosyncrasies became evident. Clothier Bill Bahr always brought his change of clothes in a separate bag so that they never touched his smelly hockey gear. Goalie Jack Merrick couldn't care less about such niceties; he never washed his equipment and when he pulled his alternate jersey from his hockey bag it smelled so bad, "it would bring tears to your eyes." Ray Perrey was a little hard of hearing and took a lot of abuse when he missed the punch line of a joke. And Dave Killam was so slow getting out of his gear at the end of a game that everybody else would have stripped, showered and changed before Killam had even untied a skate lace; he would "rehash the game, tell a few stories and savour the dressing room atmosphere."

On the ice, the Mixers' playing styles emerged. The team came to depend on Bill Bahr, who'd played some junior hockey as a teenager, as well as two later additions to the team, brothers Bruce and Barney Folkersen. Barney was extremely competitive and yelled at his teammates, especially his brother, when they made mistakes.

In contrast, netminder Jack Merrick never took a game seriously; he claimed his best defence was "to get the hell out of the way!" The Mixers figured they had to score at least seven or eight goals in just about every game because usually the opposition was good for five or six goals against Jack.

There was one intangible asset the Mixers came to depend on—the spirit of Morris Zuk. Zuk was one of the originals who had helped to organize the team in 1977. From day one, he never missed a game and was always on time. Perhaps more than any other team member, Morris Zuk was dedicated to oldtimers' hockey and the Mixers. That dedication may have come from a childhood in Wakaw, Saskatchewan, and the Zuk household where kids gathered regularly for road hockey in the summer and ice hockey in the winter. It might have come from a close friendship with his younger brother Wayne, who had played for the WHA Edmonton Oilers and eventually played a few games as an oldtimer as Morris's defence partner.

It may have developed as a personal antidote to the stress and pressure of running the financial affairs (and later owning) a successful sheet metal business in Saskatoon.

Wherever Morris's passion for hockey came from, that passion was not reflected in his hockey equipment. Despite his comfortable lifestyle and job, Zuk always used to say of his nearly bladeless, rivetless skates, "Oh, they'll do me one more year."

Morris Zuk was a solid, though not dazzling defenceman. He tended to be on the quiet side, offering only the occasional joke or good-natured jab at his teammates. Even on the ice he wasn't terribly vocal. But when his team was down a goal or two, Zuk would encourage his teammates by calling out, "Use the magic, boys. It's time to use the Mixer magic."

While Morris's "magic" didn't always save the day, it usually buoyed the Mixers' spirits, even in the most hopeless situations. But Zuk gave the team more than inspirational words.

"We took a road trip to Minot, North Dakota," Rich Meier recalls. "We had a forty-eight-passenger school bus then. We had a five-gallon pail for a bathroom in the back of the bus. Of course, we were having a few 'pops' along the way. And as it got darker and darker, no one could see what he was doing back there. We were thoroughly disgusted the next morning when everything was frozen to the bus floor.

"Morris said, 'Never again!' He had the boys bring the bus to Harding Industries where he worked and had a full bathroom put into the back of the bus. All of a sudden we had a bona fide travelling bus....We could then take our wives and all the kids along with us. And of course if you go as a group, you get closer as a group. Then, win or lose, what happens is, it's a family outing, a social event."

Wives and families were welcome to participate in just about every aspect of the club's social itinerary—from travelling aboard the remodelled bus, to cheering in the stands, to joining the victors (or losers) in the dressing room.

"When we were on a tournament and the wives wanted to come in," Meier remembers, "one of the women would take somebody's cologne and dash it around or spray some deodorant around the room and into some guy's hockey bags.

They could usually only take it for a minute or two, then they were out of there....One of my fondest memories was each January (three or four of us all celebrated birthdays in January) the door would open and the kids would all stream in to their dads and sing 'Happy Birthday.'"

When the Mixers' season was over Bill Bahr, Dennis Krochak and John McLeod organized and staged the annual Mixers' wives banquet at the Sheraton Cavalier in Saskatoon. They would decorate a convention room at the hotel with balloons, crepe streamers and even a blow-up of the Mixers' logo—a stocky guy on skates drinking from a champagne glass nearly as large as he was. On the blow-up were cut-out stars with pictures of each Mixer team member. And if Rich Meier was feeling ambitious, he would assemble pictures taken during the year and present a half-hour slide show of the year in review.

The evening was strictly a formal affair, with roses presented to the wives at the door, flaming hip of beef served, presentation of awards, introduction of the wives, liqueurs, cigars and dancing afterward. It was the Mixers' way of "paying tribute to the wives," says Meier, "for putting up with us all year.

"It was ladies' night. It became their night. But in addition, because of the contact twice a week and on tournaments where the team jells and the players become a closer group of friends, the women began to feel that too. And the wives also recognized how much fun they could have. They started joining all the crazy things we did as a team."

At one of the Mixers' banquets for the wives, Connie Nillson, Arvid's wife, presented each couple with an album of the year's highlights and high jinks—photographs of the games they had played, the places they had visited for tournaments and the dressing room shenanigans that had gone on that season. She even wrote a poem which included these lines:

> Arvid and I have made many new friends.
> So I really feel hockey does blend.
> It joins the young and the old
> And gets us out into the cold.

The next season will soon be here again.
As we all know they play even when it rains.
But a hockey wife I have become
And glad to be like one of their chums.

Iain MacLean was another original oldtimer in Saskatoon.
Like Rich Meier and company, Iain MacLean had shown up
for the first oldtimers' games at the tiny Lions Arena back in
the mid-1970s. And like Meier, MacLean and a number of
his friends soon wanted more ice time and joined Ron Wallace
who had put together another oldtimers' group—the Eastview Flyers.

However, long before he was a Flyer, Iain MacLean was a
Blackhawk. When Iain's parents moved to Saskatoon after the
Second World War (his father took a teaching position with
the School for the Deaf), the family settled in an area south of
the University of Saskatchewan. From as far back as anyone
in organized Saskatoon school hockey can remember, if you
grew up and played your hockey south of the university, you
wore a Chicago Blackhawks sweater. Just like Saskatoon kids
in Mayfair wore New York Rangers sweaters, in Westmount
Boston Bruins sweaters, in City Park Toronto Maple Leafs
sweaters, in Nutana Montreal Canadiens sweaters and in the
downtown area Detroit Red Wings sweaters.

So, back in the 1950s, whether he wanted to or not, Iain
MacLean and his identical twin brother Alaistair became peewees wearing the colours of the Chicago Blackhawks. In those
days, Alaistair and Iain played shinny on the outdoor ice surface at Victoria Public School early in the morning, over lunch
and after school. "It was a really intimidating form of shinny,"
says Alaistair, "with kids ranging in age from eight to twenty."

"Just skates, gloves, sticks. No full equipment," adds Iain.
"We had goaltenders; you'd alternate holding a goal stick in
goal. But no raising. And if you wanted to keep the puck,
there was only one way to do it. You learned how to stickhandle. It was real scrub pick-up hockey."

However, Saskatoon peewees got their chance to shine on
Friday nights. From six to ten o'clock the city's Kinsmen
organized a city-wide league on the only indoor ice surface in

the city, the Saskatoon Arena. Here, the traditional rivalries of the six-team NHL were played out by eleven-year-olds. That is, of course, if your peewee card was signed. Kinsmen hockey had a built-in system of youth discipline. No peewee player could compete on Friday night unless his school teacher, his Sunday school teacher and his parents had signed his card indicating unsatisfactory, fair, good or excellent behaviour for the week.

"One unsatisfactory and you didn't play. Two fairs and you didn't play," recalls Alaistair. In the 1955–56 season the MacLean twins must have been angels at home, school and church because they were ever present (and brilliant) on the ice. In the Kinsmen peewee championship game in April, the Saskatoon *StarPhoenix* reported that "the MacLean twins, Al and Iain, figured prominently in the clinching victory for the Hawks. Al scored three times and brother Iain came up with one goal and an assist...as they defeated the Canadiens 5–2."

"We won the championship," Iain recalls, "and they used to have a chicken pot pie banquet at the Bessborough Hotel. They usually had a hockey star come out to it. And that was the first time I ever saw Gordie Howe in person....He seemed huge. He filled his entire suit. I mean, he had no neck; his shoulder started from just below his ears. He was standing over us signing autographs, and it occurred to me that if he leaned forward he would have split his suit jacket all the way down his back. I had never seen anybody physically that large and that strong."

"And it was a coin toss between my brother and me, as to who would be the most valuable player on the team that year," says Alaistair. "I won. And I got the jacket, a cloth jacket with the big black and red Chicago Blackhawks Indian logo on the chest. It was a classic!"

As successful as the MacLean twins were in school-age and even university-level sports (Iain played basketball for the University of Saskatchewan Huskies and Alaistair played hockey for the Saskatoon Junior Quakers), neither put athletics ahead of education. Alaistair studied law and joined a legal firm in Regina, while Iain got a degree in education and ultimately became university secretary at the University of Saskatchewan in Saskatoon. When oldtimers' hockey emerged in the mid-1970s, they both rediscovered the sport.

Iain MacLean was first exposed to oldtimers at the Gordie Howe Arena in Saskatoon. On winter Sunday afternoons from 4:30 to six o'clock, a group gathered to play some pick-up. For Iain it must have seemed like the scrub shinny he and his brother played as kids. No raising. No goalies. Just a sixth skater who stood in net for five minutes and then moved forward to be replaced by a teammate. Twice MacLean broke his skate blade in net trying to stop those hard shots along the ice. But he really took to it. Even when he periodically joined a more competitive tournament team—the Eastview Flyers—he kept that Sunday afternoon appointment at the Gordie Howe Arena.

Alaistair hadn't worn his hockey skates in ten years when he began playing as a spare for tournament teams, including one based at the RCMP barracks in Regina. That team was originally called the Regina Bisons but eventually became known as Hicke's Hookers because they were led by former Montreal Canadiens right-winger Bill Hicke. Just like the River Heights Mixers, Hicke's Hookers thrived on road trips with players, wives and children in a forty-eight-passenger bus, and holidays planned around oldtimers' tournaments in Saskatoon, Edmonton and Victoria.

But it's when the MacLeans play oldtimers together that they have the most fun. And both Iain and Alaistair go out of their way to make sure that happens. At the beginning of each oldtimers' season, winter and summer, each brother sends the other his hockey schedule. When Iain travels to Regina to meet with University of Regina officials, he makes certain the trip includes enough time to join Alaistair for his Thursday night game; similarly, Alaistair "can't remember a winter when I've travelled to Saskatoon and not played hockey with Iain. I schedule my life around my hockey."

When the two MacLeans get together on the ice—even now, beyond their prime—the chemistry is nearly perfect. They understand and employ the principles of the game. Playing shinny together as kids honed their stickhandling and skating skills. The Kinsmen peewee league gave them discipline. And the oldtimers' experience has taught them that it's easier to pass the puck than to skate with it. Maybe because they were born twelve minutes apart on November 21, 1941, they've always sensed they had something extra. If it wasn't evident before, it became crystal clear one Sunday morning when the MacLeans joined an oldtimers' pick-up match at Exhibition Stadium in Saskatoon.

"It was nearly unconscious," explains Iain. "It began when we were very early into the game. Without looking I knew that if I had seen Al a second or a second-and-a-half ago in a particular spot, a second or a second-and-a-half later, I could throw a blind pass and he'd be right where I expected him to be. I couldn't do it with any other player but I could do it with Al."

"We hadn't played together in maybe twenty years," says Alaistair.

"The two of us came down on two defencemen and went in opposite directions," Iain continues. "We crisscrossed at the blueline. Now what a normal player would do would be to try to get in *front* of the net. But I knew Al was coming all the way *around* the net. So I went to my left and I fed a speed pass to the right-hand side of the net. And he came around the net, got there the same time as the puck did and shot it in. The goalie was down and out."

"Shot it into the open net," nods Alaistair.

"We did this sort of thing all game long," Iain adds. "And by the time that game was over, the opposition was just dumbfounded. It was fun."

Richard Schroh took great pleasure in playing with Iain MacLean. The jocular and diminutive netminder used to describe the "elder" MacLean as "Iain with the five-foot arm and the seven-foot stick." They played together in the early days of the Eastview Flyers oldtimers. Schroh relished having Iain and another defenceman, Gordie Cook, in front of him because "with Iain and Gordie on defence, for me it was like sitting in a rocking chair back there. Their long reach helped me block a lot more shots and cover a bigger area."

Schroh hadn't planned to be a goaltender. The oldest of

nine children growing up on a farm near Kerrobert, Saskatchewan, Richard saw himself more as a defenceman than a goalie. But when he moved to Saskatoon he did neither. Instead, he found himself coaching minor league baseball and hockey. In the 1960s, Ron Wallace, an executive with the Saskatchewan Minor Hockey Association, invited Schroh and other coaching fathers to play pick-up hockey after their sons' games.

"We played at night after eight o'clock," Schroh says. "We just used the outdoor rinks. We had a change shack and we'd just use the phone and say, 'Hey, we've got some ice time tonight,' and we'd get a couple of teams together.

"It was pretty rough hockey. Lots of body contact and slapshots. No referees. Not like the oldtimers' rules. In fact, we even developed some of the rules that [the COHA] later wrote into its rule book....We soon took body checking away from the boards and then finally got rid of it all together and eventually got rid of slapshots too....Anyway, we'd play for an hour and a half, an hour if it was cold."

Schroh soon discovered he was destined to be a goalie. It had nothing to do with talent and everything to do with circumstance. As a regular convenor of the impromptu coaches' games, he generally lugged the required goal pads, gloves and chest protector to the change shack for the evening. Inevitably, the designated goalie wouldn't show up, so goaltending fell to the least talented skater of the bunch. Schroh qualified. Finally, one night, about 1979, he arrived and announced, "I don't care what you guys think. I'm tired of carrying this stuff. So if I have to carry it all the time, I might as well play goal all the time."

Richard Schroh actually fit the goalie mould perfectly. His height (even on skates) gave him that Gump Worsley demeanour. To defend against feeling he was the goat in a loss, Schroh always referred to his goaltending gear as his "tools of ignorance." His scientific explanation for a goal scored on his glove side was, "I used to put the glove out and the puck was always in there. Now I put the glove out and it's behind me." However, he was also quick to remind his teammates that "the fastest hands in the world are a goaltender's when he forgets his can [jockstrap and cup]." He didn't mind being called "Sieve" as long as no adjectives preceded the name.

Joking aside, goalies in the early oldtimers' game were just as vulnerable to injury as the pros. During one of his first winters as the team's unofficial goalie, Schroh wore only a plastic mask for protection. One night he took a shot in the face. The mask broke, cut his eye and broke his cheekbone. He feared he would lose his eye or at least have to have surgery to rebuild the socket. Fortunately, his eye repaired itself. Now only occasionally does he close his good eye, look down the rink and see "a hundred guys skating toward me. Worse, about twenty-five pucks. And I don't know which is the real one."

But Richard Schroh's contribution to oldtimers' hockey wasn't limited to his willingness to volunteer, his good-natured clowning on and off the ice or his abilities (good or bad) between the pipes. In the 1980s, when Saskatoon's oldest indoor arena, Exhibition Stadium, suddenly needed someone to maintain the ice surface, Richard Schroh jumped in.

Here was a facility that began life during the First World War as an army barracks, then became a curling rink and finally was turned into a hockey arena. It had seen the likes of Gordie Howe, Glenn Hall, Ed Van Impe and Keith Magnuson. But what it needed desperately in the 1980s was good ice for all the minor, recreational and oldtimers' hockey being played there. While his netminding talents might be questioned, Richard Schroh had all the skills he needed for the stadium job. He was a qualified millwright, a machinist, a licensed mechanic, a high-pressure welder, a gas fitter and, best of all, an improviser.

Instead of ordering a $50,000 Zamboni, Schroh went out and bought a 44 Massey tractor, made a three-point hitch for it, upgraded its hydraulic system and installed a box behind with a cutter blade, a chain to pick up the snow and a tank to flood the ice surface with water, all in one operation.

The oldtimers'-goalie-cum-ice-maintenance-man also learned the science of ice cleaning. Schroh learned to keep the ice high in the centre of the pad (which usually had the greatest wear). He took two to three hours each week to plane the ice lengthwise, widthwise and diagonally to a true level. And, perhaps selfishly, he made sure that his tractor-drawn ice-cleaner put down only as much water in each goal crease as he shaved off snow, "because," says Schroh, "that's where water settles.

"I've played games where three-quarters of the way through the game, there's still a puddle underneath me—and it wasn't just from my sweating in goal either."

Schroh's penchant for improvising and his attention to detail paid off. The 190-foot by eighty-five-foot ice surface at the Exhibition became the preferred rink. Not only was the ice surface fully booked on weeknights and weekends during the winter, it was also receiving regular daytime bookings from the police, CNR workers and Air Canada employees who wanted to play a little recreational hockey over their lunch hour or on weekday afternoons. So, while he didn't improve his game in goal much in those early years, within a couple of seasons Richard Schroh had given Exhibition Stadium a reputation for "the best ice in Saskatoon."

By 1985 oldtimers' hockey in Canada was officially ten years old. The COHA under executive director Larry Regan and a handful of staff was firmly established in Ottawa, growing and gaining credibility with players, teams, sports federations and corporate sponsors. John Gouett and Gerry Aherne were still involved but mostly as organizers of international tournaments.

That October, the curtain went up on a booming old-timers' hockey season in Saskatoon. The local oldtimers' association had about twenty teams registered and, thanks to Gord Wintermute, the oldtimers' referee association had enough certified officials to ref their games. Hans Nickel was making plans for the ninth annual Nu Central tournament. Iain and Alaistair MacLean had already planned which old-timers' games each could attend in the other's city that autumn. Goalie Richard Schroh was working on his ad libs for the dressing room.

The River Heights Mixers headed to Archibald Arena for one of their first scrimmages of the season. As usual Morris

Zuk was among the first in the dressing room. John McLeod's European-style hockey helmet still sported a spike on top (Zuk had fashioned it at his sheet metal business) making McLeod look like a Prussian soldier. Jack Merrick's equipment, unwashed all summer, had its usual sensory impact even if his goaltending didn't. However, he did have a new crop of jokes for his teammates and as usual when he laughed, his face went red, his eyes squinted and his potbelly rolled with laughter. Everybody else was there—Skip, Nordie, the crazy Slovaks and the Hun (Rich Meier).

On the ice, his teammates continued to kid Morris Zuk about his rivetless and now squeaky skates. He still hadn't bothered to get a new pair or even replace the blades. But they dropped the puck and the game was the thing.

"Then somebody noticed Morris skating toward the bench," Meier recalls. "The game was going on and Morris was skating toward the bench. And maybe six feet in front of the box he collapsed."

The game stopped and players gathered round. Zuk was gasping for air. Someone thought he might be choking on something. On his knees, Meier checked for an obstruction in Morris's throat and started giving him mouth-to-mouth resuscitation. A firefighter from the other team began pushing in rhythm on Zuk's chest until an ambulance arrived. Meier thought he could feel a pulse.

As they placed Zuk in the back of the ambulance, Skip Wright, his skates still on, climbed in beside Morris. The paramedics protested but Wright insisted he wanted to make sure they did the best for his friend.

Most of the Mixers just ripped off their skates and followed the ambulance to the hospital. Rich Meier was partly in shock and feeling the physical after-effects of trying to resuscitate his teammate. He quickly cleaned up and phoned the Zuk family.

When Wayne Zuk, Morris's younger brother, got the call, he figured the injury must be serious and hurried to the hospital. He found Meier and the other Mixers waiting. In a smaller adjoining room Wayne met with doctors and Morris's wife, Marian, and "then I went in to see him. There was

Morris, dressed in his Mixer uniform, lying on the table. And something came back to me.

"Morris had once said, 'If I can't play hockey, what the hell's the use of living?' That comment flashed back to me the moment I saw him in his hockey gear. It was all so devastating on the one hand—wife and two children—but on the other, he had died doing something he loved."

They believe he died of an aneurysm.

It was October 8. Morris Zuk had celebrated his forty-second birthday with his family the day before. His brother Wayne had given him a new hockey stick as a birthday present but Morris never got to use it. Wayne Zuk admits he had difficulty relating to his brother's passion for oldtimers.

"These guys were a unique phenomenon," says Wayne Zuk. "I had played some fairly good hockey and then I catch wind of oldtimers. At first, I couldn't understand. They were far too serious on the ice for me. They wanted to play in tournaments every week and three games a week in the league. I couldn't keep up.

"But Morris and I played maybe three games together. It was neat, playing defence together, backing him up, feeding passes to him…like Mark and Marty playing with Gordie Howe. Morris was my closest friend."

At Morris Zuk's funeral, the River Heights Mixers were there en masse. The eulogy included stories about Morris's exploits with the team. The players and their wives helped organize the ceremony and the reception after. Years later, the friendships between Morris's family and the Mixers remain close.

The Mixers retired Zuk's number seven sweater. The Mixer wives published a cookbook, using Morris's familiar phrase of encouragement as its title *Mixer Magic*. And each year since Morris's death, the Mixers ask referee Gord Wintermute to choose a Saskatoon oldtimer who, like Morris Zuk, "most exemplifies the spirit of oldtimers' fair play, sportsmanship and camaraderie."

Iain MacLean and Richard Schroh have been among the recipients.

FOUR

"In the Kingdom"

Depending on the source believed, Canada's official winter sport owes its creation to a half dozen different cultures and civilizations. In 500 B.C., the Greeks apparently played a form of shinny. Ancient Danes and twelfth-century Anglo-Saxons are supposed to have attached bones to their feet, skated on ice and chased a ball with field hockey sticks. Eighteenth-century Dutch art shows figures with bone skates and wooden sticks. Siberian sources report Russian boys batting "an orange ball about the frozen taiga...using splintered sticks." In Ireland the game was called "hurley," in Scotland "shinty" and in England "bandy."

While the marriage of these two pastimes—skating and field games—is not purely Canadian, its offspring—the game of hockey—is, although argument persists as to who played the game first and where. The theory that hockey was born in Kingston, Ontario (the International Hockey Hall of Fame and Museum is located there), is based on the diaries of a man named Horsey; in 1847 he wrote that "most of the soldier boys were quite at home on skates. They could cut the figure eight and other fancy figures, but shinny was their first delight."

Montreal claims to be the cradle of hockey because the first rules of the game were drawn up there. Broadcaster Foster Hewitt wrote in his memoirs that, "Montreal authorities emphatically declare that their city was the original home of ice hockey. They do not deny that shinny was earlier played at Kingston, but they definitely assert that the first game of pure ice hockey was played in Montreal at Victoria Skating Rink on March 3, 1875." But this argument is muddied by the revelation that James Creighton, an engineer and the author of the rules for that first game in Montreal, had merely imported the game as he had seen it in his native Halifax. And some Haligonians claim that during the eighteenth century Mic-macs and British troops played a form of hockey, called "wicket," on the Dartmouth Lakes and Halifax Harbour with eight men on each team chasing a puck made of rounded wood.

However, all three cities—Kingston, Montreal and Halifax—have recently been knocked out of contention by discoveries made in the nineteenth-century reminiscences of Thomas Chandler Haliburton of Nova Scotia (best known as a judge, a provincial MLA and the creator of Sam Slick). Haliburton recalled his schooldays and play at King's College near Windsor, Nova Scotia: "And boys let out racin', yelpin', hollerin' and whoopin' like mad with pleasure, and the playground, and the game [of] hurley on the long pond on the ice."

This recollection puts the first recorded instance of hockey being played in Canada at about 1800, fully thirty years earlier than the earliest recorded date in Halifax. Remarkably, Haliburton's boyhood "long pond" still exists. Today it's known as Long Pond, a slough located in the back forty of Nova Scotia farmer Howard Dill. Six generations of Dills have lived, raised cattle and harvested fruit and vegetables (including Howard's world-famous Atlantic Giant pumpkins) beside that pond. And that's where Howard as a boy learned to skate and prepare himself for the hard-fought games of the Windsor church league in the 1950s.

One of Howard Dill's neighbours in town has long been fascinated by Long Pond. As a boy, Garth Vaughan played hockey on the frozen pond; it was where Vaughan and his childhood friends imagined they were Syl Apps, Gordie Drillon and other Leafs defending the Gardens' ice against the Bruins' high-flying Kraut Line of Bobby Bauer, Milt Schmidt and Woody Dumart. After Haliburton's memories of "hurley on the long pond," were reprinted, Vaughan, now a retired surgeon, and Howard Dill realized the significance of the site. Together they formed the Windsor Hockey Heritage Society to champion their cause and have the world acknowledge once and for all that Windsor is indeed "the birthplace of hockey."

"Oh, we can talk about organized hockey and its start in Montreal leading to the NHL," says Vaughan. "That's one era. But just as fascinating is the era of development, the unorganized hockey that started on the ponds and arenas where they made up their own rules as they went along, which kids still do."

Whether hockey was born on Long Pond, playing the game simply for the game's sake predominated there. It flourishes today in shinny, in street hockey and in oldtimers' hockey. For what is oldtimers' hockey but adults picking up the hockey traditions and styles they enjoyed as youths? It's shinny, just a little slower. It's house league play for the camaraderie. It's COHA tournament competition without the do-or-die pressure of the seventh game of the Stanley Cup Playoffs. It's the commonest form of hockey being played today—in neighbourhood arenas, on creeks and ponds, on outdoor rinks that park workers maintain, and even sometimes on the manicured ice surfaces of a Gardens, Forum, Stadium or Coliseum.

It's recreational hockey.

In fact, what began with a handful of schoolboys on that King's College pond just after the turn of the nineteenth century can be found as adult recreational "oldtimers" hockey right across the country.

In the words of one rec hockey player, "Just like they say in *Golf in the Kingdom*, that somewhere in the world a golf ball at all times is in flight, in the kingdom of oldtimers' hockey, at any time of day or night, somewhere in Canada, a puck is sliding across some ice in a hockey game."

LONDON, ONTARIO

Every Monday morning, just about the time the inhabitants of most London offices are brewing their first cup of liquid inspiration, two of the six teams known as the Huff n' Puffs are taking to the ice at the Earl Nichols Arena on the south side of the city. There'll be plenty of time for coffee after the game at the doughnut shop down the street. Right now, hockey is their inspiration.

"If I've got a game at 8:30 in the morning," says Emile Benedetti, "I'm up at six o'clock. I have my wholesome breakfast—orange juice, banana, cereal and all that crap. It's what my doctor calls my regimen."

"Benny," as his teammates call him, is seventy years old. In 1943, when he was nineteen, Benedetti left his home in northern Ontario and joined the RCAF. He developed tuberculosis overseas and was discharged home to recover. Even years after the war, while working at a veterans' hospital in London, Benedetti says, "I didn't do a hell of a lot. I wasn't able to. Doctors told me, 'No exercise...the treatment is to rest.'

"In fact, the first time I was out with the Huff n' Puffs, I'm out in the middle of the ice thinking, 'What the hell are you doing out here anyway?'"

The fact is, Benny was right at home. Nobody in this morning league is in his prime. None is younger than fifty-five and most are in their sixties. Fourteen are over seventy. Benedetti's linemates, Jack Wilson and Ted Froats, are sixty-eight and seventy-one respectively. Together they're known as the Fossil Line. Froats, like Benedetti, is an air force veteran who survived two years in a German POW camp. After the war he spent thirty-two years in sales and retired in 1985.

"I was one of the originals," says Froats. "I had played a bit before the war, minor hockey and junior, and intermediate after the war in Kirkland Lake. But back then, in the late forties, I would never have thought I'd be playing now."

The idea came to Froats and his friend Al Finch who met regularly to pleasure skate in London. Eventually the two gathered eleven retired friends, rented some arena ice and in 1986 launched Huff n' Puff Hockey. At first, they rented the ice for an hour. As their numbers swelled, they rented a second hour at another arena. Today about 100 skaters and a handful of goalies show up three times a week year round.

"At first it was just shinny, like you used to play as a kid on the pond," says another of the originals, seventy-year-old Doug Good, another air force veteran. For him the best part of Huff n' Puff hockey was the freedom to make mistakes. Nobody was as sharp on his skates or with his stick as he used to be. Reflexes were much slower. Players fell down a lot. The toughest part for Good was remembering not to use the body because "when guys came in over the blueline, I just wanted to throw my hip into them. Well, you can't do that."

About a year after Huff n' Puff began, a guy showed up with skates, shinpads, a grey sweater, a motorcycle helmet and one of those hybrid hockey sticks with a wooden shaft and a plastic blade, the kind used in road hockey. When he joined Huff n' Puff, in 1987, Charles Crawford hadn't played hockey in twenty years. "Spike" Crawford, as he came to be known, had been an air force career man. He joined in 1941, was posted to Lahr, Germany, in May, 1945, and was discharged in 1970.

"We played hockey in Germany," says Crawford, "but never won a game all season." In 1959, when he was posted to the RCAF station at Clinton, Ontario, Crawford tried to organize a hockey team with his fellow servicemen. But "most of them were around forty years old and said they were too old to play hockey." Today, at seventy-five, Spike has given up the motorcycle helmet. He mostly wears newer equipment although he hasn't given up his original 1950s-vintage Eaton's Gordie Howe signature gloves. He backs up the Fossil Line on defence. He claims, "I'm playing better hockey than I ever have in my life."

Bob Kendall is another Huff n' Puff regular. While younger than many in the league, fifty-nine-year-old Kendall also remembers scrub hockey during his RCAF career. In the early 1960s, he was posted to a radar station on the Gulf of St. Lawrence at Moisie, near Sept-Îles. They played on an outdoor rink where temperatures were often minus forty and where, the story goes, if the puck stopped on the ice, the wind would actually drive it backwards.

"It was so cold," remembers Kendall, "that they brought in a house trailer for the dressing room and the bench. When you came off the ice, you went right into the trailer. And you looked out the window to see when it was your turn to go back out on the ice."

Kendall jumped on the oldtimers' hockey bandwagon early, in 1976, by joining the London Oldtimers. In 1978, he launched the ten-team Southwestern Ontario Oldtimers' Hockey League, which included teams from Windsor to Woodstock and from St. Thomas to Seaforth. While all teams had to be card-carrying members of the Canadian Oldtimers' Hockey Association, "there were no trophies and no playoffs," says Kendall, "so there wouldn't be any bad feelings or hard competition. You want to win the game at the time you're playing, but to this day, with over eighty teams in the league, there are no playoffs and no reports go into the papers."

When he turned fifty-five, Bob Kendall also joined the Huff n' Puffs and brought that same friendly style of competition with him to the Monday, Wednesday and Friday games.

In recent years, Huff n' Puff hockey has become a family affair. Wives, sons and daughters join the organization to play in slow pitch, horseshoe, tennis, badminton and volleyball tournaments, as well as to line dance and enjoy picnics. Still, Spike's wife, Sadie Crawford, says he's too old for hockey. She's got ample evidence to make her case. Two of the original Huff n' Puffs, Al Finch and Ed Loney, died of heart attacks on the ice.

"You can't worry about it," says Benedetti. "If I worried about that, I wouldn't be playing at all....This stuff may not help you live longer, but you live better. I think it's better to wear out than rust out."

"At our age you look at things differently," agrees Doug Good, who was playing with Al Finch the day he collapsed and died. "I look at it this way. He was out there, he was enjoying what he was doing. If he didn't, he wouldn't have been there. Tomorrow it could be you."

"A few years ago, after my buddy Duke Woods died of cancer," says Bob Kendall, "I was diagnosed with something I thought was cancer. I started getting my affairs in order and told my wife, Barb, if I die, I want my epitaph to read, 'Gone to play hockey with the Duke.'"

A somewhat fatalistic attitude is common among Huff n'

Puffers. Most players fondly remember how, on days he wasn't playing, one of their club members—a local undertaker—would stand along the arena boards. He never said a word. He'd just stand there wearing a telephone company baseball cap that sported a slogan with special meaning for him and his teammates: "Call before you dig."

SHAWVILLE, QUEBEC

If not in body, certainly in spirit oldtimers' hockey is alive and well in Shawville, Quebec. Ask Royce Richardson and he'll tell you. He's known as "Mr. Oldtimers' Hockey" in this part of the Ottawa Valley. It was one of the joys of his life.

"It just started," says Richardson modestly. "Oldtimers just started because we had some good hockey players kickin' around who wanted to play. And Bryan Murray was our first coach."

In 1977, before he landed his NHL coaching and managing positions, Bryan Murray was home in Shawville between jobs, as they say. He had been coaching tier two Junior A hockey and felt he was being overlooked by major Junior A clubs. So he took a year off and coached a group of oldtimers instead.

"We played the system," Richardson says, remembering Murray's coaching style, "the system you use when you don't have that many players....Check them and check them. Never give [the opposition] anything. Keep the game close, until the last period, and beat them near the end."

In this small town of 1,640 people, making your opportunities is a way of life. The tradition began when Irish and Scottish settlers first pioneered the area, then known as Clarendon, in the early nineteenth century. It was the case when Royce Richardson's family first came to town in 1943. That's when Royce's father, Ebert Richardson, left a farm outside Shawville to manage the local dairy in town. The elder Richardson also bought and operated the local arena.

Even though his father ran the rink, Royce and his hockey chums were hard pressed to play there because it cost $3.50 an hour to rent. And with natural ice, the arena could only accommodate one game a night. One night was taken by the town's junior club, the Shawville Pontiacs. Another was reserved for the Senior B Pontiacs. Pleasure skating and practices took up the rest. That left some after-school hockey and the afternoons when Royce and his friends skipped school to play hockey by sneaking into the darkened arena.

"We used to get in by the side boarded-up windows," recalls Shawville resident Albert Armstrong. "We'd open up the windows for light. We never turned on the lights....And Royce's father knew we were there. He just left us long enough, then came in and shouted, 'Hey, what're you guys doing in here?' But he never called our parents."

Albert Armstrong's family came to Shawville about the same time as the Richardsons, but Albert's connection with the town goes back to one Captain John Armstrong, who was awarded a parcel of land for his service in the British army in 1821. As boys in Shawville, Albert and Royce remember how hockey-crazed the town was. After all, this was the home of the "Shawville Express," Frank Finnigan, who scored in the Ottawa Senators' 1927 Stanley Cup win, the last NHL championship Ottawa won before the franchise was moved to St. Louis in 1934.

"I remember going up and down the streets of Shawville ringing that bell," says Armstrong, "making sure everybody knew there was a hockey game on that night. You were like a town crier. It took about an hour but by then everybody knew. It was just a way of life here."

Like all kids in Shawville, Royce and Albert dreamed of wearing the town colours on the ice. Royce did in the Junior B league and Albert in Junior C. Briefly, in 1966, they played together as Seniors with the Pontiacs. But their proudest moments wearing the gold, black, red and white jersey with the Indian-head logo of the Shawville Pontiacs on the front were after the birth of their oldtimers' team in 1977.

Right from the beginning, coach Murray said, "we'll get about twenty guys, play some shinny, get sanctioned by the COHA and do some tournaments." This plan was slightly more adventuresome than these oldtimers were prepared for. Most had lost or given away their hockey gear. Many hadn't played in years. Still, those Tuesday night practices became reunions for a generation of senior league hockey players.

There was Carson Ryan, who had moved to Shawville from Pembroke to play for the Senior Pontiacs; he worked for Hilton Mines. Goalie Brian Poupore and defenceman Bill Kuehl had also left Pembroke to play senior hockey in Shawville; Poupore landed a job with a paper company, while Kuehl took over the Clarendon Hotel in Shawville. Cletus Newberry and Jim Carmichael had both goaltended in the senior league. Civil servant Fred Desebrais had played senior hockey in Quyon. Carpenter Bob Findlay played senior in Bristol. Tom Fraser, who coached senior, had a refrigeration business in Shawville. Insurance agent Chris McColgan played in Renfrew. Peter MacIntosh, Kervin Burman and Ivan Saunders worked for the Consolidated Bathurst paper mill in Portage. Dave Pilgrim and Ron Armitage were farmers in the Quyon area. Jack Graham was a banker in Bristol. Don Lavallee was a lawyer in Shawville. And Dick Meisner ran the Stedman's in Shawville. They all joined GM parts manager Royce Richardson and electrician Albert Armstrong to form the Pontiac Old Timers.

Very quickly and very smoothly, the resurrected Pontiacs found their legs at the Shawville arena Tuesday nights. Old rivalries faded. New friendships began. And routines, regimens, superstitions and idiosyncrasies were soon established among teammates. In the Shawville dressing room, for example, goalie Carmichael always sat just inside the door and took up three spaces. But nobody argued. His teammates also gave Bill Kuehl plenty of room, but not for the same reason.

"Billy put his hockey gear in his kit bag at the start of the year," says Albert Armstrong, "and never took it out of the car till the end of the year....His stuff was always frozen; he'd have to pry the socks and underwear apart to get it on....One time he left his bag in my car. I took my stuff in because I didn't want it to freeze so I took in Billy's too. They were both stinking so bad, my wife washed everything.

"Next week, I walk the 300 yards from my house to the rink with Billy's and my stuff. It was all nice and warm from being in the house. Billy grabs his stuff and says, 'Holy Geez! That's the first time I've ever put on warm equipment!'"

Some members of the Pontiacs hung their socks a certain way along the bench. Others sat beside the same player they had the last time the team won. Bob Findlay and Tom Fraser would be busily ribbing teammates, saying, "I hope you don't play with me tonight," or "Will I have to carry you again?" But Fraser's teammates got the last laugh one night when the 300-pound, six-foot-one-inch oldtimer leapt over the boards and his skate blades collapsed under the impact.

Meanwhile, not saying a word most nights, Ivan Saunders would pull out his sharpening stone and carefully smooth the rough edges of his skate blades. Saunders would always catch Armstrong taping his stick from the toe to the heel and would always tell him, "You don't tape your stick that way....You tape from heel to toe." Armstrong also taped his groin before games, presumably he did so without being corrected by his teammates.

Team captain Royce Richardson always sat beside the shower, because nobody else wanted the spot with water on the floor. But he didn't mind. Richardson readily accepted his role as convenor, road manager, oldest team member and team captain. Off the ice, in a back room of Bill Kuehl's hotel, Richardson usually chaired meetings about what tournaments to attend and how to raise the funds to get there. In 1979, the Pontiacs decided they would go to the Sixth Annual COHA National Oldtimers' Hockey Tournament in Vancouver. To finance part of the trip, team members agreed to paint the exterior of the three-story agricultural building at the Shawville Exhibition grounds, a job that meant working summer nights and weekends and some individual acts of bravery.

"Right in the middle of the domed roof of the building," recalls Albert Armstrong, "there was a bit of a steeple. And the only way to paint this part was to hang outside the steeple by a rope....Dave Pilgrim was the only one able to do it. With a rope attached around his waist, he just painted himself around. Kept going around in a circle and painted."

By the time the September fair opened in Shawville, its agriculture building sported a new coat of paint. And by the time

March rolled around, the Pontiacs had the funds to get to Vancouver. They made it to the quarter-finals in the D Division.

"We always played to win," says Richardson. "But when the game was over, 'Hey, let's go have a beer, guys.'"

The Pontiacs' easygoing, take-it-as-it-comes style was evident both on and off the ice. In 1986, the Pontiacs travelled to southwestern Ontario for an oldtimers' tournament in St. Thomas. Everything went smoothly until game four, when only five Pontiac players arrived for the start of the game. The rest were locked out of their motel rooms. By the time they retrieved their gear and made it onto the ice, the game was half an hour old.

"We had the five guys," remembers Armstrong, "and we just played it slow and easy. We passed the puck around, didn't do a whole lot of skating and we held them. I guess we were a goal ahead. As soon as we had the full team, they scored a goal on us....But we won the A side of the tournament, a trophy and $400."

Unfortunately, the St. Thomas tournament was the Pontiacs' last. And not long after, the team gave up its Tuesday night ice time as well. Not out of apathy. On the contrary. Just the way, as kids, they had rung the bell to gather the community at the old Richardson arena and had always cheered on their Pontiac Juniors and Seniors, this community-minded group of oldtimers decided to give up its own game for the sake of hockey's future in Shawville.

It was clear that oldtimers' hockey was the only hockey left in town. Shawville's tradition of strong representation up and down the Ottawa Valley was reduced to a group of aging hockey players. If something wasn't done, Pontiac hockey would disappear when the oldtimers did.

In the late 1980s, the team boldly relaunched a Shawville junior hockey program on its own. It organized fund-raisers, sold advertising, raised commercial signs in the arena and staged golf tournaments. In addition, each Pontiac Old Timer signed a promissory note for a thousand dollars. Tom Fraser became coach, Albert Armstrong became president and Royce Richardson became director of the new Junior B Shawville Pontiacs.

Today, the Shawville Junior program has a budget between
$60,000 and $70,000 per year. It draws between 12,000 and
15,000 fans and is thriving just like the old days.

Now, when Royce Richardson makes his way to the
Shawville arena each Tuesday night, it's to see the Juniors, not
the oldtimers.

"And yet, the arena's not busy every night," says Albert
Armstrong. "Saturday evening eighteen years ago nobody
wanted to play hockey. There were too many things to do.
Now Saturday night is quiet in this town. If the teenagers
don't want to use it, we could get ice time around seven
o'clock for us oldtimers...."

NORTH YORK, ONTARIO

In the Grandravine Arena at the northwestern edge of
Metropolitan Toronto, the North Metro League runs a full
schedule of games on Monday evenings. One of the teams on
the ice just after the 9:30 scrape is the Newtonbrook Stars.
The players vary in age and occupation. There's a firefighter,
a police officer, the manager of an office supply store and a
number of businesspeople.

Their Monday night hockey provides a full game's worth of
vigorous exercise, close friendships in a team of some years'
standing and the delicious distraction of not having to deal
with the pressures of life for several hours. One, however, who
cannot seem to completely escape the workplace is a player
on Newtonbrook's defence—the forty-two-year-old president
of the Ontario Women's Hockey Association.

"Most league games we play," explains Fran Rider,
"nobody is in the rink. But very often I'll be sitting on the
bench trying to catch my breath. And somebody will
approach me and ask a question like, 'I've got a player here, is
she eligible to play in this tournament?' or 'What's the interpretation on this new rule?'

"The administrative part of my job is about 4,000 hours a
year....And even though it's sometimes hard to focus on the
game, I do it to get away from the troubles. Usually, when I
come back after a game, I can face them easier."

Fran Rider's hockey and real life are sometimes difficult to separate. She's been involved in women's hockey for twenty-five years (eleven years as president of the OWHA) while the association experienced both victory and defeat. During her involvement with women's hockey, Rider has seen it emerge from a novelty act to respectability. It gained status at the Canadian Amateur Hockey Association in 1982. Its annual Dominion Tournament in Brampton, Ontario, now attracts nearly 200 teams. Without official backing from the International Ice Hockey Federation, in 1987, the OWHA welcomed the first Women's World Hockey Tournament, including teams from Holland, Japan, Sweden, Switzerland, the United States and Canada. Then, in 1990, it helped stage the first fully sanctioned IIHF Women's World Championship in Ottawa. During the same period, it endured the International Olympic Committee's procrastination over introducing women's hockey as a full-fledged Olympic event. That will finally happen in 1998.

"There is something very special about female hockey," Fran Rider has written. "During the game we compete. After the game we co-operate. Together we have won. As a team, we have won...credibility for female hockey and the opportunity to be part of the 1998 Olympic Games in Nagano, Japan."

Unlike some men's hockey, which has turning pro as its ultimate goal, all women's hockey remains an amateur pursuit. Players participate strictly for the fun of the game. In fact, one of the founders of the Brampton Canadettes Hockey Club, Roy Morris, had specific objectives for his and other women's hockey teams:

Hockey can be an excellent means of exercise for the body and mind. Strive to obtain it.
Hockey is a group activity and can bring you new friends. Appreciate them.
Hockey is an association of groups that bind you together. Guard it.

An article about the Brampton Canadettes first attracted Fran Rider to hockey. In 1968, Fran attended her first women's hockey practice. It was horribly intimidating. Until then, she had only skated on figure skates. The concept of wearing hockey gloves and holding a hockey stick was foreign. She had no idea how to put on all the hockey equipment, "except for the garter belt. That I did know how to put on.

"And yet, they couldn't do enough to help you," remembers Rider. "They helped you put on the gear. There were all ages on a team, anywhere from fourteen to forty. And people that had played for a long time were teamed up with people that had never played.

"It was fun. I was terrible. But everybody was so supportive. If you stopped a puck they were as excited as if you had scored a goal....I think that first year I learned the most about teamwork and what to do as much without the puck as with the puck. When you're on the ice or on the bench, you're playing a role on the team. You're always contributing."

By the early 1980s, when Fran Rider was in her thirties, women's hockey began taking over her life. She was donating time to the Canadettes and the association, assisting coaches, sitting on committees, scorekeeping or timekeeping at games and organizing tournaments. Her volunteer commitment quickly rose to eight and ten hours a day. While physically draining, the work was spiritually satisfying.

What Fran realized, both as a senior player and as an administrator with experience, was that those early days with Roy Morris, the Canadettes and those intimidating practices had given her some positive and practical knowledge; how to tackle something new, how to get along with others and how to solve problems. But it wasn't until December, 1992, that she realized just how well that education would serve her.

Since 1988, Fran had been a regular with the Newtonbrook Stars, taking her shift on defence each Monday night at Grandravine Arena. The games were a welcome lift and escape for her. She would don her number twelve sweater, in honour of Ron Stewart, her favourite Maple Leaf from the 1960s, and lose herself in the game. The Stars weren't that successful at first. But that didn't matter. It was, after all, the friendships and the ice time that Fran enjoyed most. Then, just before New Year's, 1992, the Stars entered a Mississauga tournament. On the final evening of the tourney, Fran and the Stars won the Senior C championship, complete with gold medals and a team photograph. It was a memorable night.

It was one o'clock when Fran and Jann Bower, the Stars' coach, piled equipment into the car and left the arena. Heading off for a late night coffee, the two women came upon a taxi at the side of the road. As they approached they could see figures moving around the cab in the dark. A fight was going on and the cab driver was getting the worst of it.

After a moment's hesitation, Fran and Jann decided to help. By the time they reached the cabby, two of his attackers had run off into the bush; the third had jumped into the cab and gone speeding off into the darkness. Still feeling uneasy about getting involved, the women dialed 911 on their car phone and handed it through their car window so that the semi-conscious cabby could describe his attackers to police. Just then, the stolen cab reappeared, racing up behind them. The women threw open their car door, screamed at the cab driver to jump in on top of their hockey equipment and off they sped, trying to elude the stolen cab.

The two women couldn't believe what was happening to them. Just minutes before, they had been in the friendly confines of a winning dressing room, savouring their tournament victory. Now, nearly frightened out of their wits, they were speeding through the night. A battered man was lying on the back seat of their car and another man was pursuing them in a stolen taxi cab.

Finally a police cruiser came into view. Then another. The women stopped their car. The stolen cab raced past them and the two cruisers began to chase the cab. Before long seven cruisers and two unmarked police vehicles converged and the resulting roadblock finally stopped the thief.

"It was absolutely bizarre," remembers Fran Rider. "You're so high from winning a championship game. And then this happens. Who cared about hockey at a moment like that?

"But we have always said women's hockey gives us life skills and prepares us for things, to be ready to deal with anything. Well, we made some split-second decisions under a lot of pressure that night—on and off the ice. I guess it all paid off."

SAINT JOHN, NEW BRUNSWICK

On this hockey night, Dennis Boyle's father is dying of cancer. His wife Trish is about to give birth to their second child. The sluggish economy in New Brunswick is causing no end of woes among family and friends. The winter has been abnormally bleak. And his work has been particularly stressful lately. But tonight at the Stu Hurley Arena in the east end of Saint John, none of this is on his mind.

"Here, there's no birth, no death, no hard times," says Boyle, "just the puck, the net and me."

If life is a blur for Dennis Boyle, it's his own fault. He's a community booster. He manages the famous Flying Fathers hockey club. He's a devoted family man and a lawyer with a cellular phone. His Waterloo Street law practice is one of the busiest and it follows him wherever he goes—except to the ice rink.

"My job is high pressure. I'm dealing with people's lives. It's an ulcer-infested environment....But when I go out on the ice, I don't have my cellular with me. I can't be reached. For an hour there's no stress. No mortgages. No people in jail. It's a total escape to a place where I'm comfortable, I'm competent. I'm safe."

Hockey has always been a sanctuary for Dennis Boyle. As the eldest of twelve children, Dennis often took on a parental role, helping his mother and father keep the Boyle household running smoothly. But when he had time to himself it generally led to a hockey game, either road hockey on Demont Street (he and his chums called themselves "the Demons") or shinny at the Beaconsfield outdoor rink, where a hundred kids chased pucks around until it was dark or their mothers called them home for supper.

Organized hockey in Saint John was then pretty disorganized. Dennis's parochial school had little ice time, even less coaching and one set of sweaters that only fit the bantams. What motivated him, however, was the advice of his uncle, Jack Boyle (one-time star of the Intermediate League Saint John Moosehead Brewers): "If you're a good skater, you can make any hockey team." So Dennis tried speed skating. In junior high school he won city-wide skating sprints three years in a row; in Grade 12 he qualified for the Quebec Winter Games. He maintained his speed on skates but played only university intramural and some industrial hockey before hanging up the skates, he thought, for good.

It wasn't until a dozen years after graduating from law school and returning home to Saint John that Dennis Boyle rediscovered his passion for hockey in something called the "HB and NW."

"The Has Beens and Never Weres. That's the way we were listed [with the city's recreation department]," says University of New Brunswick at Saint John chemistry professor Carl Tompkins. "Two teams. Twenty players. Two colours of sweaters we got on a deal through a sporting goods store....No checking. No slapshots. Referees only occasionally. Every Tuesday night from eight o'clock to nine o'clock at the Charles Gorman Arena. And anybody could play—teachers, doctors, lawyers, anybody."

Dennis Boyle scared up some gear and joined Tompkins's group. That season he also played competitive hockey in the first Atlantic Canada Law Society Hockey Tournament. The second year, he scored the goal that put his team into the finals, quite an achievement for a man who insists, "I can count the goals I score in a season on the thumbs of one hand." He had reconnected to the rhythm of the game and was soon helping to organize the annual lawyers' tournament as well as a Thursday night lawyers' league from 10:30 to midnight at Hurley Arena in east Saint John.

"I froth at the mouth just thinking about it," admits John MacGillivray, Boyle's defencemate on Thursday nights. "It's a perfect level of hockey for me. I can keep up. I can make passes, receive passes, get an occasional breakaway and all the things that get your blood pumping. I think I play better hockey now at thirty-seven than I did as a kid."

MacGillivray played goal as a boy growing up in east Saint John because he couldn't keep up. He was so self-conscious about his lack of skating skills that he was embarrassed to go pleasure skating with his girlfriends. Not until he attended law school when he decided to try intramural hockey did he overcome his fear of skating out front. While he admitted he was the worst player in the league, he was also having more fun than anyone else, and that's what drew him to Boyle's Thursday oldtimers' games.

In friendly, no body checking, no slapshot hockey, John MacGillivray had the time and room to develop the skating skills that had eluded him as a child. Despite having no formal hockey training, he learned to carry the puck and soon discovered dekes and fakes.

"Instead of aspiring to the NHL," says MacGillivray, "I have aspired to being able to play oldtimers' hockey and not have people realize that I didn't play hockey through my adolescence."

Forty-one-year-old Norm Bossé is another late bloomer. Raised in Maine, as a teenager he preferred soccer and basketball, but he too discovered hockey as an adult and admits, "I just wanted to see if I could skate, stickhandle, take a breakaway and put it in the net sometimes. It's funny, but I would never have envisioned I'd be doing this."

Dennis Boyle's lawyers' hockey league is not only lawyers. Teachers, priests, civic workers, doctors, business owners and even a professional musician are regulars at Thursday night hockey at Hurley Arena. At 200 pounds and six feet, Chris Buckley doesn't look like a violist in the Saint John String Quartet. He doesn't look like a hockey player either. But he's both.

"Hockey is Canadian," says Buckley, "and if you're Canadian, it doesn't really matter what you do for a living. You still play."

Much like the others, Chris Buckley was separated from hockey for some time. He played on natural ice as a boy growing up east of Saint John but gave up the game for ten years while studying music in England. When he returned to Canada, Chris picked up the thread of the game through his family, playing shinny with his brothers each Christmas.

The passion for hockey came back.

First he joined a gentlemen's league—competitive hockey without body checking. It was a rocky start. His unplanned pirouettes on skates and clumsy tumbles on the ice were little more than "an entertainment sideshow" for his teammates. But he persisted and soon squeezed Dennis Boyle's league into his busy schedule as a musician. On Thursday evenings he would rehearse with the quartet from seven o'clock until 9:45 and then race to the Hurley Arena in time for the game, often carrying his viola into the dressing room with his hockey gear to keep it from freezing in his car.

"For the first two years," says Buckley, "it seemed like after every hockey game I was going to bed with an ice pack on a hip, an elbow or an ankle. Occasionally I'll pinch a finger between my stick and the ice, but nothing that'll get in the way of my job.

"It's a big excitement every time I put on the hockey gear. When a guy of my abilities can force a defenceman to cough up the puck, complete a nice pass or get an occasional goal—contribute to the team—it's an emotional high."

That same emotion binds the rest of Boyle's Thursday night regulars together. Each man understands hockey's place in his life and his place in hockey. Some could skate circles around the others, but prefer to pass and be playmakers instcad of puck hogs. Others are learning as adults the hockey skills they never knew as boys. On Thursday nights at Hurley Arena there's room for both.

That doesn't mean that everybody fits in.

"A couple of years ago," recalls Thursday night regular Steve Fowler, "this young bunch came out. There were five or six of them. They kind of got themselves isolated. They all wanted to be on the same team. They wanted to play together so they could go out and make the big flashy passing plays, go whipping down the ice and have all kinds of fun with their friends.

"At the same time, while these young guys were always racing up and down the boards scoring lots of goals, the older guys took their time and moved the puck with passes and positional hockey. After about five or six weeks of these young guys winning all the games, all of a sudden the older guys were within one or two goals. The games were getting closer and closer. The older guys jelled. What they didn't have in legs they made up for in experience, patience and a modicum of luck. These guys were out there because they love hockey and don't give a damn about wins.

"Eventually, the young guys got the message—we weren't into heavy, competitive hockey—and they moved on. Most of the Thursday night bunch are mature in attitude. They're out for fun, and part of the fun is seeing everyone else enjoy the game too."

PICKERING, ONTARIO

It's a Wednesday in January, 1995. It's a great night for hockey. The NHLPA has just settled its dispute with the NHL owners over a salary cap, draft age and free agency that kept professional hockey shut down. In twenty-six NHL cities around the continent, fans (they hope) will be flocking back to arenas soon. For about seven hundred NHL players there will be a hasty ratification vote, abbreviated training camps and a condensed forty-eight-game 1994–95 season. And for the Champlain Hawks of the over-35 senior men's hockey league, B Division, in Pickering, it's the best of all possible worlds. There'll be plenty of new grist for the conversation mill in the dressing room. And because of the rare but convenient six o'clock game time, there'll be plenty to complain about.

"You can bet we'll get a full turnout," grouses Wayne Moss, and of course that means he'll get less ice time, a precious commodity for this City of Toronto employee. "It means Greco and Walker will be here for sure." Moss laughs, but he'll be seriously annoyed if an odd number of players forces one player to go through the forward lines spelling teammates off one at a time.

This team is notoriously short of manpower, particularly when its Wednesday games fall in the later evening. Many's the night the Hawks have barely iced five skaters and a goalie because so many of the regulars have contracted what's called "the eleven o'clock flu."

There are no excuses tonight, though. Not only do municipal worker Dave Walker and department store employee Steve Greco show up but so does letter carrier Jeff Mathews. He's been away partly because of a couple of injuries but also because, like many on the team, he's got a young family and expenses that make it difficult to raise the winter playing fee— over $300 per player.

The Champlain Hawks is a team typical of thousands across the country. It's a lunch-bucket adult team. With various players and under various names, it's been in existence for about a dozen or fifteen years, more to retain its spot in the Art Thompson Wednesday night league than because of a brotherhood among its players. In fact, the team took on its current Champlain Hawks identity only because a former team member persuaded a Toronto-based graphics company to part with some sponsorship dollars and share the cost of team jackets.

However, the fiscal realities of playing adult recreational hockey don't seem to get in the way of having a good time. Tonight, there are three fifteen-minute periods of pretty competitive hockey ahead. Then there'll be chicken wings and a couple of jugs of draft beer at a nearby bar. But even before all that, opportunities abound for some good-natured verbal jabbing in the pregame dressing room. Most of the joking is directed at the best players, or those who consider themselves the best.

"Sure glad the NHL settled that free agency thing," says wholesale buyer Bob Burke. "Now they can go ahead and negotiate with Wayne."

"Don't call us, we'll call you," somebody else cracks under his breath in the far corner.

"What a bunch of crybabies those pros are," pipes up freelance accountant Boyd Parsons, and then, just for the benefit of his civic employee teammates, he adds, "It's just like fucking government workers. Think the world owes 'em a job."

There's the usual ripple of laughter and several Here-we-go-again responses around the bench. Everybody knows hard-nosed free-enterpriser Parsons is just baiting the public employees in the room. This time, no one bites.

In another corner of the room the Hawks' goalie, Al Aylesworth, is stretching. For twenty-two years Aylesworth has worked at General Motors doing assembly line maintenance on the night shift. And whenever he's not on the job, Al is playing goal. Two, three and four times a week, all year round. In the years this team has played Wednesday nights, Aylesworth has missed only a handful of games. Not moody, not flashy, he is as reliable in the nets as he is showing up each week. He's even reached an understanding with his boss at GM; he won't be penalized if he and the Hawks happen to play an eleven o'clock to midnight game.

"We're countin' on you, Al," quips banker Rick Gascoyne. "You get the shutout and we'll guarantee the tie."

"Got pucks, Al?" asks team captain Brad Mortley.

"The best kind," says Aylesworth. "Invisible ones."

As usual, nobody has a single puck in his hockey bag. So it is up to Mortley to scrounge for even one or two pucks just to warm up their goalie before the opening face-off. Mortley is among the longest-surviving members of this Wednesday night team. Perhaps for that reason, or maybe because he was away the night of the straw vote, this stocky, automotive hardware salesman is team rep. Contrary to the rest of the team's penchant for complaining, Mortley regularly arrives at the arena early, fills out the game sheet and haggles with the league management over the Hawks' outstanding fees. As with so many team reps, Mortley does his volunteer work stoically, without either recognition or the expectation of recognition. It is a trait that is at odds with his feisty, often explosive on-ice personality—one that puts him in the penalty box for body contact offences more often than anybody else on the team.

Despite their fair share of penalties, though, tonight the Hawks can do no wrong on the ice. They seem to have the jump on their division rivals, the Tudor Arms. Their passing clicks. The puck bounces their way. Everybody seems to be in the right place at the right time. There's little or no bitching on the bench; even Bill Redmond, who usually complains about defensive gaffs, can find little to fault. Wayne Moss gets plenty of ice time. And Aylesworth has a successful game in net.

Whether it's the crisp air inside the arena this January night, or the anticipation of NHL games returning next week, or maybe just because it's wings and beer night, the Champlain Hawks (who are in the middle of the standings) blow away their opposition tonight with a convincing 10–4 win.

In the dressing room after the game, heads, pads and backsides are patted. Sticks and water bottles are tossed helterskelter on the floor in the middle of the room. Amid the honest congratulations handed out to goalie Aylesworth, there are also the clichés. "Good hustle, guys." "We played well as a team." "Lots of heart out there." But then, the real voices of the players pick up right where they left off before the game.

"Yeah, good game, guys" agrees winger Steve Greco, waiting for his moment. "Too bad our D[efence] fucked up on those four goals."

"Well, we didn't see you back our side of centre all night," scolds defenceman Jeff Mathews.

"And way to go, cement hands," adds defenceman Eric Allen, poking fun at Wayne Moss's bad luck at centre most of the night. "Two breakaways and you still couldn't score."

For some—Rick Gascoyne, Brad Mortley and Vance Page—the pleasure of these first few minutes back in the dressing room is shedding skates, pads and sweaty underwear as quickly as possible. For others—Bob Burke, Barry Toner and Jeff Mathews—it's the stillness after an hour of motion and savouring the win that keep them sitting for some time before peeling off any equipment. Mathews and Dave Walker even light up cigarettes. However, the reason Boyd Parsons is slow to undress is a common complaint among oldtimers.

"This is the worst part of a game," laments Parsons. "I hate taking off this gear." He's even got an old Cooperall shell, a long pant that covers the inner padding from his hip to his ankle and makes dressing and undressing much easier than putting on garters and long hockey socks. "You know, the guy that invents a full Velcro hockey suit'll make a million bucks. I'm tellin' ya."

Tongue-in-cheek criticism and routine complaints are at the heart of this team's weekly post-game ritual, win or lose. But of course, because the Hawks have won, it's much more enjoyable. This team is fun to be around when it wins. Amid the laughs, there are also bits of business to attend to, such as who still owes playing fees, who's got names of any reliable guys who might make it out for summer hockey this year, or when the next game is.

"What time next week, Rick?" somebody asks Gascoyne because he's Mr. Time Management.

"Eight-thirty," he says without even checking the schedule.

Not ten seconds later comes the same question.

"Eight-thirty," Gascoyne repeats more emphatically.

A bit later, "Was that nine o'clock next week, Rick?"

And there's a laugh at Gascoyne's regimented banker's lifestyle. Eventually, though, there are more important matters to discuss. "Okay, boys," interrupts Brad Mortley, "wings and beer at Upper Deck?"

"Go there? For fucking budgie wings?" mocks Billy Redmond. "No way!"

However, half an hour later, Redmond and most of the other Hawks have showered, dressed and are seated around a plain table in the nearby sports bar ordering wings, french fries and jugs of draft beer. The quality of the food and drink doesn't seem to matter; every last morsel of food and drop of beer are consumed. As well, every last complaint about tonight's game—real or imagined—gets a going over. And since the NHL and the NHLPA now have a tentative agreement, the Hawks give it a going-over too.

It's all part of a night of hockey that keeps a nucleus of Champlain Hawks coming out week after week.

VANCOUVER, BRITISH COLUMBIA

Just about the time the Champlain Hawks are wolfing down the last of the budgie wings at their favourite lounge in Pickering, the Vancouver Flames are assembling at the University of British Columbia for their Wednesday night diet of old-timers' hockey.

In the mid-1960s when the B.C. lower mainland had only three indoor hockey arenas to speak of and two hometown heroes to look up to (Ottawa Senator legend Fred "Cyclone" Taylor and Montreal Canadien tough guy John Ferguson), organized adult hockey was nearly non-existent. About 1966, a handful of hockey-hungry graduate students at UBC approached the management at the newly built Thunderbird Winter Sports Complex for some ice time to play shinny.

They got Wednesday nights at eight o'clock.

"It was pure shinny," remembers Keith Morrison. "Guys went out there, split into two more or less even teams, went at it for an hour and a half, no referees, no whistles, just non-stop hockey....Some of the guys [who] were from the East had played some pretty good hockey. The rest of us played hamburger hockey—unorganized, poor quality, but fun."

Mostly Vancouverites in their mid-twenties, mostly helmet-less and wearing a motley collection of sweaters, these dozen or so originals continued to play that shinny style of hockey every Wednesday night even after they took jobs in and around the city. A decade later, when the phrase "oldtimers' hockey" was creeping into the hockey lexicon, Morrison and company were ready to make their association formal.

The team responded to a newspaper ad promoting the first Oldtimer Invitational tournament in nearby Port Coquitlam. They fit almost all the criteria. They were all over thirty-five. They had adapted to no-slapshot, non-contact hockey. The trouble was, they had no name and no uniforms. Morrison's first *Hockey Newsletter* documents the solution:

"After eleven years of deliberation and procrastination, a Uniform Committee was struck....As usual Norm [Smith] knew someone who could 'get us a deal,' which turned out to be the Atlanta Flames travelling uniform. Made in Poland, they are cheap, even if there is only one arm. Turning the Atlanta flaming 'A' crest upside down gave us the flaming 'V' crest. And a new name—the Vancouver Flames. Cost $20."

The Vancouver Flames placed fourth in Port Coquitlam.

The Flames soon became regular participants in oldtimer tournaments. Each April, the team would meet to plan the following year's itinerary. Each September, Flames' manager Keith Morrison would collect $250 from each player to pay for weekly ice time, membership in the Canadian Oldtimers' Hockey Association and tournament entry fees. During the season, the Flames would hit the road for the COHA Pacific Cup in Victoria or cartoonist Charles Schulz's Snoopy's Senior World Hockey Tournament in Santa Rosa, California. In their first decade, the Flames travelled abroad a half dozen times to play tournaments in Mexico, Europe and Australia.

And yet, as attractive and exotic as those road trips were, the essence of Flames' hockey is not tournament competition. It's the routine, the familiarity and the fun of hockey that keeps these men returning to the UBC main rink. Each Wednesday night (and eventually Monday night) twenty or so regulars show up, kibitz, pull on their pads, skates and jerseys, and hit the ice. When one side reaches five goals, the goalies switch and a new game begins.

"Flames hockey fits into my life," says Rob MacFarlane.

Born in Scotland in 1942, MacFarlane never saw a pair of skates or a hockey stick until his family emigrated to Montreal in the 1950s. There, in the shadow of every other kid's fantasy of becoming tomorrow's Elmer Lach or Rocket Richard, Rob struggled to master basic skating and playing skills. He persisted, and played varsity hockey while attending McGill, Dalhousie and UBC. And in the 1970s, his commercial law practice established, he rediscovered hockey with the Flames.

"Playing now is an escape," MacFarlane says. "You're back to having fun. Everyone realizes that the days of being great are gone. It's reasonably serious, but it's not ridiculous."

"Everybody wants to win, sure," agrees another downtown Vancouver lawyer, Roger Bourbonnais. "There's still that competitive spirit; you don't want to be embarrassed. You make a lot of mistakes but whereas before you'd get upset at yourself, you mellow. Now you accept your limitations."

Bourbonnais grew up on skates while imagining he was Jean Béliveau on the sloughs outside St. Albert, Alberta. He played junior with the Edmonton Oil Kings, winning the Memorial Cup in 1963. And in 1964, he joined Father David Bauer's first National Team bound for the Olympics.

At the Winter Olympics in Innsbruck, Austria, Bourbonnais and Team Canada finished out of the medals. Then in Grenoble, France, in 1968, they won the bronze. But after eight years in the pressure cooker of international hockey, Bourbonnais decided to turn to law, first practising in Edmonton and then in Vancouver. He coached minor league players and later scrimmaged on Sunday mornings at UBC but only when oldtimers' hockey became widespread did he suit up again for real.

"I never really got caught up in the tournament thing," he admits. "I played because I enjoyed the adrenalin. Setting up the plays. Scoring a goal once in a while. Playing with certain individuals because you knew you're going to get the puck back. Not for the competitive side of it...for the fundamentals."

When he played with the Flames, Bourbonnais often found himself alongside or squared off against Al McLean, one of his teammates from the 1964 Canadian Olympic squad. Like Roger, Al played his formative hockey years on the prairies; he remembers being scouted in New Westminster and sent "back east" to the Melville Millionaires of the Saskatchewan Junior Hockey League. But McLean left Team Canada before the 1968 Olympics, joined the Vancouver Canucks of the WHL and earned his master's degree in social work at UBC.

Naturally, McLean's experience made him a valuable commodity among Vancouver oldtimers' teams. "I hooked up with the Coquitlam Ambassadors when I was thirty-five. Their philosophy at the time was practising twice a week and playing a lot of tournaments. They even made a rule that if you didn't make all the practices you couldn't play the games.

"So I said, 'You might as well say goodbye to me.' I knew about the Flames and joined them."

Winning at all cost is not part of the Vancouver Flames' philosophy. At one point, when the Flames were contenders in the upper divisions of oldtimers' tournaments, someone suggested they get rid of the slower and/or older players to become more competitive. Flames' manager Keith Morrison would have none of it. The same thing had happened to a team he had organized in Saskatchewan. The team got hungry for tournament wins and cut their older players; they won for a while but eventually began to bicker and disbanded.

Morrison has a kind of litmus test for the Flames' competitive aspirations. After most tournaments he'll say, "You remember what happened in that second game in Victoria last year, don't you?"

Most players will respond, "No. What happened?"

"That's the point," Morrison will say. "It doesn't really matter. But did you have a good time?"

"Oh, yeah, a hell of a good time."

"Well, that's what it's all about," Morrison will say. "Unless you're going after the Stanley Cup, everything below that is just do your best and have fun."

To the Flames, having fun means that everybody is fair game. In a 1983 newsletter editorial, Morrison wrote, "The Flames are predictably unpredictable. They are not ones to display mercy." He wasn't referring to their killer instincts as hockey players, but to the humour they direct at each other on the ice and in the dressing room.

Despite his professional reputation (he argued successfully before the Supreme Court of Canada that a client should be acquitted because of a police miscalculation of time), Art Vertlieb is constantly ridiculed for being late for games and for being unable to read a clock.

Meanwhile, because of his Japanese background, Greg Kimura generally gets blamed for the Second World War. And to get on the nerves of nuclear physicists Ewart Blackmore and Rich Helmer, their teammates will refer to them as "the glow worms" and refuse to sit beside them "because they're radioactive."

One night, urologist Andy Moore made the mistake of announcing he'd just completed his first sex change operation. Of course, by the time the dressing room got finished with him, Moore's significant medical accomplishment was being described as a mere "slip of the scalpel."

Another night, the team's travel agent, Gord Rees, experimented with a new pair of sports glasses. He claimed his vision was worse than ever. Somebody suggested that Rees try them right side up for greatest effect. While his sight was improved, his reputation was scarred forever.

On his fiftieth birthday in December, 1991, Morrison, arguably the largest but not the fastest Flame, was recovering from a knee injury. He received a trophy from his teammates. It depicted a cruise ship mounted on a pedestal above the following inscription:

"Presented to Keith 'Love Boat' Morrison. This vessel proved to be too large and unmanoeuvrable to fit harmoniously in the fleet. Kept active in a figurehead position, as an example of bulk, it is currently in drydock for repairs to the left forward thruster. Though respected by all the crew, it will soon be replaced by a swifter, sleeker model, capable of short radius turns."

Although they begin each game with dreams of greatness, on occasion the Flames have looked more like the Keystone Kops. One of their most infamous escapades was at an old-timers' tournament at the North Shore Winter Club in the late 1980s. As the tourney wound down, the Flames found themselves up against the Labatt Blues, one of the better old-timers' squads in the Vancouver area. Near the end of the game, things were going pretty much according to the script. The Blues were leading the Flames 6–2. But then the Blues took a penalty, giving the Flames the man advantage. Moments later, the Flames received a penalty too.

With the teams now playing four a side, Flames' defence-man Norm Smith seized the puck. Thinking the opposition now had the man advantage, Smith retreated behind his net and stood there as if to say, "Come and get me, you guys!"

Realizing there was little sense in chasing Smith in a four-on-four situation, the Blues lined up across the Flames' blue-line and waited.

Smith's defence partner, Ken Anderson, was appalled by this squandering of a chance to catch up. He skated to the face-off circle inside his own blueline and began waving and yelling to Smith to start up the ice.

Smith stayed with his game plan and just stood there with a grin on his face.

Soon the rest of his teammates, including those on the bench, joined Anderson in shouting at Smith to move it.

With time running out, Anderson's frustration grew and he finally hurled his stick against the boards and stormed to the bench ranting, "I'm not going to play out there with that son of a bitch!"

In the confusion, another forty seconds of the penalty elapsed before someone jumped over the boards to replace Anderson. Smith finally got the message, handed off the puck to a teammate and left the ice. As Smith sheepishly sat down on the bench, Anderson let loose with a volley of four-letter adjectives describing Smith's performance. Smith responded in kind and in the ensuing melee, Smith was pushed over the boards and back onto the ice in front of the Flames' bench.

Adding insult to injury, the ref blew the whistle and penalized the Flames for having too many men on the ice. The loss to the Blues was soon forgotten, but the image of two old friends duking it out combined with the penalty was, in Keith Morrison's words, "the funniest thing the Flames have ever seen on ice."

Nevertheless, the Flames have won their fair share of tournaments over the years. Keith Morrison's den—a.k.a. the Hall of Flame—is festooned with trophies, cups, banners, plaques, medals, mementos and certificates documenting their success. Meanwhile, the team has grown to six goalies, forty-two skaters and a long waiting list of hopefuls. Turnover is minimal. This team is committed to "growing old together."

BROSSARD, QUEBEC

On a summer evening in mid-August, a group of die-hard hockey players, some clad in shorts and T-shirts, others in business clothes, leave the warm evening air for the chill of an arena in Brossard, Quebec, across the Champlain Bridge from Montreal, on the south shore of the St. Lawrence River.

Each Wednesday night since their beloved Habs won the Stanley Cup in the spring of 1993, these twenty-odd players have been chasing pucks at Les 4 Glaces. Here, members of various oldtimers' teams—the Rusty Blades, the Montreal Old Puckers and even some from one of the original oldtimers' organizations in Montreal, the Fakawie Hockey League—have been feeding their hockey addiction all summer long.

Tonight is special; the summer hockey season is nearly over, so it's time for the annual "Oldsters versus Youngsters" match.

"People think we're crazy to play hockey in the summertime," says Brook Ellis. "I tell them summer hockey is a wonderful thing. When it's hot outside, it's great to walk into a nice cool rink, work up a sweat, then afterwards, when you're good and thirsty, have a cool drink."

Hockey without end is consistent with Brook Ellis's lifestyle.

An early tournament (about 1970) at Pointe Claire, where head-gear was primitive or optional.

"Clear the track, Shack is back!" But this time he's in ref's stripes.

Bill Wilkinson of Pointe Claire was the first to call it "oldtimers' hockey."

Pat Gouett (seated right) registers teams at the First National Oldtimers' Hockey Tournament (1975) in Peterborough.

John Gouett in his Rocket Richard pose before a game at Queen's University in 1975.

Co-creators of the first oldtimers' tournament Gerry Aherne (2nd from right) and John Gouett (right) welcome reps from Saint John.

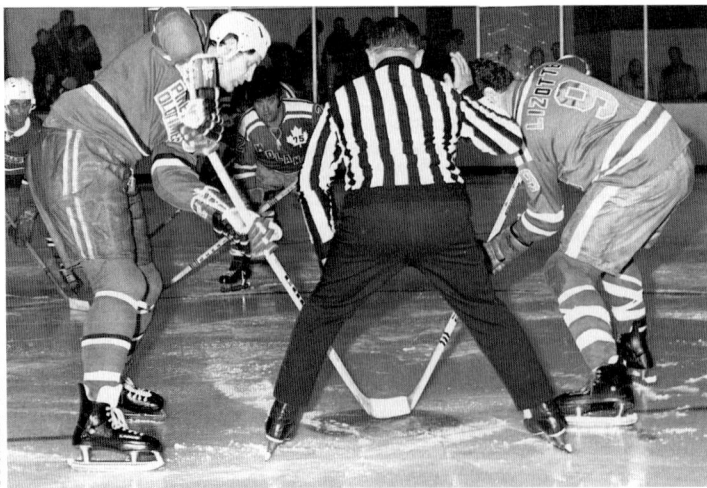

Puck is dropped at the First National tourney in the game between Pine Falls, Manitoba and Midland, Ontario.

At the First National Tournament, referee-in-chief Jim Orr said the objective of old-timers was "fun, enjoyment, exercise and fellowship."

COURTESY OLDTIMERS' HOCKEY NEWS

COURTESY DAVE TATHAM

Even goalie Greg Walker isn't wearing a mask as Grande Prairie fends off a Midland Oldtimers' rush.

COURTESY OLDTIMERS' HOCKEY NEWS

Sid Fawcett (right) of the Wolfe Island Old Timers sent in a deposit for the tournament even before he had a team assembled.

COURTESY OLDTIMERS' HOCKEY NEWS

George Hastie (right) holds D Division trophy with Sudbury coach Larry Rubic. "The team just gave me the captain title because I'm the oldest."

COURTESY OLDTIMERS' HOCKEY NEWS

Gerry Aherne escapes the pressure of tournament organizing by netminding for the Port Colborne Oldtimers (1976).

Who needs Lord Stanley's Cup? Ron Wright parades his team's D Division trophy at First Canada-U.S. Tournament at Niagara Falls in 1976.

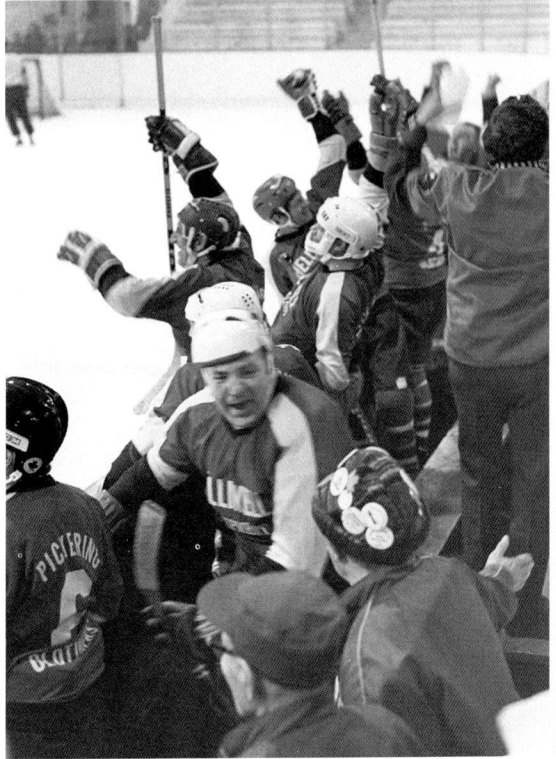

Jubilation on Scarborough-Pickering bench as they win the C Division final in Niagara Falls.

"Short on hockey talent, but long on musical ability," the Lumsden Rockers (from Saskatchewan) entertain in a hotel stairwell at the Third National tourney in Saint John, N.B.

John Gouett barnstorming on Vancouver Island, coaxing oldtimers' reps to bring their teams to the 1976 national tourney.

"World Champions" was the way the North Bay Sealtest Oldtimers were described back home when they beat Mount Royal X's for the A Division title at the First International Oldtimers' Tournament in Holland in 1976.

Twins Iain (left) and Alaistair MacLean flank their favourite target in Saskatoon, goalie Richard Schroh.

When asked to "come out and blow the whistle," Gord Wintermute almost always does.

The first meeting to organize the River Heights Mixers oldtimers was held in a change shack in Saskatoon in 1977. Rich Meier (back row, 3rd from right) and Morris Zuk (2nd from right in front row) were there.

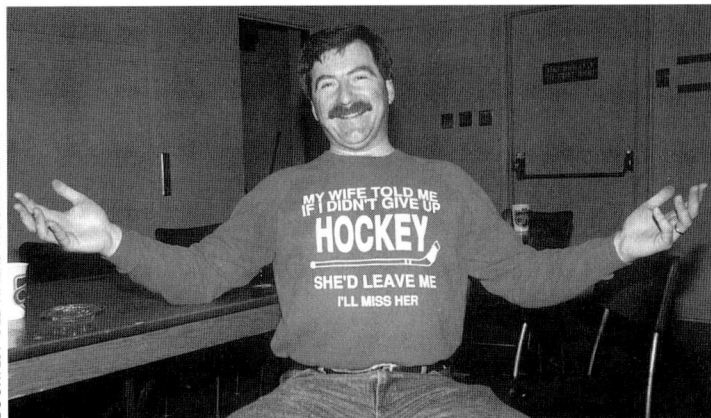

Gary Rodgers of the Niagara Falls Burnouts, displays his defiant dedication to oldtimers. (The fact is, his wife Tricia gave him the shirt.)

Oldtimers' hockey stops when a goal is scored, when a player gets hurt or when somebody loses a contact lens.

When the Golden Oldies take to the ice in Parksville, B.C., there is more than a millennium of hockey experience on skates. (front row, l to r: Eddie Taylor, Joe Ottom, Ron Butler, Howie Meeker, Bob Murrant, Scott Sherriff, Roy Reber, Tex Fandry; back row: Roy Jardine, Eddie Bird, Chuck Chestnut, Jack Harlow, Hugh MacAulay, Ray Therres, Bob Drewbrook, Florence Robertson, Mike Chestnut, Hec McLean, Merle Mundorf, Buddy Bebb, Brian Grieve, Dave Gourley, Gene Mason, Frank Robertson, Peter Kucey.)

The Saturday afternoon oldtimers' crew at Saint Mary's University in Halifax. (front row, l to r: Bill MacDonald, Dr. Brewer Auld, Paul Leydon, Robert "Puddy" Reardon, Don Murphy, Bob Dauphinee; middle row: Tusker O'Neill, Bill Bailly, Oog Jones, Ken Fellows, Lou Centa, Bill Richardson, Dr. Bob Napier; back row: Stew McInnes, Fred Gallagher, Steve Thompson; boy in front: Robbie Thompson.

Don Murphy faces a rush by his son Paul in the annual father vs. son game at Saint Mary's arena.

In borrowed Club Med jerseys and borrowed (but well spent) time, the UBC Old Birds pose at their home rink in Vancouver. (front row, l to r: Gord Robertson, Bob Hindmarsh, Lew Robinson (standing), Roy Hammond, John Thomas; back row: Jim Richards, Mike Buchanan, Paul Willing, Konrad Tittler)

From the birth of oldtimers in 1975 to its 20th anniversary, Dave "Tilt" Tatham has reported it in his *Oldtimers' Hockey News*.

Fran Rider dedicates her working life to advancing the cause of women's hockey. After hours she plays defence for the Newtonbrook Stars.

WWII comrades in arms, these three RCAF vets (l to r: Spike Crawford, Ted Froats and Ben Benedetti) are now members of Huffn' Puffs in London, Ontario.

As a high school student in the 1950s, Brook and his team-mates trekked from north Toronto to the arena in Woodbridge three times a week for hockey practice and then a fourth time on Saturdays to play their games. At age fifty-six, Ellis hasn't changed. Despite the pressures of being a vice-president at Birks Jewellers, he plays oldtimers' hockey several times a week. And he plays with a cross-section of locals he might otherwise have never met—commercial artist Paul Sicard, economist Nick Matossian and civil engineer Ken Sinclair.

"Oldtimers' hockey in the Montreal area isn't like any-where else," says Sinclair, a fifty-nine-year-old real estate development consultant. "Despite the French-English situa-tion here, I don't think I've ever seen any French-English fric-tion in a locker room, or on the ice....In Chateauguay, on the south shore, you play with some guys who can't speak English and English guys who can't speak French. We even had a couple of Mohawks from Kahnawake Reserve. Everyone got along amazingly well.

"We played a tournament there. After the game we went with all the Mohawks up to the lounge at the arena in Kah-nawake. This was just after the bridge closing and the shoot-ing at Kahnasatake. And for the first time in my life I really met these people. It was truly a turning point. All because of oldtimers."

Hockey stalwart Paul Sicard is another summer player. He got into oldtimers' hockey on the ground floor. He remem-bers sitting in a Montreal apartment in the mid-1970s, with four hockey-starved friends all scribbling down the names of potential players for a tournament team that eventually became known as the Rusty Blades.

"We started with thirty-one players," says Sicard. "Most of us were in our thirties, playing tournaments in the A Division. I designed the logo. We did some fund-raisers for charity. We even created something called Oldtimers Shampoo for jock itch and helmet itch, and sold thousands of bottles."

Over the years, a number of Montreal oldtimers' teams have raised funds for local charities. One recipient has been the Matossian Trust Fund. It was established by Nick Matossian Jr., a young man diagnosed with a brain tumour in the 1980s. After Nick's death, the SWAT (Senior Westmount All-Star Team) oldtimers picked up on the idea and organized an annual eight-team tournament.

"In four years," says Nick Sr., "we've contributed $40,000 to the Montreal Children's Hospital and Ste. Justine's Hospital for Children, enough to buy some very sophisticated and modern equipment for the neuro-surgical operating room. It shows you the kind of support you get from the people you play with."

These Montreal oldtimers are a close-knit family. Whoever they play with during the regular hockey season—the Rusty Blades, the Old Puckers, the SWAT or the old FHL—habit and camaraderie bring them back to Les 4 Glaces each summer. For twenty-five summers, nothing "short of a funeral or a marriage" has kept these hockey fanatics from driving a half-hour or more to Brossard each Wednesday night for their weekly hockey fix.

Mind you, in just his second season on the ice with the summer league, Ken Sinclair was temporarily sidelined. One night, back in the days of no helmets and no face masks, he was paired with Paul Sicard on defence. Part way through the game, Ken took a stick in the eye and immediately fell to his knees, clutching his face.

"Let me see," said Sicard, pulling Sinclair's glove away from his eye. "There's no blood."

"My eye feels like jelly," moaned Sinclair.

"It's okay, I tell you," claimed Sicard. "Let's get on with the game."

Despite Sicard's iron-man preference that his defencemate stay in the game, another of Sinclair's teammates, Bud Adams, immediately drove his injured friend to the Montreal General Hospital where he needed eleven stitches. "I remember the doctor sewing up my eyeball, as Bud Adams stood there, still in his full hockey gear, putting drops of Novocain into my eye."

Nevertheless, everybody is in attendance for this season-ending "Oldsters versus Youngsters" grudge match, the conclusion of Summer Hockey XXV. Despite his one bad eye, Ken Sinclair is there. Nick Matossian (despite a couple of formerly fractured vertebrae) and another of his sons, Christian, have arrived. Brook Ellis, the second oldest of the Oldsters is there. So are Bud Adams *et fils* Geoff. The stellar (if a little overweight) Paul Sicard has arrived. And goalie David Schulman (weak ankle ligaments, short-sightedness and all) is present and accounted for.

Everybody checks in by age, which ranges from sixty to twenty-six. Then, to determine the two sides, game convenor David Schulman simply draws a line through the middle of the list—the eldest play the youngest.

"Until about two years ago," says Schulman, "the Oldsters won all the games."

"I remember the very first game," continues Brook Ellis. "It was really fun in the dressing room. The Youngsters were convinced that they were going to thrash us.

"They got the shock of their lives. All of a sudden the game wasn't as friendly as regular summer hockey. They skated all over the darn ice. They all had big slapshots, but, because they couldn't use them in this crowd and because we could move the puck faster than they could move their young legs, we beat them handily."

"That's right," Schulman concludes, "old age and treachery will beat youth and legs every time."

Somewhere along the way, though, a light went on in the Youngsters' heads. They started using their brains instead of their legs. At the same time, all of the Oldsters hit fifty. And so, tonight's annual classic pits a wise but aging group of men against sons and other younger men who grow wiser by learning their fathers' secrets—secrets readily shared because this ice surface makes them brothers in the spirit of the game. This year, it's the Oldsters who win.

Within minutes of the end of the game, the intensity and competitive drive subside. The Youngsters run a verbal gauntlet from the Oldsters enroute to the dressing room. But between these verbal shots, pride flows through these men. The sons are amazed at their aging fathers' capabilities; the fathers are thrilled to be playing with their sons.

"It's being together," Brook Ellis explains. "You start off in the dressing room together. You're on the bench and on the ice together. Then you're back in the dressing room together. You belong to a group."

"It's the love of the game," adds Ken Sinclair. "There isn't a game in the world like it....I feel sorry for Americans who've only played baseball. They grow old and can't do it anymore. Canadians kids grow up into old men like us and can continue to play our game."

ETOBICOKE, ONTARIO

It's the seventh game of the Stanley Cup final.

Tonight's game is being played without a crowd or cameras, without referees, coaches, general managers or even a cup or trophy of any kind. And yet, all the marbles are at stake in this winner-take-all match between the Blacks and the Whites at the Westwood Arena in northwest Toronto. It's the final night of Monday night hockey for the season.

Tonight, from 9:15 to 10:30, these two teams will play one game and part of another because the rules stipulate that five goals wins a game. And most Monday nights there isn't enough time to complete a second game. So tonight—their Stanley Cup night—everything rides on the first game. Mind you, none of these regulations is written down anywhere. They're simply understood by the twenty or so players who have been part of Monday night hockey for more than fifteen years.

"The Grand Master of the league, Bobby Bendera, he'll bring out the performance sheets, all the statistics for the season," insists Ralph Ruffo of the Blacks. "He can prove that the Blacks reign supreme on Monday nights.

"These White [team] guys—all the white collars, the lawyers, etc.—they're not used to grinding and working hard. If you're a good player, you're a Black. If you're a bum, you're a White. The Blacks have proved over the years that working stiffs always come out on top."

Ruffo's comment is playful. He takes as much delight needling his regular opposition as he does playing oldtimers' hockey. In fact, this version of Monday night hockey has no standings, no statistics, no league executives to keep track of

wins, losses, goals and assists. From week to week, it's only
the players themselves who remember or forget the outcomes.
And the results are valuable only if they can be used to rub
the opposition's nose in it. Victors' spoils in this game are
bragging rights.

Ruffo's description of each team's makeup is relatively
accurate. Most players on the Whites are professionals, while
most on the Blacks run small businesses or are tradesmen.

"I'm in the service station business," explains Ruffo. "Bob's
in sporting goods. Bill MacLean sells heavy equipment for
construction. Mike Simone's family is in the fruit and veg-
etable business. Dave Sanders is a firefighter. And our goalie,
Wayne Moulton, he's an auto mechanic."

This Monday night hockey tradition actually began with
the "working stiffs." In the late 1970s, friends and acquaintances regularly gathered at either Bendera's sport and cycle
shop or at Ruffo's gas station in Toronto's west end to talk
hockey. Just like an impromptu hot stove league, everybody
recounted and embellished championships and near championships from days gone by. The storytelling and lies conjured
up memories of games played in the Humber Valley league, in
Junior B and at the Lakeshore Arena where teams from
Christie's Bakery, Campbell Soup, Continental Can and
other companies tangled on Sundays for supremacy in the
Lakeshore Industrial League. Everybody wanted to relive his
hockey memories. So, in 1976, Bob Bendera called everybody's bluff and rented ice to see who really wanted to play
again. One side wore black sweaters, the other white. And
before long, some "white collar" players were allowed to join.

"When I first started, the Blacks always won," says lawyer
John Ritchie. "The Whites were close but the Blacks always
won. Anybody that was new and was good was always put on
the Blacks. Somebody shows up and has never skated before,
guaranteed, he was assigned to the Whites."

While it's true they have some less experienced players,
including Richard Pyne, a lawyer who didn't start playing
hockey until he was an adult, Ritchie and his fellow Whites
have managed to recruit such talented oldtimers as ex-
Chicago Blackhawk Bill White and former American Hockey

Leaguer Bill Ford. Ritchie himself climbed the hockey ladder to the Junior A Toronto Marlboros under coach Turk Broda in 1963. The following season he returned to the Junior B Etobicoke Indians whose goaltender (Ken Dryden) "helped us overachieve and we'd usually make the playoffs.

"Ken and I knew each other from the time I was eleven," says Ritchie. "He was a superb athlete and a terrific goaltender." The on-ice friendship between John Ritchie and Ken Dryden began at the peewee level, survived Junior B, university and even industrial hockey. In the 1973–74 season, when Dryden temporarily left the Canadiens and moved to Toronto, Ritchie persuaded him to join the Vulcan Industrial Packagers in the Lakeshore Industrial League. But Dryden did not play goal. He played out.

"A memory of that year," says Dryden, "I was playing defence—in my goalie skates—[suddenly] the puck went out to the point. I decided to follow it. The shot came. It hit me in the pads. And all I see ahead of me is open ice.

"I think, 'Holy cow! Is this exciting!' So I take off. Well, I'm so occupied with the puck that my head is completely down. All of a sudden, this shadow comes into view and he just nails me. It was a hip check. I go up in the air and do a three-quarter gainer, nearly a complete flip. I [learned] quickly how the other half lives."

By the mid-1980s, Dryden had retired from pro hockey completely and was only playing oldtimers. He accepted John Ritchie's invitation to play in Bob Bendera's Monday night league, but because the ex-Canadien wasn't playing goal the Blacks didn't want him. Dryden joined fellow Whites John Ritchie, Bill White, Bill Ford and an outspoken businessman named Al Hume. Only when he was Hume's teammate did Ken Dryden discover that it was Al Hume who had inflicted the thundering hip check that introduced Dryden to how "the other half lives."

But of course there is no contact in Monday night hockey. Each week players pay their twenty dollars for hockey governed by the simple justice of the playing field: no referee, just arguments put forward, heard and resolved by the two battling sides. Face-offs only happen at the start of each game. Icings and centre-ice offsides are ignored. On a blue-line offside, the defensive team can choose to ignore it or protest with a shouted chorus of "Offside" from the bench or the ice.

The first side to score five goals wins the game. Both Whites and Blacks agree the best games—the most fun games—are the closest ones. Losing 5–0 isn't fun. Being skunked may temporarily fuel the good-natured needling in the dressing room, but it's still a shutout. It's still embarrassing. And nobody—not even oldtimers who watch and tolerate each other's diminishing skills—chooses to be embarrassed on the ice. After all, they come here week after week to feel good.

But not on the final night of the 1992–93 Monday night season. On Stanley Cup night, the idea isn't just to feel good. The goal is to win.

Everything else about the game is as usual. Bendera and Ruffo have brought in a few ringers to bolster the Blacks' lineup. Bill Ford, as usual, inspires his Whites by "complaining that the game is not being played to perfection." The difference about tonight, however, is the level of competitiveness.

For the first thirty to forty-five minutes of the game, the two sides trade goals. But suddenly the score reaches 4–4. One goal will win the game. The season will be over. It's sudden death. And the competitive instincts of all these players resurface.

"It's like an overtime game," recalls Dryden, "because it *is* an overtime game. Whoever scores the next goal is going to win the Stanley Cup. I couldn't believe how nervous I got."

The score remains tied for twenty or twenty-five minutes, by far the longest stretch without a goal in many games. Both sides are playing far beyond their abilities. Rushes take on an intensity seen only on this one night of the year. Desperate defencemen throw their bodies in front of shots. Then the Whites get a break and score what appears to be the winner.

"Offside! Offside!" comes the cry from the Black bench. The Whites, chiefly captain Bill Ford, argue, "Onside."

"Usually, where a goal is advocated by one side and disputed by the other side," says John Ritchie, "the side disputing usually wins." In other words, whoever whines loudest wins. The White goal is disallowed. The score remains 4–4.

Minutes later, there's a scramble in the White end. After a shot into the goal mouth, the White netminder, Moon Mullins, tries to cover the puck. He's not quite on it. The White defence can't smother the puck either. A Black forward gets his stick on it and whacks it into the net.

"No goal!" shout the White defenders.

"They claimed the whistle had gone," remembers Ralph Ruffo. "But of course," he adds condescendingly, "there is no whistle, so how could it have gone? The puck was in the net, but because of the season, the type of season they'd had, the frustration, we already had the title locked up, so we went along with it."

Finally, the Whites score a clean goal. They win the Stanley Cup and, more important, bragging rights.

"That game felt like any game I've ever played at any level," says Ken Dryden. "The feeling is the same. But, of course, it is the same. It's a game that had to be won.

"I remember feeling a bit disappointed after I won my first Stanley Cup, the other Stanley Cup, that it didn't feel really any different from all those other big games in my life. But you know, that's the great thing. When I was seven years old playing for the Humber Valley Hornets and when I'm forty-five years old on the Whites and all the time in between— with Cornell, the Canadiens and Team Canada—basically it is the same."

FISHER RIVER, MANITOBA

The residents of Fisher River, Manitoba, have always known oldtimers' hockey as inter-lake hockey. Here among the iso-lated communities located between Lake Winnipeg and Lake Manitoba, aboriginal men of all ages have long played a brand of recreational hockey that gives them the exercise they like and the contact with neighbouring communities they crave. For as long as anyone can remember, this region of the country has had an all-aboriginal hockey league with teams from Dog Creek, the Peguis Reserve and the Fisher River Reserve.

Reverend Stanley McKay, a Cree born on the Fisher River Reserve, played hockey here as both a child and an adult. McKay's grandfather introduced him to hockey in the early 1950s: he told Stan stories of George Armstrong, the famous Native captain of the Toronto Maple Leafs, and gave the boy his first pair of tube skates.

"We played shinny on a small patch of ice we cleared on the [Fisher] River," McKay recalls. "Just a couple of rubber boots for goal posts and road apples or an old pair of mitts tied together for a puck....In fact, it was better to use something other than real pucks because we didn't have shin pads, so when you got hit it didn't hurt as much."

In the 1970s, McKay came back to Fisher River to be ordained at Stevens Memorial United Church and eventually to serve in the ministry. Apart from his duties at the church, McKay coached youngsters who didn't fit into other levels of organized hockey. In his spare time, he played defence for the Fisher River Cobras, an oldtimers' team.

"We had this big ugly snake on the front of our shirts," laughs McKay, "but we had a definite team spirit."

The Cobras played one league game a week and practised at least once a week. They won their fair share of games, but winning had little to do with inherent talent. Reverend McKay believes it had more to do with the closeness of the community. Because teammates were friends, they felt at ease with each other on the ice, and every oldtimers' game was a natural expression of that relationship. The Cobras were like a family. And that family feeling permeated the inter-lake league.

"In all-Native hockey leagues there were many strong rivalries between the local reserves....But it was friendly rivalry. People knew the players on the different teams. So there was a very clear protocol for gentlemanly behaviour and good humour along with the competitive play."

The only conflict that Rev. McKay found difficult to reconcile was the scheduling of a tournament game on a Sunday morning. He never skipped a service to play hockey. But during one Sunday morning tournament game, McKay was involved in a tussle for the puck in front of the net. An opposition stick came up and clipped him over the eye. At the evening service, Rev. McKay was sporting a large bandage and a shiner. From then on he excused himself from all Sunday morning games.

Between 1993 and 1995, the years that he served as moderator of the United Church of Canada, Rev. McKay missed most Sunday morning games and indeed most games of the inter-lake league. But whether he has time to play or not, he has never lost his sense of the spirit of the game or of hockey's importance in his community.

"Oldtimers has been the best development in hockey," says Rev. McKay. "It says much for the way we organize the game early on…and for the value of recreational hockey in people's lives.…It's the kind of hockey we should have for seven- and eight-year-olds who may discover that they're not going to be competitive hockey players, but love the game."

PARKSVILLE, BRITISH COLUMBIA

As the twenty-five or so members of the Parksville Golden Oldies take to the ice at eight o'clock in the morning at the District 69 Arena on Vancouver Island, they possess more than a thousand years of hockey experience on their collective skates. Mind you, the talent may seem somewhat disguised by greying whiskers, receding hairlines, a few midriff bulges, and knee and elbow braces.

Sixty-two-year-old Eddie Taylor, whose hockey career included stops in Brandon and Flin Flon, Manitoba, and Minneapolis, in recent years has had a heart attack and two operations. Six months after his second bypass surgery in 1989, his heart specialist asked, "How're you feeling?"

"Just fine," said Taylor. "I'm playing hockey again."

"You're what?!" exclaimed the doctor.

"Playing oldtimers."

"How do you feel?"

"Great," said Taylor.

"Play every night, then," said his specialist.

Hugh MacAulay and his friend Hector MacLean started

the Golden Oldies in 1987 when the two senior citizens asked if they could play shinny at the arena just before public skating. The team, along with Monday, Wednesday and Friday scrimmages, grew from there.

Another of the originals is sixty-two-year-old Peter Kucey, a.k.a. "the Thompson Kid." Kucey has played on forty different teams in his hockey lifetime stretching from his home province of Manitoba to his current oldtimers' stomping grounds on Vancouver Island. He recently announced to his daughter, "I've made a major decision."

She held her breath.

"I can't play hockey any more—any more than once a day," he quipped.

Montreal-born Eddie "Santa Claus" Bird is seventy-two. He took up hockey when he was three, but had to give it up during the Depression when his family moved to England. He struggled back into the game in the English National League but the war ended his hockey career until the mid-1980s.

Roy Jardine came to hockey from the other direction. He was born in Manchester, England, in 1921, came to Canada soon after and learned hockey on the sloughs of eastern Saskatchewan. Père Athol Murray spotted Jardine and invited him to join his famous Notre Dame Hounds in Wilcox, Saskatchewan. He played against Elmer Lach and Doug Bentley and eventually tried out for the AHL Cleveland Barons.

As far as longevity is concerned, Frank Robertson outstrips them all. He is eighty-two but has only played hockey since 1985. The day Eddie Bird joined the Parksville Golden Oldies he went home and said to his wife, "I can't quit playing hockey."

"What do you mean, you can't quit?" asked Eileen Bird.

"There's a guy ten years older than I am. He's eighty-two and still playing. That means I've got another twenty years."

About the middle of the pack, at least in age, is the seventy-year-old mentor of the Parksville Golden Oldies. He battled his way up hockey's ladder of prestige further than any of his teammates, but Howie Meeker claims, "I played nine years in the NHL on four Stanley Cup teams. And the only time I was a professional was when I didn't have the puck. The second I had the puck, my brain stopped. Today, my brain can keep up with my feet. I'm creative now. So hockey's more fun."

During his career as a Maple Leaf, Meeker's accomplishments were plentiful—playing right wing on the second generation "Kid Line" with Vic Lynn and Teeder Kennedy; fighting with Gordie Howe (in fact beating him for the Calder Trophy as rookie of the year in 1946–47); scoring five goals against Chicago in one game; and winning four Stanley Cups with the Leafs, including helping to set up Bill Barilko's Cup-winning overtime goal against Montreal in 1951. But the moment Meeker considers his proudest occurred in his rookie season during the sixth and deciding game of the Stanley Cup playoffs against the Montreal Canadiens.

"We were leading by a goal," Meeker remembers, "with about a minute, fifteen, to go. [Turk] Broda was in net. [Jim] Thomson and [Gus] Mortson were on defence. And Hap Day put us on the ice—Kennedy, Lynn and myself. Five rookies against [Rocket] Richard, [Elmer] Lach, [Toe] Blake, [Ken] Reardon and [Glen] Harmon. They had a hell of a hockey team.

"But they had only one shot in the time we were on the ice. And I was on the ice as we won [my] first Stanley Cup."

Retiring from playing in 1954 only drove Meeker into other hockey careers: coaching, managing, broadcasting and teaching hockey school. Whether he is helping kids overcome wobbly-ankled skating, chastising the amateur associations for excluding youngsters of average size and ability from the game, or advising the professionals to clean up hockey violence, Meeker has never lost his passion and his desire to share the joys of hockey with everybody.

The first time he encountered the Golden Oldies, he realized why their game wasn't as satisfying as it could be. First, the playing calibre varied greatly, partly because of age and partly because of experience. To compensate, Meeker suggested creating A, B and C lines according to the skill level of the players and then to make sure that A players were matched on the ice with A opponents, never A against B or B against C.

Second, Meeker recognized that hockey is most fun when

you have the puck and that it's just hard work when you don't; by chasing the puck carrier and stripping him of the puck, you kill the other fellow's fun. To maximize the pleasure of the game, Meeker suggested that a team in the offensive zone be encouraged to steal the puck for a chance on goal. But when the defensive players were carrying the puck beyond their blueline, they should be allowed to move the puck through the centre ice area and into the opposition's end unmolested. A rush up the ice ends only when somebody gives the puck away or takes a shot. More players get to handle the puck and goalies get to handle more shots.

Finally, Meeker made sure that everybody got equal time on the ice. He brought along a clock with a bell set to ring every two minutes and fifteen seconds. The bell never nullified a play; if someone was rushing to the net when the bell went, the play would be completed. But then the lines would change and fresh skaters would get their shift. The Parksville Golden Oldies dubbed these their "seniors oldtimers'" rules. And they stuck.

"You play according to the ability of the players you're on the ice with," says Eddie Taylor. "I love it out there, especially seeing the way Howie helps us improve our skills because at our age you forget things."

Taylor hardly needs coaching. He skates quickly and effortlessly. Even his good friend Howie Meeker has trouble keeping up with him. But Meeker compensates by needling Taylor about passing the puck blindly to the opposition and not listening to his advice about carrying the puck.

"Never go up the middle," yells Meeker. "Go wide, Eddie. Go wide!"

"What do you mean wide?" Taylor shouts back. "I'm six feet from the boards. Do you want me on the other side of the boards?"

Meeker has often dispensed the same advice to rushing defenceman Joe Ottom. Better known as "Preacher Joe" because of his Christianity, Ottom usually takes a fair bit of friendly abuse from his teammates. Once, during a tournament, Ottom skated up the ice on a breakaway. But instead of going to the net, he headed for the corner.

"What the hell were you doing?" Eddie Taylor asked him later.

"Howie says, 'Go wide,'" said Ottom, "so I went wide."

"Well, I don't know," said Taylor, "Howie keeps trying to teach you hockey. And you keep trying to teach him religion. I don't think either one of you is going to win."

When Jim Dorman persisted in throwing passes up the centre of the ice right onto an opposing player's stick, Meeker forced Dorman to sign a promise: "I will never again pass across our own zone unless it is 100% safe. Signed, Jim Dorman. November 14, 1992."

"The very next goddamn game," says Eddie Bird, who was playing against Dorman at the time, "he put one through the middle and right onto my stick. Everybody stopped and looked at him."

However, Dorman knows how to deal with the razzing. When Meeker and the rest of his teammates began kidding him about the faux pas, Dorman simply turned down his hearing aid and became oblivious to it all.

Whether a point is taken or not doesn't really matter. By 9:15 on a Friday morning, the game is history. And each success, each mistake, each goal and each goal missed provides grist for the dressing room cut-up session. Yet, despite the ribbing and carrying-on, these solid friendships are based on a common passion for hockey.

For Roy Jardine, "the thrill of lacing up the skates has never left me." For heart surgery survivor Eddie Taylor, "hockey has saved my life." Eddie Bird won't let his wife Eileen plan winter holidays away from the island for fear he'll miss hockey, while octogenarian Frank Robertson manages to get his wife Dot out to play a few games with the Oldies each season. And despite having his name inscribed on the Stanley Cup four times, Howie Meeker still feels, "I'm having more fun at hockey now than I ever had before."

ANNAPOLIS VALLEY, NOVA SCOTIA

Almost every town in the Annapolis Valley stages an invitational hockey tournament each winter. Whether it's in Windsor, Wolfville, Kentville, Coldbrook, Berwick or Greenwood, everybody generally shows up. Sometimes prize money is at stake but often it's just for the bragging rights. The intense rivalries here—rivalries between armed forces stations, schools, clubs, and entire communities—go back decades.

Hockey pundits say that on any given day any team can win. But for a variety of reasons, hockey players from Windsor win more than their share.

"Windsor has a winning tradition in hockey," claims Frank "Junior" Moore. "Whether it's because of the old Windsor Maple Leafs who went after the Allan Cup for many years or the years of senior hockey played here, there's never been another town that can just dig down and come up with hockey like you've never seen before."

Even though he was born and raised in Kentville, forty-year-old Moore has witnessed a lot of Windsor's winning tradition himself, albeit sometimes on the losing side. When he was playing for Truro in the Nova Scotia Intermediate A League, Moore remembers a playoff series against Windsor. Just before one of Truro's home games, Moore heard that Windsor had arrived with only five forwards and three defencemen.

"This is great," said one of Moore's teammates. "Windsor's only got seven or eight guys!"

But Moore just shook his head.

"What's wrong?" asked Truro coach Johnny Hutchison.

"How many have they got?" Moore asked.

"Only a line and a half. We'll grind them into the ground."

"Nope. We're in for the game of our lives," moaned Moore.

That night, Windsor beat Truro 7–2 and eventually won the series.

In 1978, after Junior Moore had married, set up a financial consulting business and settled down in Windsor, he helped launch the Windsor Sports Club team of recreational players. The idea was to assemble players around age thirty, from in and around Windsor and to compete in gentlemen's hockey.

Whatever the level of hockey, for fifteen years the Windsor Sports Club has maintained the town's winning ways. At Lake Placid they faced a team of ex-pros and beat them. At the annual Monctonian or Greenwood Bombers invitationals, they are always placed in the A Division and come away with their fair share of trophies.

"How about that tournament in Kentville?" says Windsor car salesman Bob Dill. Dill, now forty-one, was one of the co-founders of the Windsor Sports Club team. He remembers a particular Saturday morning in Kentville when the Sports Club had only five skaters when the game began at 11:30.

"I left work at 11:30," says Dill. "Now Kentville is twenty-five miles away but I drove like a bat out of hell. Got there about 11:45. Stepped on the ice and two guys went to our bench. They hadn't had a break since the game began. We ended up getting a tie to put us into the final.

"The saying was, 'Windsor's always got another car full of players on the way.' The key word here is pride."

Bob Dill chalks up Windsor's legacy of success to an ingrained will to win. He believes that all Windsor hockey players have it and that most of them learned it on the frozen ponds. When he was a kid, Dill remembers epic hockey battles on Campbell's Pond and Long Pond (the pond his cousin, Howard Dill, claims is the birthplace of hockey in Canada) where the shinny looked more like roller derby matches than hockey.

"A lot of Windsor's good skaters were coached by Moe Smith," says Mike Hughes. At forty-two, Hughes is a teacher and respects the gift that Moe Smith gave him and several generations of Windsor hockey players. Smith's family operated a sporting goods store in town but, beginning in the mid-1950s, Moe devoted all his spare time to teaching kids how to play hockey, from shinny on the ponds to minor hockey at the Matchbox Arena downtown to the Junior B Windsor Royals in the arena at the fair grounds.

"Moe taught you the fundamentals," remembers Rod MacPherson. Born in the fishing town of Digby, Nova Scotia, MacPherson graduated from road hockey to Moe Smith's semi-organized minor hockey league when the family moved to Windsor in 1965. "He taught me how to skate, pass and shoot. But what I really learned from Moe was the desire to win.

"You just had to look at him, growling at the bench. That red face said it all. You could tell when he wasn't pleased with the way the game was going. You could see the desire in him. Moe didn't like to lose."

As well as fostering Windsor's winning tradition, Moe Smith can also be credited with beginning the practice of taking fewer players than required to games, although this practice owed more to circumstance than strategy. Many was the time Moe Smith's 1961 blue Volkswagen beetle could be seen with six or seven players (plus their equipment) inside, heading off down the road to take on the opposition in Chester, Brooklyn or even Glace Bay on the tip of Cape Breton Island.

That's still the way Windsor Sports Club oldtimers often travel. Just a couple of cars, trunks full of gear, some postgame refreshments and enough players to ice a team plus a few spares. Along with regulars Moore, Dill, Hughes and MacPherson, there will also be surveyor Bruce Lake, farmer Brian Knowles, construction worker Frank Woodman (the goalie), Halifax bar manager Roger MacKinnon, record store owner Dave Hunter, urban planner Bill Butler, memorial maker Graham Lake, trucking shipper Brad Lunn and the senior citizen of the team, hardware store owner Clarence Redden.

Fifteen years after they came together, members of the Windsor Sports Club are closer than ever. They still have the drive to win. But at the same time they remember to have a good time wherever they are.

The annual invitational oldtimers' tournament in Greenwood, Nova Scotia, is typical. Each year, the Windsor team—usually two forward lines, two defence pairs and a goalie—piles into a couple of cars and drives an hour west to Greenwood. For two dollars a night tournament players can rent a blanket, a pillow and a bunk in the barracks of the nearby Canadian Forces base. Because their roster includes former juniors, seniors and university players, the Windsor Sports Club is inevitably placed in the tournament's most competitive A Division. It doesn't seem to bother them. The only demand they make of the organizers is no game Saturday night, "because Saturday night is our night to party."

In contrast to the Sports Club's cavalier approach to the tournament, their hosts—the Greenwood Bombers—take the competition quite seriously. They usually ice four forward lines, three sets of defencemen and a couple of goalies, and they have a coach. Their pregame routine consists of strenuous stretching and skating drills even before they drop a single puck on the ice to warm up their goalie. And when shooting drill begins, every player has his own puck.

"The big joke for us," says Junior Moore, "is that they've got what seems like thousands of pucks, and we're scrounging to find a couple to warm up Frankie, our goaltender."

According to his teammates, the secret to Frankie's success is not a warm-up but "a shot of rum to settle his stomach before the game." It seems to be just what the construction worker's five-foot-eight, 280-pound frame requires. Then again, his wall-like posture in the goal mouth might be due to the fact that his skates and pads remain in his car trunk all winter long. "To get dressed," says Clarence Redden, "he bangs his skates on the floor and, honest to God, ice falls out of them."

As limited in manpower as it is, the Windsor Sports Club seems to have all the right components. Bob Dill and Junior Moore are the team's clutch goal scorers. Mike Hughes provides the speed on skates "although he couldn't break an egg with his shot." And despite having once suffered a broken leg, forward Rod MacPherson will dipsy-doodle and spin past the opposition just like Serge Savard. Brian Knowles and Graham Lake are tough to get around on defence and, "when it comes to slipping the puck through him at the blueline," says Moore, "Clarence Redden's got the biggest feet in Canada."

At any rate, the results at the Greenwood Invitational are not unexpected. The Windsor Sports Club wins their first game. They lose their second game to the favoured team from Bridgewater. But in the final game Windsor blanks Bridgewater and wins the weekend tournament.

"It's the same pattern just about every time," concludes Junior Moore. "For the first ten minutes, we're out there screwin' around, just getting things going. And they're serious. Just pumped. Then all of a sudden we just say, 'It's time to play.' We pick up the intensity and walk all over them."

The source of their success is tough to pinpoint.

Maybe it's the experience gained on Windsor's frozen shinny ponds. Or it could be the work ethic instilled in them by Moe Smith. It might be the cohesiveness from years of playing hockey together. But these Windsor oldtimers embody the essence of the game—they look to win while seeing there's more to the game than the final score.

FIVE

Faith and Charity

On the final night of the 1947–48 NHL season, Conn Smythe, the manager of the Toronto Maple Leafs, sat beaming in the team dressing room and announced to the press, "This is the greatest team I ever had."

The Leafs had just swept the Detroit Red Wings four straight in the Stanley Cup final, holding Detroit's famous Production Line (Sid Abel, Ted Lindsay and Gordie Howe) to just one point in the entire series. It had been one of Toronto's best-ever seasons. The Leafs finished in first place after the regular schedule for the first time in franchise history. They eliminated the Boston Bruins four games to one in the semifinals. Then they romped over the Red Wings, winning the fourth game 7–2 at the Detroit Olympia. After celebrating their victory in Detroit, they returned home by train the next day to a ticker-tape parade and ten thousand cheering fans. It was the first Stanley Cup parade in Toronto's history.

That final game at the Olympia was historic for other reasons as well. It was the Leafs' fifth Stanley Cup, their second of three in a row. It included the final goal in Leafs' captain Syl Apps's professional hockey career; he retired shortly after. And it featured a goal—the Leafs' seventh in the game—by a five-foot-eight, 158-pound left-wing rookie named Les Costello.

Costello's goal wasn't essential to the game's outcome but it came at a pivotal time in his life. Born in South Porcupine, Ontario, in 1928, the second son of a millwright, Les didn't skate at all until he was eight. He was scouted as a juvenile, played junior hockey on two Memorial Cup winners for St. Michael's College in Toronto and turned pro in the Leafs' farm system with the AHL Pittsburgh Hornets. In his first professional season, Costello scored thirty-two goals for the Hornets, won rookie of the year, was called up to Toronto for eight games in the 1947–48 Stanley Cup Playoffs and became part of Smythe's "greatest team."

During the NHL playoffs the next year, Costello was again called up to play for the Leafs, but he rode the bench through most of the post-season. The following year, he decided, "There was something missing in my life and in hockey I wasn't fulfilling my potential." Instead of working on his backchecking, Les was reading Catholic philosophers such as Etienne Gilson and Jacques Maritain.

In the summer of 1950, as the Leafs geared up for the new season, the Toronto coaching staff gathered in St. Catharines, Ontario, for their pre-season training camp. All veterans and prospects were expected to be there. The only apparent hold-out was Les Costello and the newspapers couldn't find him.

"He was at my house," recalls Bill Scanlon, a hockey chum from St. Mike's. "Costy was the only one missing from camp, but he said they could sit on it."

What the newspaper reporters didn't know, nor did Bill Scanlon even, was that Costello had quietly enrolled at St. Augustine's Seminary in the east end of Toronto. He had decided to try the priesthood. Remarkably, Scanlon had made the same decision, but had never told Costello.

Like Costello, Bill Scanlon hadn't taken to hockey at first. He grew up near High Park in Toronto, where most kids played as much box lacrosse as hockey. Serious hockey didn't happen in Scanlon's life until he too went to St. Michael's College in the mid-1940s. He played both Junior B and Junior A and might have gone further if he hadn't broken his leg one morning in practice at Varsity Arena. Shortly after he, like Costello, began to seriously consider the priesthood. Scanlon went to the seminary the same summer as Costello. "We were both at St. Augustine's [Seminary]," laughs Scanlon, "but didn't know it until we met in the hall."

Life at St. Augustine's was strict. Days were spent in study and prayer and exercising self-discipline. Students read scripture, studied theology and abided by the rules of the rector. Scanlon called it "a prison mentality." There weren't outlets to relieve the pressure or to balance the rigid lifestyle—except for sports.

"Any sport at the seminary was mayhem," remembers Scanlon. "There was only one place to get rid of all the things you had to get rid of, and that was playing sports. To survive you had to break the rules as much as possible. So the hockey had no referees. No rules. No holds barred.

"I remember young guys like Sal Arrigo coming in. He had played in the mercantile leagues in Toronto. He was a pretty good player. And I can remember him sitting in the centre of the rink on his ass—guys running over him—and he's saying, 'What is this all about?'

"And Costy would say, 'It's better to give than to receive, to do it to somebody before they do it to you.'"

In 1956, Bill Scanlon was ordained and began work at the parish of Lady of Peace Cathedral in Islington (in the west end of Toronto). In what spare time he had, he joined other priests every Thursday morning for shinny across town at the Ted Reeve Arena. The hockey was freewheeling, roughhouse, not refereed and, as Scanlon remembers, "a case of everybody getting rid of their frustrations" at the same time. One of the priests dubbed the group *Fratres in unnum* from Psalm 133, which says, "Behold, how good and pleasant it is when brothers dwell in unity!"

After being ordained in 1957, Les Costello returned to his home in the north, serving parishes in Noranda, Quebec, and in Kirkland Lake, Cobalt and Timmins in Ontario. In addition to the routine responsibilities of marriages, baptisms, counselling and confession, Costello immersed himself in the St. Martin de Porres Apostolate, providing food, furniture and clothing to families in need in his community. The closest he ever came to hockey in the late 1950s was coaching youth teams.

Life-and-death hockey at the seminary rink might have been the last Scanlon and Costello ever saw of each other were it not for another fellow seminarian, Brian McKee. Like

Costello, McKee had shown promise as a professional athlete, only in football, not hockey. And like Costello, McKee had left that life behind to enter St. Augustine's. After ordination McKee was assigned to the Pro-Cathedral of the Assumption Church in North Bay.

North Bay in the early 1960s was typical of many northern Ontario communities. The railway, the air base and resource industries paid most of the salaries in town. The population, then about 50,000, was mostly English-speaking but the city had a large Francophone community. Summer activities centred on nearby Lake Nipissing; in winter attention shifted to the North Bay Memorial Gardens. There was entertainment for every taste—from figure skating shows to wrestling to the home games of the NOHA Junior A North Bay Trappers.

McKee's extensive community work with young people in boys' homes, youth camps and hostels had shaped his belief that, "If you treat a boy like a man, he'll become one." He also realized that his programs required funding. He decided to combine his need to raise money with the wealth of hockey talent he remembered among his fellow seminarians, a popular hockey venue and an interest among some media friends in putting the skates back on.

"A number of us at CFCH radio had talked about getting a team together," remembers former broadcaster Terry Spearin. "We had talked about benefits and various charities…[and about] the thrills from days when our rheumatic joints weren't giving us as much trouble."

Because CFCH was the only radio station in town, the voice of Terry Spearin was as well known in North Bay as that of Foster Hewitt. Spearin hosted the early morning show, a weekly children's show and Saturday night sock hops at the arena, but above all he loved doing the colour commentary alongside CFCH play-by-play announcer Pete Handley for the North Bay Trappers' home games. One night at a Catholic Youth Organization dance, Spearin got talking with Father Brian McKee. The subject of hockey and benefits came up.

"Wouldn't it be fun to put on the skates?" Spearin said.

"Yeah, wouldn't it," McKee agreed. "Most priests I know are hockey players, for God's sake. A lot from northern

Ontario. They'd love to belt the hell out of somebody legitimately!"

"Let's do a hockey game that pits priests against the radio station," someone suggested. And so it was decided. A team of priests would play a team of radio personalities in a charity game at the North Bay Memorial Gardens in February, 1964.

Easier said than done. The broadcasters cobbled together a team of CFCH staff members, including on-air personnel such as Spearin, Handley and Greg Lawrence, along with the station manager, Reg Carne, and even the station's security guard, Johnny Klimits. Then they confronted the problem of hockey equipment and preparing for the big game. Other than old skates and a scattered assortment of pads and gloves, Spearin and his buddies had little gear and even less experience on the ice together. However, word travels quickly in a small city and soon the local air base pitched in, supplying hockey gear, sweaters and even some ice time so the newly formed "Statics" hockey club could practise.

Meanwhile, Brian McKee had called Bill Scanlon in Toronto to scare up ex-seminarians and priests from his Thursday morning league, including Fathers Pete Vallely and Paul Lennon. Closer to home, McKee contacted Les Costello in Timmins, Norm Clement in Sault Ste. Marie and Ted MacLean in Sudbury. The team of fathers even recruited a monsignor, Bernie Pappin, to join the team and a bishop, Adolph Proulx, to coach. During the lead-up to the game someone dubbed the team the "Flying Fathers" and the name stuck.

Thanks to coverage at the radio station and in the *North Bay Nugget*, word of the charity match between the Statics and the Flying Fathers spread quickly. Although the fundraising purpose of the game received plenty of attention, it was the idea of having a game between priests and laymen that captured the community's imagination. By the night of the game, February 20, 1964, the 5,000-seat North Bay Memorial Gardens was nearly sold out.

"We figured we might get a hundred people in the stands," remembers Bud Berry, a photographer for the local television station and a member of the media team. "We were sitting in the dressing room putting our equipment on before the game and one of the guys went out for a warm-up skate. He came back and told us the place was packed to the rafters. I guess every Catholic within a hundred miles had come to see the media get the hell beat out of them."

The teams emerged from their dressing rooms at game time, the Statics in their borrowed air force togs and the Flying Fathers in a set of sweaters borrowed from a local team of old-timers. Representatives of the North Bay Crippled Children's Association, referee Lou Farelli and the two centres—Msgr. Bernie Pappin and Terry McInnis—assembled for the ceremonial face-off. Alexander Carter, the archbishop of Sault Ste. Marie smiled for the camera, dropped the puck, shook hands with the dignitaries and that's when the pleasantries ended.

"I had the feeling very quickly that the game was underwritten by a higher authority," laughs Terry Spearin. "We had never seen the Fathers until that night. But it was murderers' row. These guys were the dirtiest bunch of players I had ever seen in my life.

"They were good at stickhandling, puck control, passing. They knew how to play positional hockey. And they had a goaltender who, when called upon, could stop a puck....But I remember Brian McKee taking me into the corner on a couple of occasions saying, 'Forgive me, Father,' and then just rapping me one. I remember being really knocked about, not all by clean checks...but all of them were in the name of charity, so I accepted it."

Dirty or not, the priests' superior skills quickly became obvious. The years of junior hockey at St. Mike's, the no-holds-barred scrimmages at St. Augustine's, the shinny played at Ted Reeve Arena and the dormant professional calibre talent sprinkled throughout the team all came to the fore. The Fathers were all over the Statics within minutes.

"We had grown up being extremely competitive," remembers Bill Scanlon. "If you go out, you go out to win."

"The whole thing was kind of a lark," says Les Costello, "playing against guys who were in worse shape than we were."

Scanlon and Costello each scored a pair of goals while Fathers Mike Brady and Aurel Blake each got a hat trick. And the Gardens crowd loved it. Spectators chanted "Go, Fathers, Go." They cheered every rush the Fathers made, every body-check they threw and every goal they scored. And along the way, the priests discovered ways to have some fun with their opponents, the crowd and themselves. The seed was planted for inserting gags and antics into future contests, whether or not the outcome of the game was assured. In this case, in the Fathers' inaugural game, the final score was: Flying Fathers 13–Statics 4.

In the end, though, the score didn't matter. The Crippled Children's Association took home $700. The Statics got their wish to "remember the thrills," despite their bruises. The priests discovered a new way to connect with their communities by dusting off talents they had put on the shelf. They christened a new fraternity, and a new kind of ministry, that would ultimately outlive each of them as individual oldtimer hockey players.

"I don't know if we realized it at the time," confesses Terry Spearin, "but those priests loved this opportunity to be human, to be one of the guys and to mix with people, slap backs, shake hands and not have to be clerical.

"At the same time they showed off not only their dexterity, but their great showbiz capacity. These were showmen, not just priests, but genuine entertainers."

A year later, the Flying Fathers, the Statics and the fans enjoyed a repeat performance. This time, the Gardens completely sold out—5,037 inside the arena—and had to turn away 500 more. The Children's Aid Society received the proceeds of $1,600.

For this rematch, the Flying Fathers had prepared some hockey schtick to spice up the game. In addition to making faces at the referee, taunting the opposition and generally showboating for the audience, goalie Lionel Brousseau appeared at one point in Scottish regalia—complete with kilt and tam-o'-shanter—and sat in a chair while defending the goal. There was the soon-to-be patented chase around the ice surface with a bucket of water that inevitably ended up being dumped in the faces of the opposition bench.

But the Statics were not about to be upstaged in this repeat engagement. They equipped goal judges with dark sunglasses and white canes for the assignment. And when he was awarded a penalty shot, the Statics' Bruce "Petunia" Ruggles came out dressed in a tutu and conducted a figure skating exhibition in front of the Fathers' net before shooting the puck past Father Brousseau. The Statics had also added the leading scorer from the 1940s New York Rangers, Ab DeMarco, to their roster; despite being forty-nine, DeMarco scored three times, including a goal that saw him stickhandle through the entire Flying Fathers team before flipping the puck and the stick into the net; it turned out the puck was actually tied to the stick.

The Statics still lost by about the same margin, 16–6, but somehow it didn't hurt nearly as much as the first time.

In their first year the Flying Fathers played five charity games. The second year, ten. Before long, their schedule consisted of thirty to forty games a year.

"Hey, isn't this getting to be too much?" the bishop asked the priests.

"We'll keep going until it's no more fun," McKee responded.

"Just as long as it doesn't interfere with your work," said the bishop.

As quickly as Brian McKee received invitations and requests for benefit games, the Flying Fathers made plans to be there. In the early days, they responded to the large charities, such as the Crippled Children's Association and the Children's Aid Society, and the small ones—helping a community build a church, supporting families after a mining accident or giving minor hockey a helping hand. They'd play in rinks with no washrooms or showers but the whole town would be there to watch. Afterward, the local Lions Club or Knights of Columbus or parish volunteers would hold a reception in their honour. One night, the Fathers played in North York for the children of a firefighter killed on duty; they raised $3,500. As usual, they travelled on their own time, most by car to the southern Ontario arena, and some drove 800 kilometres home overnight to lead mass in their own parishes the next day.

The physical pace was gruelling, the spiritual satisfaction constant. But at times awkward scheduling or insurmountable geography left the Fathers' ranks thin. For a charity game in Cobourg, Ontario, in 1969, only seven priests were available. Bill Scanlon called St. Augustine's to talk to Flying Father prospect Tim Shea. "I'll arrange transportation if you can get out," Scanlon promised.

"I don't know if I can get out," Shea said.

As usual St. Augustine's rules and regulations restricted students at every turn. Classes filled Monday, Tuesday, Wednesday and Friday. On Sunday seminarians prayed all day. Thursday was usually the only weekday seminarians could leave the property. Mind you, if anyone could escape St. Augustine's successfully, Tim Shea could.

Shea was always battling the odds. He was one of seven boys growing up in one of the poorer parishes of Kingston. He always cheered for underdogs; as a boy in the 1950s, Tim rooted for Eddie Litzenberger and the last-place Chicago Blackhawks. Playing shinny at Skeleton Park in Kingston, Tim was smaller and slower than his younger brother, Terry, but also more agile. He managed to score his share of goals. Despite a strong minor hockey career, he fell just short of making Kingston's junior team, the Frontenacs.

At school, Tim Shea was the class clown, always pulling impossible pranks and getting away with them. Shea regularly imitated the teacher, played catch behind the teacher's back and once skipped school to attend the girls' track meet. One Friday in Grade 13 history class, he made up an excuse for not being able to do his homework on the coming weekend. He said, "It's the opening of duck hunting season. I've never shot a gun before. And my uncle's taking me duck hunting."

"If you can bring me proof," said the sister, "you don't have to do your homework."

Over the weekend, he goofed off and then borrowed a dressed and frozen duck from his uncle's freezer for Monday's history class. By noon, when the sister asked for proof of his duck hunt, Shea pulled the now thawed and limp bird from a brown paper bag. The sister shrieked. The class exploded with laughter.

Not surprisingly, then, as a seminarian in 1969, Shea was bold enough to respond to Bill Scanlon's request that he slip away from St. Augustine's to join the Flying Fathers for their charity game. On the appointed Thursday, Scanlon arranged to have a Toronto funeral director, Bud O'Connor, pull up in front of St. Augustine's with a limousine. Shea threw his equipment inside and disappeared for the night.

The St. Augustine's escapee marvelled at the Flying Fathers' prowess on the ice, especially its star-studded first line—nimble Pete Vallely who "looked about seventy in a pair of granny glasses," Bill Scanlon "who looked as big as a linebacker," and Les Costello "who could stickhandle through anybody." Shea was paired on defence with Brian McKee, "another big guy who never wore hockey gloves, just a pair of mitts.

"I was pretty shy that first night," admits Shea. "I was still worried about getting caught. I wasn't even supposed to be there. So they put me on defence. And if I got the puck I'd just wait, give it to Costello and he'd take it down the ice. And that became my job. They knew I could hold onto the puck, skate around with it and give it to Costello. For the first five or six years that's all I ever did!"

During Tim Shea's apprenticeship as a Flying Father, the Fathers generally used few gags, choosing to play good hockey most of the time and to clown around only as a ploy against better competition or when their opponents were a lot worse. In fact, Art Appleton, the Fathers' goaltender at the time, never took his role in net lightly; even when his team-mates helped the competition en route to the priests' net, Appleton refused to let easy goals in. The Fathers' main aim was to slow the opposition down with the bucket of water gag in the first period, a pie in someone's face in the second and the Fathers' version of "The Flying Nun" in the third.

The Flying Nun stunt capitalized on a contemporary television show that starred Sally Field as a nun with the inexplicable ability to fly. The Flying Fathers' version was Sister Mary Shooter, who suddenly scooted onto the ice in a nun's habit. She would stickhandle around the ice surface with her gowns flowing. Then she would pretend someone had tripped her and be awarded a penalty shot. This show-stopping role was generally given to special guests such as former rival Ab DeMarco. Otherwise Tim Shea donned the habit and filled the role.

"One fall, the Flying Fathers had a trip to the Maritimes," says Shea. "So I went along again as Sister Mary Shooter. Except that the Halifax paper published this big picture of Sister Mary the next day and it was obvious it was me.

"That same weekend a new bishop was being installed at Grand Falls, Newfoundland, or somewhere and Father John Lamaire [of St. Augustine's] was invited to Halifax. The first morning he's in Halifax he got the newspaper and there I am on the front page. I was supposed to be back studying but there I was as Sister Mary Shooter taking my penalty shot.

"Fortunately, I was all caught up and my marks were good but [Father Lamaire] had the newspaper with my picture on the front page."

The same year the Flying Fathers found a permanent Sister Mary Shooter in Tim Shea, they also initiated one of Shea's classmates. Grant Neville had grown up in Pembroke, Ontario, in the Ottawa Valley. He learned hockey on the shinny rinks under the lights at Rotary Park. He became a rushing defenceman in public school hockey and learned how to fight in university hockey. But he realized his true hockey calling one night in 1966 at the Civic Auditorium in Oshawa.

"A group of us seminarians went out to see a Flying Fathers game," recalls Neville. "We were helping out in the dressing room. Here were these priests—'Costy' Costello, 'Skinner' Scanlon, 'Buck' McKee and Pete Vallely—all playing the game we loved for charities. And I thought, if I ever make it through the seminary, if I ever become a priest, this is what I want to do.

"Then, in 1969, they were coming through Arnprior on a tour of games. They needed a couple of players. So I joined them for the first time...I was nervous. It was like playing for the Stanley Cup. We played in front of 3,000 people, a packed house at the Arnprior Arena.

"They said, 'Don't be afraid to carry the puck. Let the other guys do the tricks, throw the water and the pies. Just look enthusiastic, join in and have fun.'" He did. And at the end of the game Grant Neville returned to the dressing room to find his gloves full of shaving cream. He knew he had arrived.

By the time Fathers Tim Shea and Grant Neville were regulars on the team, the Flying Fathers were a household name around Ontario. The team was also more showbiz conscious. They had incorporated a skating clown, Rollie, into their program to entertain the children during intermissions. Also during this time Father John Caswell realized, "We couldn't keep borrowing sweaters for our games, and we also had to have some sort of crest to depict what we were and what we were trying to do."

He approached North Bay Parks and Recreation director Sam Jacks who sketched a whimsical face with a Roman collar and halo. It became their team emblem on their sweaters and on publicity material promoting each Flying Fathers game.

While there was never a problem for the fathers paying their own way to the games and using their own days off, as the schedule became more hectic and the locations further apart, the team managers had to find ways to cover the growing expenses. Brian McKee and Bill Scanlon came up with some money-recovering ideas. They had programs printed and souvenirs made, mostly to cover the priests' gas money. Then one day, Scanlon got a call from Revenue Canada asking to see the books.

"What books?" he asked.

"Well, we've seen the figures of money the Flying Fathers are raising," the official said.

"Those are sometimes exaggerated," Scanlon suggested.

"Well, we've got this clipping out of the paper. Where's the accounting on this?"

A nervous Bill Scanlon paid the taxation people a visit and explained the Flying Fathers had no accounting system. Money was raised and money was dispensed to charity. Sometimes they saw it but mostly they didn't. The tax people seemed satisfied for the moment, despite the fact that the team's total earnings were well on the way to $500,000.

In 1970, at the invitation of the Canadian Armed Forces,

the Flying Fathers travelled to Germany to play a series of charity games against the military hockey teams stationed at Baden-Soellingen, Lahr and Düsseldorf. On the ice, the Canadian priests fared well, defeating the Soest Royal Huskies 3–2 and the Hemer Rebels 7–6, but losing to the 4 Wing Raiders 12–9. As usual, the fathers brought along a lively brand of hockey and a full bag of tricks.

"Angels in Disguise" was how the *Schwarzwälder* headlined its coverage of the Fathers' game against the Raiders in Baden-Soellingen. The tongue-in-cheek story described the 1,500 hockey fans as "the victims of a hoax...when a band of rebels disguised as men of the cloth invaded." The reporter highlighted Costello's water tossing and pie throwing, the Raiders' "protest that the glare from Scanlon's bald head was blinding their goalie...forcing him to wear a Beatle wig," and the arrival of the Flying Nun, Sister Mary Shooter, who "after some deft stickhandling to within a few feet of goalie Roger Côté, dropped her stick, jumped into Côté's arms and gave him a big kiss."

The greatest victory of the trip, however, was not scored on the ice in Germany but on the public relations front in Rome. At the end of their hockey tour, the fathers wangled a trip to the Vatican on a military chaplain's promise that he could get them in to see Pope Paul VI. When they arrived they discovered that the chaplain's plan had stalled. Les Costello immediately went into high gear. He contacted the monsignor at the American College in Rome and concocted a story about the arrival of thirteen air force chaplains from Canada. That did the trick. The bogus air force chaplains were granted an audience with the Pope.

Once inside the Vatican, however, there was dissension in the ranks. Father Steve McLellan, who was usually quite self-assured and a strong personality among the fathers, suddenly panicked. "We've got to get out of here!"

"No," said Bill Scanlon, "not now. We're in here now. We'll explain to the Holy Father when he comes what we're about."

Just then the Pope arrived and in very poor English tried to describe what an important role air force chaplains played and how proud he was of these Canadian chaplains.

When he finished, Father Bill quickly piped up, "Holy Father, we are all priests. We are not armed forces chaplains. We made up that story to get in here. But we're guests of the Canadian Armed Forces in Europe. And we're here playing benefit hockey games." Pulling out a hockey stick which the Flying Fathers had all signed, he continued, "We have something to give you."

The Pope took the stick upside down and didn't seem to understand the gift until Scanlon retrieved it from him and showed him how it was used.

"Oh, yes," exclaimed Pope Paul, "Canada...ice hockey."

With that, Les Costello, who had been surprisingly quiet, jumped in. He blithely addressed the Holy Father as "Pope" and innocently suggested, "If you have no other use for it, you could use it to stir your spaghetti!" With that the floodgates were opened. Costello shook the Pope's hand and told him his name, where he lived and that he, the Pope, was doing a wonderful job for the church.

What saved the entire audience and turned a potential public relations disaster into a coup was the arrival of the official Vatican photographer. Word of their audience had preceded the Flying Fathers' return to Canada where church officials waited with apprehension. But when the Fathers produced the pictures of a smiling pontiff holding his brand-new hockey stick courtesy of Canada's Flying Fathers, the whole endeavour received official blessing. Even *The Canadian Register*, the national Catholic weekly, headlined their story, "Flying Fathers Score in Rome."

"Les is incredible," concludes Scanlon. "He could meet the King of England or the Prime Minister of Canada and he'd treat them the same as the guy that's cleaning the arena. Everybody was equal in Costy's eyes. No pretence. And he was just himself when he met the Pope."

The Flying Fathers weren't afraid to poke fun at anything and anybody inside or outside the church. This tendency became clearer and clearer as the team's reputation for good-natured clowning and oldtime hockey spread. Community and oldtimers' teams were lining up to play the Fathers. But not all the priests could make it to all the games. On occasion the Flying Fathers had to import talent, creating another opportunity for fun at the expense of a religious ritual.

One of the first regular outsiders to join the Flying Fathers' roster as a fill-in was ex-NHLer Dick Duff. While his being a non-cleric might have seemed to water down the team's original all-priest premise, Brian McKee made it work for them. Early in the game, McKee would stop the play to point out that due to a number of weddings and funerals several of the regular Flying Fathers couldn't be present and that the team had conscripted Dick Duff. Amid cheers and applause, Duff would come to centre ice to be ordained.

In all seriousness, Father McKee would gather the other Flying Fathers around. He'd say to the crowd, "May I have silence please…"

Duff would kneel down with reverence and humility.

McKee would place a father's beret on Duff's head and a black robe around his shoulders and say, "In the name of the Father, the Son and the Holy Spirit, I ordain you a Flying Father."

Duff would then receive a splash of "holy water."

And as McKee made the sign of the cross, another father would sneak up behind Duff and throw a pie into his face. The audience loved it. Because it was done early in the first period, it always got the whole evening off to a rollicking start.

Tim Shea later refined the gag so that the first player on the opposing team to score a goal would receive the ordination, the splash of holy water and the pie in the face. This act was particularly valuable for the Flying Fathers if they ran into a team of junior players or a hot oldtimers' team. It inevitably slowed the momentum of the game, threw a good team off balance and at the very least gave the aging Fathers a chance to catch their breath.

The more games the Fathers played, the more slapstick and irreverent they became. During the 1970s, as Tim Shea and Grant Neville began to assume more of the managing duties for the team, Neville invited some of his Ottawa Valley friends to join or to substitute for priests who couldn't play. One family, the Smiths, supplied three players: Father Basil Smith, Pat Smith who succeeded Rollie the Clown and Ernie

Smith who says he was recruited because "hockey and horses are my disease."

One night during the second period of a charity match in the Ottawa Valley, Ernie Smith (doing the honours as Sister Mary Shooter) came barrelling onto the ice on horseback. An expert rodeo rider, Smith had attached sharp cork studs to the shoes on his horse's hooves and out they came at a full gallop. After several circuits of the rink to get the crowd up out of their seats, Smith lassoed the opposition's goaltender, yanked him out of the goal crease and replaced him with his horse "Penance," complete with hockey stick, chest protector and goalie pads on his front legs.

Once Penance was ready to play, Tim Shea grabbed a public address microphone and conducted an interview with him.

"Does the opposition have a chance?" Shea asked.

Penance shook his head wildly from side to side.

"Will the Flying Fathers win the game?"

Penance nodded his head.

"Why?" said Shea.

And Penance knelt down on his front legs as Shea interpreted, "Because they pray."

If that didn't bring the house down, the Fathers would actually let Penance play goal for a few minutes. And if Penance happened to make a deposit or two on the ice, so much the better.

By the mid-1970s, Penance was following a pretty tough act in goal. The Flying Fathers' new goaltender was a wild and irreverent comic in his own right. Oblate Father Vaughan Quinn was more likely to grab Penance's tail for a free ride around the arena as stand there and be upstaged by a horse in goalie pads. Whereas Art Appleton would refuse to allow any opposition player to score, no matter how big the potential laugh, Quinn would milk a gag for all it was worth. The goal be damned.

Vaughan Quinn nearly didn't make it to the Flying Fathers at all or to the priesthood or even to adulthood. He was one of those gifted people who had it all but wanted none of it. Born the second son of a prosperous doctor in Westmount in Montreal, Quinn enjoyed a childhood that included his own backyard skating rink and tickets to the Forum to see the Canadiens. As a kid, Quinn was overweight and not a good skater so the others made him a goalie. By the time he finished high school, even though he never studied, his marks were high enough that he'd been offered hockey scholarships to six American universities. He turned them all down because, "I wasn't going to be a hockey bum!"

Nevertheless, Quinn didn't desert athletics and he never did things by half. He mixed Golden Gloves boxing, semi-pro football, hockey—and booze. In 1952, by the age of nineteen he and Charlie Hodge were alternating as opposition goalie for the Canadiens' practices. Elmer Lach and Butch Bouchard were still playing and rookie Bernie Geoffrion was starting to experiment with the slapshot. Then he tried three years of medical school, one year of advertising and finally, because he wanted a bigger challenge, he joined the Oblate Fathers. He went through a year of novitiate, three years of philosophy, four years of theology, took his vows—poverty, obedience, chastity and perseverance—and was ordained in December, 1963.

While Quinn exchanged priestly duties for sports, he didn't leave the drinking behind. Within six months he was too drunk to say Mass, blacked out while hearing confession, brawled in bars at night and was constantly in and out of hospital. His superiors ordered him to diocesan confinement. Three years later he emerged from a rehabilitation centre in Michigan openly describing himself as "ex-CIA—Catholic, Irish and alcoholic," and dedicated himself to treating skid row alcoholics. By the late 1960s, Father Quinn had taken over the ramshackle Sacred Heart Rehabilitation Center in Detroit and turned it into one of the largest and most successful detoxification facilities of its kind.

In 1973 Quinn turned forty. He hadn't worn his goalie pads in a decade. He heard about industrial hockey in the Detroit area and decided to come out of retirement to play some serious hockey. First it was every Wednesday with the priests. Then it was Canadian priests versus American priests. Then one day in 1975 Father Jack Costello (Les's cousin) called about a Flying Fathers game across the Detroit River. Could he be the substitute goalie?

"My first game with the Flying Fathers was in Windsor," remembers Quinn. "I'm standing there in the net minding my own business when this horse, a bloody horse, comes running out from behind the net across the ice. And I look and all of a sudden there's a nun coming down on me. It's Ernie and Penance. I didn't know what was going on."

It didn't take very long for him to fit in. Quinn's extroverted personality, his wisecracks and his talent for taking things over the top moved the Flying Fathers to new heights. Within a few months of his Windsor debut, Quinn was at home in the Flying Fathers' net. As each game began, Quinn thumbed his nose at the opposition, clowned with the spectators and hammed it up around the net, juggling balls, doing figure eights in the face-off circle or climbing on top of the net for a nap.

"We worked at coming up with plenty of gimmicks," says Quinn. "Tim Shea decided we should have a mascot, a teddy bear named Edward St. Bear. At times, just to distract the opposition, I'll get the crowd chanting, 'We want Edward.' Sometimes I'll turn the net around or I'll install this four-by-six piece of Plexiglas so the other team can't score. After the first guy's taken a pie in the face, I'll go over to their bench and tell the rest of them, 'You better watch out because you don't know what's going to happen to the next guy that puts a puck past me.' And if we're down by five goals, we'll form a football front line, hike a football, throw it in their net and claim six points."

Quinn calls this form of hockey "divine intervention. We almost always win because God's on our side." Whatever it was, it was working. Each time the Fathers appeared, audiences knew they could expect irreverence, plenty of good hockey and some nonsense along the way. Very soon the public and the press were calling the Flying Fathers "the Harlem Globetrotters of hockey."

But as Shea often points out, "The Globetrotters didn't take any chances. They played against a team that knew what the routine was. They had their own referees and announcers.

We were playing teams who didn't have a clue what we were up to. So to keep things from going wrong, I printed up a sheet for the referee and the announcer so that they had some idea what was going to happen next."

As the Flying Fathers neared the end of their second decade, their "ministry on ice" continued to grow. Brian McKee had retired from the team and Grant Neville now handled recruiting and booking the team into twenty or more games a year. Tim Shea and Vaughan Quinn kept dreaming up new gags and gimmicks. During this period, the team raised nearly $2 million for charity.

Through two decades, the bread-and-butter work of carrying on parish duties most of the year and taking vacation time to raise money for charity as a hockey team continued. Playing tours took them farther afield—to the prairies, the Pacific coast and Atlantic Canada, as well as to Europe and the United States. At the same time, the Flying Fathers' roster began to expand outside its original Ontario roots.

On a trip to Michigan and Minnesota in 1980, the team welcomed seminary student and former Junior A prospect Bill Brennan, originally from Bath, New Brunswick.

One night during their 1983 tour, clown Pat "Smitty" Smith couldn't make it to a game. His nephew Pat Lunney, a farrier from the Ottawa Valley, filled in and eventually became the second to play the Smitty the Clown character.

In 1987, when Vaughan Quinn got hurt before a game in Kitchener, Ontario, Norm Roberts, a theology student from the University of Toronto, played net for the Fathers. Since Quinn was leaving the goal mouth more and more during each game to create havoc around the arena, eventually Roberts became the Fathers' seventh player on the ice, the team's serious goaltender.

The next year, 1988, again in Kitchener, John MacPherson, another seminarian from Fredericton, New Brunswick, joined the team.

And in 1990, when the Flying Fathers toured western Canada, recently ordained priest Sheldon Olekson took all his vacation time to travel from Prince Albert, Saskatchewan, to join the team for nine games in ten days.

"My first game with the Flying Fathers, in fact, the first time I'd ever seen them," says Olekson, another one-time junior prospect, "was in the Calgary Saddledome. I walked into this NHL rink where even the team bathroom is bigger than most dressing rooms we go to...and I think, 'Wow. This is big time!'

"The first guy I meet is [former Calgary Flame] Jim Peplinski. And I think, 'Is he playing against us. God, I hope not.' He says, 'No. I'm your ref.' And they told me I wouldn't have to do any tricks, just get in on the other team. I played that game in Calgary, then Medicine Hat, Lethbridge and Trail, B.C.

"In Trail, I'm sitting in this fancy restaurant in a suit and tie. I'm next to Ernie Smith. And someone comes over and hits him in the face with a pie. Then he took the rest of the pie and nailed me over the head with it. I was ready to punch his lights out. But that was my initiation into the Flying Fathers. I guess they liked me. I fit in. I was as nuts as they were."

Perhaps the reason Olekson, Brennan, Roberts and MacPherson fit in so well was the brand of hockey the Flying Fathers played. It was rollicking but it was gentlemen's play. Sometimes it was rough on the boards and in the corners, but it was oldtimers' rules. It was hockey for the fun of it, a sharp contrast to the hockey each of them had played as young professional prospects.

In 1974, when Bill Brennan went to the training camp of the Major Junior A team in Sherbrooke, Quebec, he felt he had the desire and strength to play. But this was during the goon years when a two-hundred-pound player was expected to be an enforcer to make the team. He refused. Similarly, at a tryout for the junior team in Prince Albert in 1979, the coaches wanted the six-foot-two-inch Sheldon Olekson to be "a big bruising defenceman," not play the finesse hockey he preferred. He dropped out of the game.

"What I like about the Flying Fathers," says Olekson, "is that we have some good talent. We've got guys who can really pass the puck...like you make your cut and, crack, the puck's right there. That's the finesse hockey I enjoy.

"And regularly there's gags to remind the guys that this

isn't the NHL. It's for fun. And if you take it too seriously, you're going to get a pie.

"There's an art to throwing a pie, you know. We use real whipped cream. Shaving cream can burn the eyes. And not plastic or aluminum plates. Real whipped cream and paper pie plates. Father Jack [Costello] who does the ordination of an opposition player, he likes to hear the pop when a pie hits someone. He says it's his style. Others like slowly placing the pie on the person's face and then sliding it up on to the top of their head like a hat. There are those who rub it from ear to ear. It's pie-ology. It's something you develop as a Flying Father."

The pies, the flying nuns, the horses in goal, the buckets of water, the football scrimmage on skates and the finesse hockey were all preferable to the kind of game their prospective Junior A coaches had expected of them. Yet the Flying Fathers gave these young and middle-aged priests much more than lively recreation on their vacation time away from their parishes. It gave them a sense of belonging and an opportunity to let down their hair. On the road they played cards all night, wrestled with each other, had a few beers in the dressing room and played practical jokes.

The Flying Fathers phenomenon also became a ministry unto itself, particularly at the post-game receptions. These gatherings—sometimes in the arena banquet hall or a local church basement—allowed the town fathers to stand up and thank the Flying Fathers and vice versa. But beyond that anything could happen and often did.

The priests took the opportunity to spin yarns, sing songs and tell jokes, mostly putdowns of fellow priests, teammates, or members of the opposing team.

"You know Johnny MacPherson," says Father Quinn, holding the mike. "Just before he was ordained, he's completing an essay on celibacy and whether or not priests should be able to marry."

"No kidding," says Les Costello.

"And he puts the question in a letter to the Pope," continues Quinn. "And the Pope writes back and says, 'Yes, priests may soon be able to marry, provided they are over seventy-five and have a letter from their parents.'"

Among other reception business, a rookie with the Fathers was expected to sing a song or recite a poem. It helped train the newest members of the team to think on their feet. The best Bill Brennan could do when he was called upon to perform something at his inaugural reception was sing "Mary Had a Little Lamb." His first time up, Norm Roberts quickly concocted a monologue about the Fathers' oldest and most revered member, Les Costello, "who is ninety-three today." He then led the reception singing "Happy Birthday."

While all the nonsense was going on in the centre of the room, priests and townspeople would mingle in the corners. Here was where the Flying Fathers' real ministry was at work. Sometimes a parishioner wanted to complain about the local priest. Someone else would need help sorting out a bad marriage or an interpretation of church doctrine. Whatever it was, the talk seemed to pour out of people during these sessions. "Because they know you are a priest," says Sheldon Olekson, "and because they know you are in town and out, they can share their guts with you and will probably never see you again. So it's a type of ministry that likely wouldn't happen if you lived there."

This travelling ministry was often at its best when the Fathers worked with young people. When they met with troubled kids before or after their games, Fathers Costello and Roberts would break the ice by having the uptight teenagers sing "Twinkle, Twinkle, Little Star," complete with hand and body actions. By getting the young people to laugh at themselves and each other, the Fathers broke down barriers and helped them talk about their problems.

Father Quinn met a reformed alcoholic after a game one night and she described how her fourteen-year-old son only spoke to her to criticize her. "By some fluke, he got to be your stick boy in Duluth, Minnesota," the woman told him. "He came home that night after taking care of your sticks and Edward St. Bear, and he said, 'Gee, mom, it's okay because you're an alcoholic like Father Quinn.' And now we're talking to each other again."

In their first thirty years of "playing and praying for a better world," the Flying Fathers have accumulated many firsts as oldtimers, hockey players and ambassadors for Canada and the priesthood. They have played nearly a thousand games for charity and won nearly all of them. Their record is five games in one day. During one trip across Canada and the U.S., they played sixteen games in fifteen cities in twenty days and travelled 14,000 miles. The largest crowd they drew was 15,396 at Vancouver's Pacific Coliseum. A single game at the Montreal Forum in 1984 raised $50,000 for the Shriners Hospital. During a charity game at Maple Leaf Gardens in 1985, nearly 14,000 spectators watched the Flying Fathers play the Maple Leaf Alumni. Leaf owner Harold Ballard turned over all gate receipts and proceeds from concessions that day, and the event raised $240,000 for cancer research.

Nevertheless, the Fathers may not have their greatest impact on a packed Pacific Coliseum or the Canadian Cancer Society. This band of globetrotting, hockey-playing priests leave their most indelible impressions away from heavily populated areas, away from the huge charity events and out of the sight of cameras and reporters, in smaller, out-of-the-way places such as Huntsville, Alabama, or Inuvik, Northwest Territories, or Lahr, Germany. That's where people never forget their visit. Nor do the Fathers.

In December, 1986, the Fathers made a series of stops in aboriginal communities along the shoreline of James Bay in nothern Ontario. The first town was Moosonee and most of the Flying Fathers arrived in a twenty-passenger plane. As usual, it had been an eventful trip. During the flight, Pat "Smitty the Clown" Lunney slipped into the cockpit and convinced the pilot to put the plane into an unscheduled nosedive. Grant Neville and Moncton priest Peter McKee were sitting in the front row without their seatbelts on; the last thing they remember before they hit the wall in front of them was the sound of Smitty shouting "Yahoo!" from the cockpit.

A short time later, a smaller, four-seater airplane from Timmins also landed in Moosonee. Its passengers included Fathers Les Costello, Dan Bagley and Darcy Quinn, who was filling in on the team for this trip. The smaller plane's flight had been eventful as well. The cabin was poorly heated and turbulence had prompted fatalistic remarks from Costello, such as, "If we ever make it, I'll get down on my knees and kiss the ground," and "If I have to go down, who better with than my two linemates."

At the Moosonee airport, the Fathers disembarked and filed passed a group of locals standing on the tarmac. The Fathers thought they were passengers waiting for the next flight out. In fact, they were the welcoming committee but because neither group knew the other they passed like ships in the night. It was the Fathers' introduction to a shy people in a remarkable community.

Moosonee is actually two communities. The neighbouring community of Moose Factory on an island in the river dates back to the Swampy Cree. In 1673, Moose Factory became the first permanent English-speaking settlement in Ontario. Moosonee, on the mainland, came into existence in 1903 when the French established a post of the Revillon Frères Trading Company there.

And so, these two towns have remained two solitudes: Moose Factory is a Native reserve on an island. The residents speak English and are primarily Anglican. Moosonee on the mainland is of French heritage and is primarily Catholic.

What has traditionally brought the two communities together is hockey and, lately, building a new Moosonee Community Arena. In fact, the Flying Fathers were there to officially open the new facility with a charity match against the local oldtimers' hockey team, the Moosonee Bombardiers, who were, except for the goalie, entirely Native.

"I was the only non-Indian member of the team," says Mike Malott, then a teacher in Moosonee. "And that's only because I was the oldest guy still playing goal. So when they needed a backup in goal, I said 'Sure.' But these guys were terrific hockey players. They were used to skating on the river at thirty degrees below zero. They could skate all night."

It was out of respect for his teammates that Mike Malott was recruited to contact the Flying Fathers. The community wanted some kind of an event to officially open the Moosonee arena, something that would attract people from all parts of the community including Catholics, Moosonee residents and hockey fans. The Flying Fathers seemed the obvious choice and the Bombardiers their likely opposition.

The Bombardiers had heard of the Flying Fathers, and knew they had some former pros, outstanding juniors and Senior A calibre players. They also knew they were parish priests with a pocketful of practical jokes. But the Bombardiers had talent too, including players such as Snowball Gunner, who had tried out for the Vancouver Canucks, but had packed up and come home when he missed his family, and former junior prospect Tommy Moore.

In contrast to the shy welcoming committee at the airport, most of the community was primed for the event. Children drew posters advertising the game. The wives of the Bombardier oldtimers decorated the Flying Fathers' dressing room at the arena with balloons and streamers. The local air base provided chairs so that Native elders could sit right at rink side. The visiting priests were billeted in community homes, including at the private quarters of Bishop Jules Leguerrier who remembers their visit as "a true highlight for Moosonee."

On the night of December 8, most of the citizens of both Moose Factory and Moosonee were at the arena. Nearly 2,000 people and all the dignitaries, including MP John Mac-Dougall, were there. As they settled into their seats, the emcee, Andy Faries, described the background to the event and sang "O Canada" in English and Cree. Bishop Leguerrier offered "thanks for the gift of hockey and humour and the sense of community that bring us together." He dropped the puck at centre ice and the Flying Fathers' entertainment machine took over.

The game wasn't a minute old when Vaughan Quinn paraded Edward St. Bear around the ice surface. He started his patter with the crowd behind the net, inviting them to "guess whether the next puck will go to the stick side? The glove side? Or if it's coming right down the middle, just tell me to duck."

The home side's Sam Whiskeychan scored the first Bombardier goal and accordingly was ordained with holy water and a pie in the face. Referees Vern Mortson, Charlie Cheechoo and Robert Tyre received their share of whipped cream. Sister Mary Shooter made an appearance. And Mike Malott made the fatal mistake of borrowing Edward St. Bear when Vaughan Quinn wasn't looking. "The next thing I knew, they were charging up to my end pushing their net. They took the bear back and boxed me in between the two nets and then pails of water were suddenly flying at me."

As the game progressed, the crowd got more and more enthusiastic. Their Bombardiers were still in contention. By the third period when the Fathers led by only a goal, 10–9, they pulled their football scrimmage trick, advanced up the ice in a line and scored a touchdown and conversion to defeat the Bombardiers 17–9. The evening had raised some $2,500 toward the construction of a new hospital to serve both Moosonee and Moose Factory.

The Fathers had enough energy to bring along guitars and sing at the traditional reception that followed and at the schools the next day. The local children and their teachers were a little reluctant to join in but they sat and listened to the songs and watched and enjoyed the Fathers' antics. Whether they were greeted by uproarious laughter from the bleachers, or the restrained smiles of children a classroom, the Fathers knew they were getting through. Their mission was succeeding.

For a day, the Flying Fathers' ministry on skates had brought this northern Ontario community together—its Native elders, its religious leaders, its politicians and its citizens—to celebrate what they had in common. They love their traditions. They love their way of life. They love their new facility. They love their hockey. And those wild hockey-playing priests had helped them celebrate all of it under one roof that December night.

"The Cree people have a phrase to describe 'those who are respected and trusted,'" says Mike Malott. "They say, '*Kaa gis tae li ma kaa noo ow chik.*' They believe the good that you do will be shown by the way you fish or hunt or work or provide for your family or play hockey."

Like Conn Smythe's 1947–48 "greatest ever" Toronto Maple Leafs, the first championship team Les Costello ever played for, these Flying Fathers oldtimers are worthy of a community's highest praise: "Those who are respected."

SIX

The Greying of the Game

In February, 1971, Helen Hirschfeld found her husband Bert sitting on the back steps of their Cork Street bungalow in Halifax. Sweat was pouring off his face and he had pains in the chest. He was close to passing out. Helen called their family doctor who told her to rush him to Victoria General Hospital in downtown Halifax.

Halfway there Bert told his wife, "You might as well stop and turn around. The pain's gone."

Helen didn't listen and drove on as quickly as she could.

On the way from the parking lot to the emergency ward, Bert collapsed. His heart stopped. Inside the ward, they got it going again with electric shock paddles. Emergency staff jump-started his heart two more times on the way to intensive care. He spent six weeks in hospital and celebrated his forty-second birthday in a hospital bed.

As with many men facing a long road to recovery, Bert Hirschfeld completely altered his lifestyle. He quit smoking. He stopped drinking. And he began walking to trim down his 214-pound body. On his first trip outside, he made it to the corner but had to sit on the curb to get his breath back before he could return home. He refused to give up. Soon Hirschfeld was walking two to three miles a day and weighed 180 pounds. That's when he found out about a group playing shinny at the Halifax Forum on Sundays.

"First I asked if I could referee the games until I felt stronger," remembers Hirschfeld. "I did that for two or three

Sundays. They warned me to take it easy because I had played competitive hockey. It was really frustrating. I used to depend on my speed. You know, you try to do things you know you should be able to do. And the legs just rebel."

Among those playing pick-up was Douglas "Dugger" McNeil with whom Hirschfeld had played in the Montreal Canadiens' farm system in the late 1940s. And McNeil wasn't surprised at Hirschfeld's comeback. As far as he was concerned, Bert never did anything halfway. He always skated hard, played hard and fired the puck hard. One Sunday, after Hirschfeld had graduated from referee to puck carrier, McNeil recalls seeing Hirschfeld grab the puck, dart for the net and then tumble to the ice. McNeil rushed over to him thinking he'd suffered another heart attack. He bent down and asked, "Bert, are you all right?"

"Yeah. Oh yeah. I'm okay," said Hirschfeld.

"Well, what is it?"

"My goddamn back," Hirschfeld moaned. He had a disk problem and had thrown his back out. But he was soon back on his feet and going flat out again.

Defeat is not in Hirschfeld's vocabulary. As a kid growing up in the west end of Halifax, Bert played every sport—baseball, football, basketball, track and field, swimming, rowing and hockey. In the mid-1940s Hirschfeld and McNeil both signed "C" forms with Montreal, promising their hockey playing rights to the Canadiens in return for "a stack of five twenty-dollar bills." They played junior with the powerful Halifax Saint Mary's Juniors, winning the Maritime crown three seasons in a row, until being invited to Montreal's training camp in 1949; Dugger became a member of Montreal's Senior Royals and Bert a member of the Junior Royals.

"It was the biggest thrill of my hockey career," recalls Hirschfeld. "Montreal had never won the Memorial Cup. When [Frank] Selke joined the organization, he promised management that within three years [the Junior Royals] would win the Memorial Cup. This was his third year."

The Royals' 1949 season was historic from start to finish. During the regular season, Hirschfeld and his teammates won the Quebec Junior League championship by turning aside teams with such players as Bernie Geoffrion and Jacques Plante. In the Eastern Canada playoffs they defeated Hap Emms's highly favoured Barrie Flyers whose roster included Leo Labine and Stan Long. Then, in the Memorial Cup finals, against the Western champs, the Brandon Wheat Kings, the Junior Royals played a full eight games (Game 5 was cancelled when two overtime periods carried the game into Sunday, violating local by-laws that forbade work on Sundays).

"It was the sixteenth of May," recalls Hirschfeld, when the Royals, using Winnipeg as their home rink, prepared for the final game. "The fire department was spraying the inside of the building to keep the arena as cool as possible. Even so, the ice became desperately thin as the evening's game progressed.

"By the end of the second period we were trailing the game 4 to 2. In a desperation move, coach Tag Miller rested some of the guys due to the heat and fatigue. That left two lines—one with Dickie Moore, Bill Rattray and Neale Langill, the other with Gordie Knutson at centre and Bobby Frampton and me on the wings.

"We found it so warm oxygen was supplied on the bench to us for the first time. Experimenting with it in that final game, we found it aided our breathing (until someone tramped on the line and cut it in the third period). We came back strong, winning that clincher by a 6 to 4 score, with our line accounting for all of our tallies—Knutson with two, Frampton with one and me with a hat trick.

"It was a storybook ending—pictures, parades and stacks of wires. Back in Montreal they met us at the station. There must have been 10,000 people. They drove us through the streets in convertibles, took us to the Forum with thousands of people there. We went to City Hall and signed the book and the mayor gave us rings."

After the Memorial Cup, Bert Hirschfeld's NHL career was something of an anticlimax. He spent most of the next season with the Cincinnati Mohawks of the American Hockey League. He was called up in the spring of 1950 to join the Canadiens but felt "less confident" playing with the likes of Rocket Richard, Elmer Lach, Bill Durnan and Butch Bouchard. He played thirty-eight games in all with the Habs before he returned to the AHL. Then it was back home to the Maritimes for Senior League hockey and, beginning in 1956, a long career as a firefighter with the Halifax Fire Department.

It's not surprising, with hockey in his blood from having played every level of the game and years of action as a firefighter, that Hirschfeld eagerly strapped on the blades in the 1970s. He wanted both to rehabilitate his heart and to feel the adrenalin of hockey again. About the time that Bert Hirschfeld stopped refereeing the Sunday shinny games and started to play, oldtimers' hockey—with referees, no slapshots and no bodychecking—was getting its legs across the country. The Sunday morning gang in Halifax wasn't able to mount a team in time for the First Annual National Oldtimers' Hockey Tournament in Peterborough in 1975 but, soon after, McNeil and his friends started a Halifax oldtimers' hockey league that played every Monday night at the Centennial Arena.

"We got some sweaters from the local IGA," remembers Dugger McNeil, "The sponsors didn't put a lot of money into it. In fact, the guys mostly paid their own way. But it kept a lot of guys involved in the game. That was the thing."

The Monday night league started off small with a couple of armed forces teams, some locally sponsored teams and mostly younger men earning pocket money as referees. Soon though, because of their former professionals, the IGA Oldtimers became the team to beat. As well as Dugger McNeil and Bert Hirschfeld, the team had ex-New York Ranger Kelly Burnett and former Senior League players Bob Bowness and Gerald Hessian.

"The goal in the league," says McNeil, "was to beat us. We'd go through a season unbeaten. And the next year, all these teams started to strengthen. We operated under the COHA rules that classified oldtimers as thirty-five. All our guys were at least forty but we were still agile enough to play fairly well. We would go to some tournaments and we'd always be up in the A category against some pretty competitive teams. I didn't mind playing against them but it was starting to get a lot tougher chasing thirty-five-year-olds around the rink.

"I remember one tournament in particular. We seemed to be the [team] on the block to beat. We wound up in the final

game. I remember Bert had already had his heart attack and
somebody took him out pretty roughly on the boards. I could
just see it in his face—that old competitive spirit came out.
Bert looked to see who it was and the minute he saw this guy
coming with his head down, Bert just let him have it. But
that's what happens. We got competitive. We were right back
in Montreal or with the Saint Mary's Juniors again."

In later years, McNeil's IGA Oldtimers sported not only
some of the most respected hockey players in Halifax but also
a who's who of the local corporate and political worlds. The
regulars included Ron Locke, a top General Motors salesman; Bob MacDonald, who ran Locke's GM dealership;
Rowlie Perry, a Halifax coroner; a former federal cabinet
minister, Stewart McInnes; and the former premier of Nova
Scotia, Gerald Regan.

As usual among oldtimers, social or political position stood
for nothing in the dressing room. Perry the coroner often told
Locke the salesman that he was always on the lookout at the
morgue for a new pair of legs for him. The two politicians
were the favourite targets of plenty of heckling, both on and
off the ice. One night after the team suffered a 10–0 loss Hessian wondered aloud whether the team might do better if it
got rid of McInnes and Regan by getting them re-elected.

"I never was a good hockey player," confirms Gerald Regan.
"And I'm still not. But I'm a wildly enthusiastic one. If I get a
pass, I try to give it back to the guy in a good position and
head for the net. I skate my wing—left-wing—and I cover my
position, but you can't make a silk purse out of a sow's ear."

Despite his disclaimers of proficiency, Regan grew up with
hockey all around him. He played shinny on the frozen ponds
of Windsor, Nova Scotia, where he was born in 1929. He
watched wartime games between the naval training base team
from Cornwallis, the Stanley air force station squad and the
hometown Windsor army camp team. He fondly remembers
that the on-ice brawling among the fans and the players was
often so continuous, "They would play the national anthem
to get everybody to stop fighting and stand at attention; one
night they played the anthem three times."

Even though he was never an outstanding player, Gerald

Regan was never far from the game. He paid his way through university and law school by doing play-by-play radio broadcasts of Annapolis Valley League games and senior hockey games from the South Shore League; he even scouted part-time for the Boston Bruins.

When he was elected premier of the province in 1970, he quickly put together a Legislature oldtimers' team. Cabinet minister Walter Fitzgerald was centre, leader of the opposition John Buchanan played right-wing and Regan himself was the left-winger. During the 1970s the Legislature team played a dozen charity games a year against the Flying Fathers, former juniors and even NHL oldtimers. Whatever the format, whenever the game took place, Regan was there.

Regan says, "I love the game. It's as exciting as anything I've been involved in, as exciting as being premier."

Whether it was shinny, recreational hockey or minor league, Haligonians played a lot of their hockey outdoors at places like Frog Pond, on "the swamp" near Saint Mary's University, on the North West Arm (an inlet of ocean water that almost always froze) or on Chocolate Lake, a freshwater lake just inland from the Arm.

"They ran our minor hockey on Chocolate Lake," confirms Dugger McNeil. He remembers getting his first pair of skates for Christmas when he was eight or nine, a pair of tube skates made by Star Manufacturing in Dartmouth. "At that time, we used to meet at different houses almost every night. There would always be a plate of sandwiches, then we used to go and play hockey out on the lake."

The hockey played outdoors focused on the fundamentals. At the swamp, youngsters learned basic skating skills from a sports enthusiast named Jim McDonald while the kids at Chocolate Lake were organized and coached by a volunteer named Nick Diggon. MacDonald and Diggon emphasized non-stop skating, stickhandling through a crowd and passing the puck to a teammate in open ice. Team play was primary, scoring was secondary.

It was in that spirit that a number of Haligonians organized a unique recreational league in the winter of 1964. Most had played shinny together on the ponds and lakes around Halifax as well as their first organized hockey in the City Commons School League, where the seasons weren't terribly long and the coaching was haphazard. In one instance, the St. Thomas Aquinas team was coached by the school janitor. Probably the most sophisticated game played was with the various inter-faculty, intercollegiate or junior teams of either Saint Mary's University or Dalhousie University.

This was the path Don Murphy had taken. When his team won the Halifax City Commons School hockey championship around 1938, they were treated to a banquet at Russell's Tea Room complete with "bean supper and a piece of pie, a school crest with 'champions' written on it and the presentation of the City Commons School cup. It was quite exciting.

"Senior hockey paid my way through university. But in my final year I quit hockey and did nothing athletically for eleven years. [Then] I had a serious attack of rheumatoid arthritis that hospitalized me for over a month. I felt terrible. My ankles were so big I couldn't get rubber boots on and the pain in my neck was excruciating. It was 1963. I remember lying in bed fearing deformity of my feet and ankles and worrying to myself, 'Thirty-five years old and crippled. How do I support a wife and six kids?'"

Six months later, during a checkup, his doctor observed, "You used to be an athlete."

"Yes. I used to play sports," said Murphy.

"My advice to you is to get active again. And I don't mean bowling."

That's when Don Murphy, by now a solicitor for the City of Halifax, discovered a group of lawyers and doctors interested in the idea of some "challenge hockey." Even though that game never materialized, a seed was planted and during the winter of 1964 he and a number of friends rented the ice at Saint Mary's University arena one Saturday afternoon between four and five o'clock.

Most of those who assembled that first Saturday had barely enough equipment to cover their vital extremities—elbow pads, shin pads, cup and jock strap. For that reason and because the ability level in the group varied from novice to semi-professional, Murphy's Saturday afternoon bunch developed a number of simple game rules.

After the first couple of games with goalies in net and some pretty wild slapshots, they decided to "banish goaltenders." Instead, each side put a sixth skater with an ordinary stick in net. Raises and slapshots were prohibited so the only way to score was by passing or stickhandling around the sixth man in the net.

Next, to keep the game from becoming too intense, certain aggressive and more talented players were forbidden to wear protective equipment. This removed the false sense of security some players might have with a full suit of armour. It also eliminated bodychecking and, ultimately, the need for referees.

With no slapshots, no lifting the puck, no goalies, only the bare essentials in equipment, no body contact and no refs, the Saturday afternoon league had, in their view, come up with a handicapping system that pared away the downside of competitive hockey without taking away the competition.

"Our fundamental principles," explains Murphy, "are one: nobody gets hurt; two: we're here for the fun of it; and three: winning."

"It seemed to work," agrees sixty-eight-year-old Tusker O'Neill. "And being the oldest guy, I just gravitated into picking the teams. We had sweaters—white sweaters versus coloured sweaters—and I just threw guys the sweaters. "

Like Don Murphy, Frank "Tusker" O'Neill had enjoyed a moment of glory in 1939 when his edition of the St. Thomas Aquinas team won the Halifax City Commons School hockey championship. Later, when he was playing junior hockey, the tall and husky O'Neill was spotted by Maple Leaf defenceman Bob Goldham, who suggested he try out for St. Michael's in Toronto. O'Neill vetoed that idea and instead went to Saint Mary's University to study engineering. The only other hockey he played was as an import (at $35 a game) for the Chester Basin Ravens of the South Shore Senior Hockey League.

"In those days I often had guys who'd try to knock my head off," says the six-foot-tall O'Neill. "I didn't have a temper so all I had to do was hold them till they simmered down. In our Saturday league, you don't want it to get that intense, like the Stanley Cup or something. And even though there are no referees, if a play is blatantly offside or the puck is lifted on the guy in net, we decide among ourselves whether it counts or not."

In the beginning, the group could expect only a dozen or fourteen players to show up each Saturday, six or eight players per side, but the nucleus who showed up for the weekly Whites-versus-Colours game was stable. As well as Murphy and O'Neill, there was Bill MacDonald, a hospital administrator; Ken Fellows, an official with the income tax department; Bill Bailly, head of the province's liquor commission; electrical engineer Fred Gallagher; and Bob Napier, the doctor who had told Murphy to "get active again" the previous year. With each successful season, the pressure to admit new members grew.

"We had a young mayor, about thirty-four, in Halifax then," recalls Don Murphy. "He'd played university hockey. He was a good goal scorer, but a bull of a man weighing about 235 and a good fighter. Well, Mayor Walter Fitzgerald was putting the pressure on me to join our league, basically because he was my boss. So I told him I'd have to put his name before the committee. Of course, there wasn't one.

"We turned him down because he was too young, too strong and because of his disposition—he hadn't been away from [competitive hockey] long enough.

"He was on me for three years. And we finally took a chance on him. Well, he was a great addition to the dressing room. He's never hurt anybody. He took a playful approach. However, prior to his coming, the score was never an issue. Once Walter got there, he kept a record of every goal and he was constantly reminding you what the score was."

The mayor attracted other politicians, civil servants and professionals. Over the years the Saturday crew has included federal cabinet minister Stewart McInnes; Lou Centa and Doug Tobin, both provincial deputy ministers; lawyers John Barker and Danny Gallivan Jr.; air force officer Robert "Puddy" Reardon; urologist Brewer Auld; drug company representative Donny Grant; former premier Gerald Regan; and a fellow in the security business, Bob Dauphinee.

"Dauphinee is our resident singler [bachelor]," says Fred Gallagher. "A bunch of our hockey guys play cards on Friday night and sometimes the parties go on till two in the morning. So we always kid Dauphinee about not leaving the circle at centre ice and not backchecking 'cause he had such a rough Friday night."

Gallagher is another "Haligonian right to the core," born, raised and educated in Halifax. As a kid during the war, Fred played goal each Sunday morning, when hordes of army, navy and air force servicemen took to Lawrence Street in their uniforms to play road hockey; a local lady would regularly call the police to break up the game. In the 1950s, Gallagher played university hockey where he met Bill Bailly. For a while he and Bailly also played in the South Shore League, "where he demonstrated tremendous moves," says Don Murphy. "In fact, he could go in on an NHL goaltender and the guy would get an awful shock from the moves Freddy has." Gallagher also played juvenile hockey with the Halifax Toppers (later the Atlantics), and he played with Walter Fitzgerald and Donny Grant.

For Gallagher, the Saturday afternoon recreational hockey game at Saint Mary's arena rekindled all of these hockey friendships and has for nearly thirty years. That four to five o'clock ice time is one of Halifax's longest-standing ice rentals. Saint Mary's treats it as permanent as do the players. Only serious injury keeps them away. Lou Centa has had to give the game up because of two hip replacements. Tusker O'Neill had an operation for an aneurysm and has a blood clot in his leg so he's had to drop out. Puddy Reardon gave up playing because of bad knees but he still comes out to referee now and then.

Dr. Bob Napier collapsed with a mild heart attack one Saturday afternoon during the game. "It looked like he just sort of lost his balance and slid across the ice," recalls Gallagher. "Dr. Brewer Auld, a urologist in the city, and Donny Grant started giving him CPR and I ran out into the street with my skates on to guide the ambulance in. They slapped a resuscitator on him. Brewer went with him, skates and all. And he was back playing with us two weeks later." Napier died of a subsequent attack.

Generally, however, most of the Saturday afternoon skaters have survived the aches and pains that always accompany old-timers' hockey. Through the years they have also come to tolerate Tusker's way of choosing teammates each week, Fitzgerald's incessant scorekeeping and Dauphinee's excuses for not backchecking. "We've had the odd altercation," admits Gallagher, "like the time Bill Bailly got a little too aggressive. Donny Murphy grabbed Bailly's stick and told him if he did that again he'd break it over his head and then flung the stick up in the stands.

"But it was nothing serious. We're all still around for a beer at the end of the game. You're not supposed to have beer in a dressing room but we do take a minimum amount in—a case—and most have a beer or two and sit around for an hour....We'll still be there when the iceman, Ken Slaunwhite, comes along, bangs on the door and tells us to get the hell out...because there's an intercollegiate game behind us and players are waiting to get into the room."

Some cherished traditions have developed with the Halifax Saint Mary's group: a number of years ago, when they found they had spare ice time, the oldtimers invited their sons to play. The fathers-versus-sons games usually took place between Christmas and New Year's and included, among others, Dugger McNeil and his son Ross, Jack Edwards and his son John, and Don Murphy and his son Paul.

"I'd say we started playing these games when Paul was a teenager, twenty years ago," says Don Murphy. "Back then it wasn't a problem because we were just playing a bunch of kids. We had been playing. We were in fairly good shape and were really just playing with them. The fathers would usually win.

"But as they got older, we had to cheat because these young guys were getting too good."

"It was a different kind of revenge of the cradle," laughs Paul Murphy.

Murphy Jr. first put on skates at age three or four and learned to skate on one of those hotbeds of Halifax recreational hockey—Frog Pond. With his father's constant encouragement, Paul got a heavy dose of organized minor hockey in the 1960s and even went to a local hockey school run by Halifax native and former Boston Bruin, Wayne Maxner. But his real teacher was his father, Don, who taught him to "work harder than the next guy, always get to the puck first and never stop skating."

At medical school, Paul played intramural sports but stuck mostly to B level hockey through his playing career. Not until the 1990s when he was in his mid-thirties and living in Cape Breton did Paul Murphy pick up hockey again. He soon found himself playing one night a week with teachers, another night with miners and then one Christmas when he came home to Halifax he was physically and mentally ready for the annual fathers-versus-sons game.

"I was more or less in shape," remembers Paul Murphy. "But I had to remember that [our fathers] had been playing hockey since before I was born. And they knew how to get the puck, keep it and not go into a corner and come out without it.

"There was no hitting, no lifting the puck, no slapshots. And you get lulled into the idea that this is a casual game. But once you agree to those terms, there's nothing casual about it.

"So here was my chance. I'm in on a breakaway against Don. And there was no way he was going to stop me this time. I pulled to the right. And he's backing up as we cross the blueline. And I gave that extra burst—the one he was always telling me about—and I put the hand down to get his stick and got around him. The goaltender wasn't even a factor at that point. All I had to do was get around Don and I was home free. I'll never forget that."

"I attribute it to the fact I weighed 193 pounds," rationalizes Don Murphy, "when I usually play at 180."

Paul concludes, "I don't think we've ever directly competed on any other level. It was kind of bittersweet. I'd rather never beat him. He's the one who taught me, inspired me, and this is that one time when everything came together and I just had to go for it. Now that I've done it once, well, we'll see what happens next year."

"It was the thirteen pounds," repeats Don Murphy, "so, yes, we'll see what happens next year."

Murphy Sr. is quite serious. Despite his dedication to a

recreational brand of hockey, he's still passionate about the game and remaining in it. Gerald Regan says, "Don Murphy is the only guy I know and play hockey with that still thinks he's going to make the National Hockey League." Now at retirement age, Murphy himself envisages living out the reverse of the one time Participaction commercial—a seventy-year-old Canadian physically equal to a twenty-seven-year-old Swede.

"When I was forty-eight," says Murphy, "I was asked in the dressing room how much longer did I think I'd be playing. I knew how much longer I would be playing. But I was afraid to tell a thirty-five-year-old because he'd think I was nuts.

"My goal was twenty-five more years. I know it's unheard of to play hockey at seventy-three. I knew I'd be playing that long but I wouldn't tell them."

At the opposite end of the country, at a university campus more than a hundred years younger than Saint Mary's but on an ice surface steeped in Canadian hockey history, another group of hockey players assembles for their weekly oldtimers' game. Like Don Murphy's Saturday afternoon group in Halifax, these University of British Columbia alumni and their assorted friends have been gathering each week on the west side of Vancouver at UBC's Thunderbird Winter Sports Centre for many years.

It's a Monday evening in mid-May, 1993. Vancouverites have just enjoyed their first cloudless day since mid-March. Gardens in Kitsilano, Stanley Park and the University Endowment Lands are in full bloom. Cyclists in spandex suits and Vuarnets are everywhere. Outside the Sports Centre, the temperature has warmed to twenty-two-degrees Celsius. But inside the arena dressing rooms, the talk is all hockey.

"Who's gonna win the conference final?" asks businessman Konrad Tittler. Later tonight the L.A. Kings, having knocked their beloved Vancouver Canucks out of the Stanley Cup Playoffs, meet Toronto at Maple Leaf Gardens in Game 1 of the Campbell Conference championship.

"Who cares?" says an affable Mike Buchanan. "If they played here, we'd show 'em how it's done."

There's a chorus of guffaws and a few shouts of, "Sure, Mike, sure."

Buchanan is actually the only one of the group who ever made it to the NHL or, as he describes it, "had a cup of coffee with the Chicago Blackhawks." He played one game in the 1951–52 season. The others—university deans, professors, doctors, business executives and consultants—have known only minor league hockey, a bit of junior or senior hockey and oldtimers.

Around the room, from an assortment of battered nylon and duffel bags, emerges a variety of protective equipment, some of it state of the art, some of it incredibly out of step with the sophisticated 1990s game they're about to play. While some players have bulky CCM and Jofa elbow and shin pads, others are content to use nearly worn-out and flimsy felt-edged pads that date back thirty or forty years. Some wear crash-resistant plastic Cooper and CCM helmets with steel cage or clear visor attached; others pull out antiquated headgear that consists of little more than three leather pads loosely laced together à la Butch Goring. The fellow who comes out to drop the puck for the game is John Protti; he's over seventy and still uses an ancient pair of tube skates.

Added to the stench of unwashed T-shirts and longjohns is the aroma of liniment as several of these UBC alumni try to soothe and inspire aging shoulder, arm and leg muscles before taking to the ice.

"Ah, the sweet smell of wintergreen," sighs Ron Neufeld, the director of UBC's Faculty of Educational Psychology and Special Ed. "As hockey players back in Grande Prairie, we thought the smell of wintergreen was a come-on."

More laughter and kidding.

It's almost six o'clock as the last laces are tied, sticks taped and jerseys donned. Half the players wear white sweaters, the other half gold, each with lettering on the front that identifies the team as the "UBC Old Birds," a tongue-in-cheek variation of the UBC varsity logo—the Thunderbirds. The Thunderbirds' emblem goes back to the 1950s but the complex these oldtimers are playing in dates back to the arrival of a historic team of the 1960s.

In October, 1963, the Thunderbird Winter Sports Complex officially opened with an exhibition game between the Seattle Totems of the Western Professional Hockey League and Canada's Olympic team. After winning 3–1 over Seattle in front of a sell-out crowd, UBC coach Father David Bauer launched the National Team plan which became the model for Canada's participation in international hockey. The Sports Complex became the Olympic team's permanent home. While no Olympic gold came from Father Bauer's plan, some talented professionals did, players such as Brian Conacher, George Swarbrick, Terry Clancy and Gary Dineen.

The same year the Nationals moved onto the Thunderbird ice surface, so did a forty-five-year-old geography instructor named Lewis Robinson. Professor Robinson took time that year to bring his children to pleasure skate at the new arena and to dabble in the game he had learned as a kid on Church Street in Windsor, Ontario, in the 1920s. Lew had played high school hockey and intramural hockey for the Arts 40 team at the University of Western Ontario; in fact, in his graduating year he scored the winning goal in the game against the Med 40 team. But between then and 1973 he played no organized hockey at all.

"I was head of the [UBC] geography department then," recalls Robinson, "when some of the geography students invited me out to play. I had had a heart attack at age fifty and this was a few years later. I started playing with them one afternoon a week. I remember scoring my first goal with them and I said, 'It's my first goal in thirty-three years.'"

Just like Bert Hirschfeld and Don Murphy, Lew Robinson turned to his favourite sport to rehabilitate his ailing body. And like Murphy's Saturday afternoon league, the UBC afternoon geography league fashioned a few rules to keep the fun in the game. Players kept a three-minute egg timer on the bench and with every turn of the egg timer someone blew a whistle to change lines. Each team put its best players on one line and its less experienced players on the second so that the first line always played against the first line and the second against the second. These rules were particularly helpful for the hockey novices in the geography group—young British and Jamaican students who had never played the game before. Robinson spent extra mornings tutoring them in the basic skills of the game so that "raw kids who were wobbling around the ice in September could actually play the game by March."

In his seventies (and now on the ice with the second line of the alumni group), Robinson plays his position as methodically as he did when he scored the game winner for the UWO Arts 40 team. Although his speed has diminished, he still floats along the boards from blueline to blueline, taking headman passes, intercepting the puck in the neutral zone and feeding his faster centre for breaks in on net. He admits he could never stickhandle around anyone but he always had a strong, accurate shot. If somebody put the puck on his stick he knew what to do with it.

On the ice, Mike Buchanan mounts a rush from his own end. He flips the puck to Robinson waiting in the centre ice area. Robinson finishes a textbook give-and-go to Buchanan who slips past the opposition defenders and scores with a wrist shot high to the stick side. Exhausted by that rush and goal, Buchanan comes to the bench for a rest and to receive praise and cheap shots from his teammates.

"What'd you do? Take an extra spoonful of Geritol?" quips one.

"Don't tell me you're on steroids," another kids.

"It's really like watching a game in slow motion," Buchanan admits.

"No, no. It was just like a Ray Bourque rush," protests his teammate, Konrad Tittler, "except that Bourque's are a lot better."

Tittler himself would love to be able to stage a rush like defenceman Ray Bourque. Or Bobby Orr. Or Denis Potvin. But especially like Doug Harvey. Tittler always admired the calm, self-assured style of the Canadiens' Hall of Famer. Harvey won the James Norris Memorial Trophy seven times as the best defenceman in the game back in the 1950s and early '60s. He helped the Canadiens bring home the Stanley Cup five consecutive seasons, "because," in Tittler's view, "he was the guy back there who did it right in order to let the forwards freewheel. It's sort of a quarterbacking position if it's done right. I wished I could play like Harvey. I wished that I could control the game like that."

In the beginning, the game controlled Konrad Tittler. In 1937 when he was four, Konrad tried skating on schoolyard ice in the north end of Winnipeg; his ankles hurt so much afterward that he cried all the way home and vowed never to skate again. But as a teenager he joined the Canadian Ukrainian Athletic Club and learned hockey from club volunteers until injuries sidelined him when he was about eighteen. That's when Konrad Tittler began taking control of the game as a coach. His first year he coached a team of twelve-year-olds to the Manitoba championship. The next year he coached Bantam A's and B's to provincial championships, and the year following his midget team won the Manitoba championship. In all he coached or managed ten Manitoba championship teams, all while studying to become an engineer.

About his coaching days he says, "It was just the joy of accomplishment for me. I was busy going to school, under pressure to get my reports in, and all the drudgery that goes with trying to get a degree. Then [about 1957] I gave it up, not voluntarily. I cold-cocked a referee and I was suspended. And I never went back to coaching hockey. I finished engineering and lost hockey."

Tittler moved to the Pacific coast in the early 1960s and was coaxed into a recreational hockey league by, of all people, Olympic sprinter Harry Jerome. But Tittler felt he played so ineptly that he dropped hockey again. By 1988, he was thirty to forty pounds overweight. He'd become a heavy drinker consuming half a bottle of scotch most days after work. Then he met Bob Hindmarsh, the athletic director at UBC.

"Why don't you come out and play some hockey with us?" asked Hindmarsh.

"I'm in my fifties," laughed Tittler. "You don't play hockey when you're in your fifties."

"We've got this Monday night group," said Hindmarsh. "They're not very good. Just some professors and friends. And there's this fellow, about sixty-seven, Lew Robinson, who runs it."

Tittler reluctantly agreed to give hockey one last chance, this time with a bunch of oldtimers playing the oldtimers' game—no contact, no slapshots, hockey just for fun.

He arrived late that first Monday night. He was carrying borrowed equipment because after the Jerome episode he had thrown out all his gear. The rest of the players were already on the ice. Tittler watched them a moment. Hindmarsh was right. They weren't very good, some barely able to skate, most just banging the puck around the ice. He debated whether to bother, shrugged, went into the dressing room, changed, came out on the ice and by his third or fourth shift decided to upgrade his opinion of the calibre of play.

"I got the puck behind the net," says Tittler, "and thought, 'Here we go.' I cut up the middle. I felt like Cournoyer. I felt my hair was blowing back like Cournoyer.

"I finally took a second to put my head up because I'd been staring at the puck. I looked around and everyone was casually skating beside me. It was my first day back to hockey. So I recognized where I was. I thought I was leaving them all behind but there they were, skating with me. I felt as if I were flying. Perception is a wonderful thing."

By the end of that rush up the ice, Konrad Tittler had come home to hockey. The adrenalin was flowing through him. And, like so many pursuits in his life, once involved Konrad Tittler became fully committed, committed to becoming "one of the best sixty-year-old hockey players in the world." Like so many other oldtimers, Tittler reformed his lifestyle. He replaced the Scotch bottle with a sociable beer after Monday night games. He shed the extra pounds and began to feel virile and fit again. And he began to enjoy some of the best friendships of his life.

On one of Tittler's first nights out with the Old Birds, Jim Richards, the dean of agricultural sciences at UBC, recognized him. When they talked about their backgrounds, they realized they were about the same age and had met during a game in Winnipeg thirty-five years earlier. The following Monday night, Richards brought along a newspaper clipping from a 1953 edition of the *Winnipeg Tribune*, that recapped a playoff game between the West Winnipeg Orioles and the St.

Boniface Canadiens. The article recorded Richards's goal for the Orioles and the Canadiens' coach—Konrad Tittler.

More than just that playoff match, though, Richards and Tittler had a great deal in common when they joined the Old Birds. As a hockey player, Richards, also like Tittler, had all the tools of the game; he was big, dominated his position on ice, and played a "reasonably cerebral" game. But also like Tittler, Richards had put education above hockey, stopped playing to coach, encountered physical problems and eventually turned to oldtimers' hockey to relieve his sore back and his hectic schedule. For Richards, Monday hockey is a distraction from the rigours of the dean's office. It's a way of refocusing his energy and maintaining his fitness. It's time he protects selfishly.

For Tittler, oldtimers' hockey has been even more valuable. In 1991, when recession pushed his chemical business to the brink of bankruptcy, "the only thing that kept me able to go to work was playing more and more hockey.

"I didn't have to talk about my problems," Tittler says. "For a few hours every time I was out there, I knew I didn't have to think about it. Here were all these guys with a different focus. It's a different place where lawyers don't talk about law and businessmen don't talk about business. It's a place where no matter what's going on in your life, you can find friendship and fun. We just talk about the thing we enjoy—hockey and pretending to be kids again. It's a tremendous escape.

"I might have cracked up the way things were going. But I hung in there. I had to play more and more in order to stay balanced. It paid off."

Part of the escape too is that oldtimers don't have to explain to each other who they are—labourers or professionals, high income earners or low, successes or failures. In groups like the Monday night league, it doesn't even matter how proficient your game is. John Thomas grew up during the 1950s in Victoria where there was no ice and no hockey. The family didn't even watch *Hockey Night in Canada*.

"I started to play hockey at thirty-eight," says Thomas, an Environment Canada technologist. "I just started going to lunch-hour hockey, skating with a hockey stick in my hands. I had no idea what to do with it.

"Eventually, I started coming out to scrimmage at UBC on Mondays. I had hand-me-down everything when I started. I could hardly stand on my skates. I could hardly do anything. They still let me come out and play. Now I'm pretty much up on what's going on in hockey. But if I had a chance to go downtown and watch a final game in the Stanley Cup or come out and scrimmage with the guys, I'd rather scrimmage anytime!"

Paul Willing's story is similar. He was born in 1946 but didn't learn to skate until 1971 when he and his family settled in Port Alice at the north end of Vancouver Island. The community had just built a rink. His wife bought him a pair of skates and he played his first hockey with a team of volunteer firefighters. Even when the family moved to Vancouver so Paul could work in animal sciences at UBC's agricultural department, his children were far better at playing hockey than he was. His eldest son was playing Junior B while his other son and daughter were playing bantam rep hockey.

"I've always had a reputation for being easygoing," says Willing. "In other words, I could go out and play with them and not in any way, shape or form be a threat. I'm able to play as intensely as the rest of the guys. But there's no pressure."

Despite all his hockey expertise, his teammates have no expectations of Stu Robertson either. Born in 1929, Robertson grew up playing shinny on community rinks in Edmonton during the Depression. He played junior hockey in New Westminster, senior hockey in Kelowna and, after the Second World War, as a professional in several European leagues. For him, the play's the thing. "Making the good pass…making the good set-up for a goal. It's better than getting the goal itself."

While Paul Willing's wife got him into hockey, Gordon Robertson's wife got him out. In 1966, when he was thirty-nine and running his own general practice in Vancouver, Robertson found himself getting banged up regularly in the Royal City League, an industrial league in New Westminster. His wife forced him to quit until the mid-1970s, when old-timers came along. Playing with the Old Birds now, says Robertson, "it's like a rebirth."

"That's right," echoes Mike Buchanan. "Just because you get older doesn't mean those fires still aren't there."

For Mike Buchanan the fire was lit back in the 1930s when he and his twin brother Neil played shinny on the Rideau River near Ottawa and in a neighbourhood league dreamed up by a Canadian army captain named Gus Long. Captain Long's league played on a rink in a vacant lot, complete with bluelines, a loud speaker and lights for night games. From that house league of about twenty-five kids came NHLers Bill Dineen who played on two Cup winners with Detroit, former Bruin Phil Maloney and the Cullen brothers, Barry and Brian, who both played with the Leafs.

Toronto appeared to be the Buchanan brothers' NHL destination too; at sixteen they both signed Leaf "C" forms at Maple Leaf Gardens "in the office of God himself," Conn Smythe. While they both excelled in Junior A—Neil for the Ottawa Montaguards and Mike for Ottawa St. Patrick's College and then the Galt Blackhawks—only Mike got a shot at the NHL with Chicago.

During the one game he played as a pro, Mike Buchanan was paired on defence with Bill Gadsby. The Hawks' opponents that night were the Boston Bruins who had Bill Quackenbush, Real Chevrefils, Bill Ezinicki, Leo Labine, Woody Dumart, George Sullivan and Milt Schmidt. It was a rough game in which Bep Guidolin was thrown out for fighting.

Defencemen took face-offs in those days. So at one point in the game Buchanan lined up against Milt Schmidt. At the drop of the puck, he quickly (and, he thought, too easily) took Schmidt out of the play. The veteran just looked at Buchanan as if making a mental note.

A few shifts later, the two met again in a face-off. In an instant, Buchanan remembers being on his ass and hearing Schmidt say, "Welcome to the pros, rookie."

Even though his NHL record shows no goals, no assists and no penalties, Buchanan wouldn't change a thing about his shot at the pros. He got plenty from hockey—a university education, two NCAA hockey championships and even a season in Europe playing for the Wembley Lions of the English Hockey League. However his body took a lot of punishment.

He tore up his knee during an exhibition game against the Detroit Red Wings. He broke his jaw against the U.S. Olympic team in England. And in a game between his Fort Wayne Komets and Cincinnati, "I lined up Donny Marshall, hit him with my shoulder, but I was off balance…and I could tell for the next thirty years when it was going to rain by the pain in my shoulder.

"For eighteen years I never skated," says Buchanan. Then, in 1975, he started refereeing minor hockey and coaching youngsters at Vancouver's Arbutus Club, and playing for the Vancouver Canuck Oldtimers and eventually with the UBC Old Birds. "I had a stroke and the doctors strongly urged me not to play. But I had to get back to the exercise and being with the guys. I realize in my sixties that the old body can't take it anymore. It's a deterrent. But you just skate through the pain."

One of the Old Birds' goalies is the kid of the group. Steve Crombie was born in 1957. His relatively short hockey career began in 1968 in peewee when he played left-wing. But Crombie was soon attracted to the goalie's position for two reasons; goalies got more ice time and they usually don't get checked. He developed his goaltending skills principally under Mike Buchanan's tutelage at the Arbutus Club.

"Mike started a hockey school with the Vancouver Canucks in 1970, the first year they were in the NHL," recalls Crombie. "Mike came out to our practices and gave us tips on conditioning. He used to say to me, 'As a goalie you can't flop around on the ice. You've got to be smart, scientific. Come out, challenge the shooter, stand up and play the angles.'"

That advice served him well. In the 1970s Crombie played in the West Coast Junior B league, tried for an NCAA athletic scholarship, but played senior hockey in B.C. instead. He moved to Ottawa as a journalist to cover Parliament Hill for Canadian Press. In 1990 he returned to Vancouver to work in the UBC media relations and publications department and two years later started playing oldtimers with the Old Birds each Monday.

The perspective of a younger goalie playing hockey with a bunch of middle-aged and senior citizens is unique. Crombie never ceases to be astonished by what he sees. The dressing room is full of constant hockey chatter, not about the NHL, but about their own prowess and pratfalls. They argue over who will pass today, who will score the most goals and who's going to screw up. On the ice, despite the varying abilities from one man to the next, enthusiasm for the game unites them. Even when it gets scrambly in front of the net, it's still serious business—to a point. Through it all is a child-like passion for the fun of each rush up and down the ice.

"I'm an anomaly out there," admits Crombie. "I'm thirty-five. The other goalie is sixty-six. Lew Robinson is in his seventies. Most players are in their mid to late fifties. And they have this thing about playing with younger players. I'm terrified they're going to come up one day and say, 'Gee, Steve, it's been great having you, but this other guy is our age.'"

The Monday night scrimmage is winding down at UBC's Thunderbird Winter Sports Centre.

Stu Robertson has made his share of pretty passes. Mike Buchanan has completed his once-a-night successful end-to-end rush and will pay for it when his knee begins to ache. Konrad Tittler has enjoyed ribbing his own teammates as much as the opposition. It's par for the course.

There's one last rush from the white-sweatered Old Birds. Buchanan, sensing an opportunity to get back at Tittler for his Ray Bourque remark, sets Tittler up for a breakaway on goalie Steve Crombie. Tittler knows he'll have to be sharp to beat the netminder, even this late in the game. But this time Crombie outsmarts him and comes up with the puck. There's a chorus of moans at the missed breakaway.

"How come you didn't score?" teases Buchanan. "It was a perfect set-up."

"Ah, I didn't feel like it," says Tittler. "But I know he was shitting himself about my shot."

More guffaws at Tittler's nerve.

In the dressing room, weary bodies hit the benches. Some of the Old Birds peel off their gear as if it was on fire. In seconds, these aging and sweaty bodies are wearing nothing but jock straps or shorts. Others won't bother to strip for up to half an hour, partly out of fatigue, partly to savour these minutes. Much of the conversation in the room is drowned out by the cacophony of jokes, laughter and verbal shots. There's plenty of unfinished business from an hour's scrimmage on UBC ice. Most of the chatter is indecipherable except for the routine question that pierces the din. "What was the score?" somebody asks.

"One-one," shouts Lew Robinson. No matter what the score was, that's what Lew always says. This from a man with a peculiar sense of mortality. Robinson plans to die on the ice...but preferably after scoring the winning goal.

SEVEN

Hamburger Hockey

Nearly a decade after he retired from the Montreal Canadiens' goal crease, Ken Dryden embarked on a cross-country odyssey in search of the essence of hockey. During the winter of 1988–89, he and a television production crew visited Saskatchewan and spent many days and nights sitting in cafés, kitchens, bleachers and dressing rooms listening to people as passionate about hockey as he was talk about their game.

As well as shadowing NHL hopeful Kevin Kaminski and telling the story of SaskPlace, the arena that hockey promoter Bill Hunter built for Saskatoon when he expected the St. Louis Blues to move there, Dryden visited some lesser-known hotbeds of hockey in Saskatchewan. He watched young boys play shinny on a slough in the French-speaking town of St. Denis. He visited the Red Bull Cafe in Radisson to find out how important the town's hockey arena was to its survival. And he arranged to meet with a group of oldtimers hockey players in Saskatoon.

His contact was Guy Vanderhaeghe—short story writer, novelist and Governor-General's Award winner—whose passion was recreational hockey. For nearly ten years Vanderhaeghe, along with a handful of legal-aid lawyers and friends, had played shinny at various arenas around Saskatoon. However, the first time Dryden talked about interviewing and video-taping Guy's oldtimers, Vanderhaeghe took it with a grain of salt. He never really expected Dryden or his crew to show up at the Kinsmen Arena for their Sunday night scrimmage.

But two weeks before Dryden's intended visit, Vanderhaeghe got a call from a television producer asking permis-
sion to shoot their game. The following Sunday night,
Vanderhaeghe decided to make the announcement in the
dressing room. He had recently had a brushcut and was taking a lot of ribbing over it, when he dropped his bombshell.

"Excuse me. Excuse me," Vanderhaeghe began. "I was
wondering...Ken Dryden has asked if he could come and
play hockey with us next week and bring a film crew."

For a moment, nobody said a word. Vanderhaeghe remembers watching his teammates' eyes shifting back and forth;
each player was waiting for someone else to react.

Finally Adrian Ewins, a thirty-six-year-old reporter for the
Western Producer, and with every bone a Montreal Canadiens
fan, blurted out, "What the fuck is the matter with you guys?
Ken Dryden not good enough for you? Who the fuck do you
want, Gretzky?"

Amid the ensuing buzz, Vanderhaeghe recalls seeing con-
sternation on his teammates' faces. They knew he was dia-
betic and that during some of their oldtimers' games he
would have to retire to the bench for a rest and a carton of
fruit juice to replenish his blood sugar. But this time, Vanderhaeghe felt, his teammates were looking at him as if their
friend was falling apart right before their eyes.

In this atmosphere of disbelief, one of Guy's oldest buddies, lawyer Danny Shapiro, wisecracked to Vanderhaeghe,
"After a speech like that, I can see why you had your hair cut
short...so they could attach electrodes to your head!"

On the appointed night—the following Sunday—Vanderhaeghe's credibility remained in question. Dryden's crew was
behind schedule. All Vanderhaeghe's hockey buddies sat and
fidgeted in the dressing room. Guy admits he was sweating
buckets.

"Right, Vanderhaeghe," someone said. "This week Dryden's
coming to play with us. Who's coming next week, Al Pacino?"

Finally, Ken Dryden walked through the dressing room
door. Everything stopped. You could have heard a pin drop as
all heads turned in his direction. Before Dryden had a
chance to sit down, Canadiens worshipper Adrian Ewins was

at his side recounting each of Dryden's Stanley Cup wins and the entire series against the Soviets. Dryden turned to Vanderhaeghe and said, "This guy knows more about my life than I do."

While Vanderhaeghe felt redeemed, the results on television were less satisfying. When the six-part series, *Ken Dryden's Home Game*, aired on CBC Television, the images of the Sunday night scrimmage were not flattering. The segment featuring Vanderhaeghe and his hockey buddies "appeared with sixty-seven-year-old female hockey players and handicapped skaters. And I later found out," laughs Vanderhaeghe, "that our appearance being labelled as oldtimers' hockey actually got a letter of protest. I think it was from some guy who played oldtimers in Ontario and [he] was outraged at the idea that we should be thought to represent oldtimers since we were so pitifully inadequate....

"We did realize the truth on film, though. We *were* pretty bad."

Guy Vanderhaeghe is the first to admit he's no hockey star. Born in 1951 in the southern Saskatchewan town of Esterhazy, Guy learned the game as a boy playing church hockey. While the minister/coach taught the boys sportsmanship and good behaviour, "he didn't have a clue what offside meant and half the time sent too many players on the ice at once." In 1957, potash was discovered near Esterhazy. The International Minerals Corporation moved in, the population boomed, an arena was built and Esterhazy got a Junior B hockey team. At age fourteen, Guy's hockey future came to an abrupt end because "all the best players went into junior hockey...and the rest of us got left behind."

After university, Vanderhaeghe started writing, teaching and researching in Saskatoon where outdoor rinks were routinely empty on Sunday mornings. He and a number of friends, women and men "who like me had limited athletic gifts," decided to play co-ed hockey. They wore no fancy protective equipment. Just skates, sticks and a tennis ball on the outdoor ice surface. Exercise was really the purpose.

Like-minded and similarly skilled adults gravitated to the group. By the time Vanderhaeghe was thirty (1981) the group had joined forces with some legal-aid lawyers in the city and was regularly renting ice on Sundays at indoor arenas around Saskatoon. Within a few years, the heart of the Saskatoon Legal Aid Hockey Club consisted of Vanderhaeghe, lawyers Danny Shapiro, Sam Beckie and Roger Kergoat, Ewins and Steve Lewis, a research executive with the Saskatchewan Department of Health.

What made the association of people jell was the brand of hockey and the evolution of their game. Much like Don Murphy's Saturday afternoon group in Halifax, and Lew Robinson's geography league in Vancouver, the Saskatoon Legal Aid bunch developed its own "rules of tradition," rules intended to reduce the chance of injury and to keep the game under control.

There is, of course, no body contact or slapshots. There are no refs, just the honour system. Two-line passes aren't called back. The only face-off is at the beginning of the game. After a goal is scored, the team scored against skates and passes freely as far as centre ice. Because there are no goalies, a sixth player stands in the net and to protect his ankles the puck cannot be raised. To prevent long shots from deflecting up into people's faces, players aren't allowed to shoot until they are past the face-off circles. And to keep anyone with a full head of steam from crashing into the end boards, any player with a breakaway can be chased to a certain point but is then given his breakaway unmolested. These are the unwritten but acknowledged regulations of the game, spelled out to newcomers and, like the rules of children's games, abided by because of peer pressure.

Other traditions have evolved. To determine sides, all players throw their sticks into the circle at centre ice at the beginning of the game. Then Adrian Ewins skates through centre ice separating the sticks willy-nilly but equally to each side of centre. Everybody carries a white sweater and a dark one so when sticks are retrieved one group becomes "the whites," the other "the darks."

Equipment traditions have been determined by injuries. Only when Roger Kergoat fell and broke his elbow did elbow pads become regular hockey gear. And the week after Steve

Lewis had his front teeth knocked out in a game, there was "a sudden proliferation of helmets with visors. We learned over time how to protect ourselves....That doesn't mean we don't play hard," says Vanderhaeghe.

Playing oldtimers provides a balance in Vanderhaeghe's life. He writes mostly fiction; his hockey and friendships are real. His writing is done mostly in isolation; his Sunday night games regularly put him in touch with a variety of people who are generally outside writing and the arts. His work doesn't provide instant gratification; scoring goals to win a game is an immediately visible accomplishment. Perhaps best of all, old-timers' hockey is a distraction.

"It takes me out of the world of my head," shrugs Vander-haeghe. "As a writer, I live inside my head most of the time. When I'm playing hockey, it's one of the few moments I'm not pursued by the imaginary world I'm trying to create. It's banished. When I have a breakaway I'm not thinking about anything but that moment....Hockey allows me to shut my head off."

Yet Vanderhaeghe's hockey is its own imaginary world.

"In our games, it's sort of an odd business. People think of themselves in roles. Danny Shapiro is the Phil Esposito type ...cruising in front of the net with the scoring touch...Adrian thinks of himself as sort of the Gretzky player...real heads-up player, good puck handler and he distributes the puck.... He's not interested in scoring. Steve Lewis and I think of ourselves as the Bob Gainey type of player...always forechecking, digging in the corners, almost defensive specialists....

"This is all relative, of course...I have a reputation for going hard for the net. In fact people say I've got a screw loose the way I break for the net. I don't care. You can hit me with the puck anywhere, off my ass, off an elbow, the helmet...I play hard...a decent passer, but I've got hands of stone. The puck hits my stick and immediately skitters off into a corner...or onto the opponent's stick.

"But everybody thinks of themselves as being a certain kind of player. And, after twelve years, that's part of the mythology of all of us."

It's Wednesday night, almost 10:30. Manuel, the Zamboni operator at the Kitsilano Community Centre Ice Rink in Vancouver, has just finished scraping the ice for the next rental of the night. From a corridor behind the team benches on the east side of the arena he can already hear the clatter of hockey players making their way to his now pristine ice surface. About twenty hockey players are ready to play. They too have created their own hockey mythology. Manuel knows most of them. They've been renting ice at the Kits Rink for about fifteen years, almost as long as the arena has been open.

The Zamboni gate closes.

The players spill out onto the ice. They are fully equipped except for one piece of gear—they are not yet wearing sweaters. Nevertheless, amid the continuing chatter, they begin to skate, stretching groin muscles, bending backwards and forwards at the waist, twisting from side to side and generally limbering up all the hockey-playing muscles that have been idle for seven days.

They circle the ice beneath a sign that reads "Rules for Safer Skating," which prohibits skating at excessive speeds, cutting in and out, and loitering along the boards. These twenty skaters, who range in age from about twenty to late-fifties, have been guilty of many odd practices over the years but none of them is listed on that sign.

The noise level begins to rise as pucks are tossed onto the ice. Sticks deliver the first slapshots of the night into the side and end boards. There's no real value in slapping a puck into the boards like this; it's done for the sensory satisfaction of connecting wood to rubber and the sound of the puck crashing into the boards.

The two goalies hit the ice simultaneously. They stretch and bend in seclusion at opposite ends of the arena. When each arrives at his appointed net for the evening, he begins scraping his goal skates from side to side at right angles to the goal line; the thin layer of snow that results provides some friction for sliding back and forth across the goal mouth. That done, each goalie plants himself in front of the net for shots from the first players eager to warm him up with pucks.

But the warm-up is short-lived.

Before long, a player at centre is slapping his stick on the ice. "Let's go!" he shouts. He *is* wearing a sweater—a dark red jersey (the Chicago Blackhawks' road colours). This is one of the two team captains for the night, forty-eight-year-old free-lance photographer Al Harvey, nicknamed "Sir Real," and he's contemplating his options. Scanning the sweaterless bodies at centre ice just as intently is forty-four-year-old fund-raiser Murray Hamilton, nicknamed "Lash." He's the opposing team captain tonight and he's wearing a predominantly white jersey (Chicago's home colours).

On the front of both men's jerseys is a crest showing a side view of a bright yellow hamburger bun with a meat patty and ketchup inside. The white letters "HHL" are superimposed on top. This is the custom-made logo of the Hamburger Hockey League of Vancouver. A game will commence shortly between the HHL-whites and the HHL-reds.

"Shadow!" says Al Harvey, launching the pregame draft. He's chosen electrician Ken Ford.

"What, no coin toss, Real?" smiles Murray Hamilton. There has never been a coin toss at the beginning of these regular matches. Hamilton just likes to rev up the evening's rivalry. "Fine. Then, I've got Terry." Terry is a non-regular who has come out tonight, but he's young, strong and recognized as the best defenceman of the group.

"Q," says Harvey, pointing to lawyer Bryan Burke. Harvey is apparently going for puck-chasers and scorers.

"Krutov," counters Hamilton. Krutov is Rod Reid, a farmer and a bear of a player. Hamilton is obviously stacking his side with bigger, defensive players.

"Weez."

"Santa."

"Pecker."

"Skippy."

Back and forth it goes until Harvey and Hamilton have taken an equal number of players, each trying to outsmart the other. With the sides chosen, the players go to the team benches to grab the correct colour jersey—red for Real's team, white for Lash's team. But the battle of wits isn't over. Gavin Roy, a draftsman, is late reaching the ice. His nickname is "The Train" because of both his runaway-train-like rushes and his booming shot.

"Train," shouts Hamilton, "put on a white sweater."

"No way, Lash," says Harvey. "You had last pick. He's mine."

The debate is tongue-in-cheek but heated because, as with every HHL Wednesday night game, there's a five-dollar bet riding on the outcome. Al Harvey loses the argument. Train puts on his white HHL jersey and joins Murray Hamilton's side.

Neither side really has an advantage over the other. While some of the HHL oldtimers are decent skaters, most are not. While some of the Burgers, as they call themselves, can put the puck in the net, most cannot. And while some of the players have hockey experience to fall back on, most do not. The majority of the HHL players have spent all of their lives in the Vancouver area, which before the Canucks' NHL franchise was awarded in 1970 boasted only a handful of indoor ice rinks. Hockey has never been the focus of winter life here. The only hockey these men have played in their lives is purely amateur, basic and low calibre. They've always described their brand of the game as "hamburger hockey."

"I didn't know how to skate until I was twenty-six," admits Harvey. "My brother [Bill "The Sarge" Harvey] took me to a Canadiens-Canucks game in 1971–72. I fell in love with the game and went out the next morning to learn how to skate, just so I could learn how to play hockey."

At the time Al Harvey was slinging beer with his friend Ted Schultz at a downtown Vancouver cabaret known as Your Father's Moustache. One Sunday night—their night off—they rented some ice at the University of British Columbia to play pick-up with a bunch of shinny players from the Keg and Cleaver restaurant on Vancouver's north shore. Hamburger hockey was born.

"Everybody was pretty wobbly," remembers Harvey.

"We had crummy old equipment," adds Ted Schultz who also didn't learn to skate until he was a freelance handyman in his twenties. "I had no basic hockey skills. And the only ice time we could get at UBC was from 12:30 to 2:00 in the morning....For years, I remember, we had to canvass for somebody actually going to UBC who could rent the ice for us in his name."

Chasing elusive contacts, roaming from one far-flung arena to another and enduring ungodly ice time were just a few of the barriers these hockey-starved Vancouverites had to overcome. One night in the mid-1970s, all the regulars showed up for shinny at an arena in Riley Park. Al Harvey had come directly to the rink from a photo job, locked his camera gear in his Volkswagen and dashed in to play. Shortly after their game began, they noticed a guy in the stands watching. "A fan," they thought. He turned out to be a sentry for a local gang that broke into Real's bug and stole $5,000 worth of photo equipment.

Things were no smoother on the ice. After the restaurant matches, Al Harvey, his brother Bill, Bryan Burke, Ken Ford, Kent Bitz, Vic Shoji, Ted Schultz (by now known as "The Grump)" and various other recruits took on a team of hairdressers in West Vancouver. Harvey ran himself ragged trying to find enough ringers each week to make sure the Burgers didn't lose to the hairdressers. He decided that the game was more fun when the Burgers just played among themselves, not against other teams. In 1977–78, they found regular ice time on Wednesdays at the rink in Kitsilano and the Hamburger Hockey League finally had a permanent home.

HHL rules are straightforward. Only light body contact. No slapshots when a player is in traffic on the ice, only when he's one on one with the goalie. There are no referees and face-offs occur only after a goal. The basic principle is that everybody should have a good time and nobody should get hurt.

Tonight, Sir Real's red sweaters draw first blood. Surveyor Gilles Gagne breaks into the open, winds up once and fakes a slapshot once, twice, before banging it home. A cheer goes up on Al Harvey's bench.

"Typical French-Canadian," shouts someone on Lash's white team. "Has to make it look spectacular."

Moments later, Shadow (Ken Ford) gets a break and scores a second goal for Harvey's red squad.

Then it's Weez's turn. John Ritchie is a North Vancouver

video producer, who earned his nickname by hogging the puck and weaselling around the ice with it. He mounts a rush on the white net only to run into big white defenceman Rod Reid. Krutov bear hugs Weez to the ice with a thud.

But Weez is up just as quickly, tips the puck past a few more white defenders and whacks an off-balance shot into the net. It's a typical Hamburger goal, a fluke deflected off a stick, a skate, an arm or a leg. It's not pretty but all Weez and his red squad care about is that it's in.

"We're known as the uncoachables," says Ted Schultz.

"We have some good individual players," says goalie Vic Shoji. "But as a team we're lousy, hopeless. Not many of us played organized hockey. As youngsters, we were never coached. We don't know how to play zones, where a winger or a defenceman should be positioned. The first tournament we went to, nobody knew how to line up for a face-off. We had guys standing on the wrong side of the ice."

Shoji is old enough to remember the internment of his Japanese-Canadian family during the Second World War. In 1942, when Vic was three, the federal and B.C. governments confiscated his father's successful paper box manufacturing business in Vancouver and shipped the family to an abandonned gold mining town in the interior. After the war, the Shojis resettled in Revelstoke and Vic reclaimed his childhood, learning to play hockey in his boots with sticks made from barrel staves. When he started playing goal, Vic used sheet metal stove pipes to protect his arms and legs. In fact, Vic developed such a knack for scrounging that his Hamburgers Hockey buddies dubbed him "Trader Vic."

"When the HHL began," says Shoji, "our brand of hockey was so awful that goalies that did come out would play maybe one or two games and become so bored and frustrated with it that they never came back again. So we sometimes ended up with one goalie at one end and a pylon or somebody else stuck in net at the other end.

"For some reason I always ended up in net....In those days, because there were so few hockey places around Vancouver, I played with goalie pads meant for six-year-olds that only came to below my knees. I had these little gloves I could barely get my hands into. And I wrapped towels around my arms....Every time I stepped into goal with this derelict equipment on, I always came home with bruises all over my body. Out of self-preservation, I finally started buying my own equipment."

In 1983, Al Harvey bought a bungalow in Kitsilano, just five minutes from the Kits Rink. Because no oldtimers' hockey game is complete without a good long post-mortem, Harvey's house—dubbed "The Real Estate"—quickly became the Burgers' hangout. Goings-on in everything from the HHL to the NHL were discussed around the kitchen table. Real always had cold beer in the fridge and spare beds when hockey talk consumed most of the night. When Harvey decided to renovate the place, Vic Shoji, by now a building contractor, moved in to supervise construction; by the time the renovation was complete, Trader had become a permanent resident.

The Real Estate was only one of many traditions members of the HHL created for the enjoyment of their game and their fraternity. The team wrote a Latin motto: *Hockum cum summa arte non ludamus sed bachamus bene*, which roughly translated means, "We can't play hockey but we sure can stay up late and drink." While the bungalow on West 16th Avenue provided a kind of headquarters in which HHL members could uphold their motto, the team felt it also needed a mobile equivalent.

So, when it wasn't hauling construction equipment and material around, Trader Vic's 1975 Chevy cargo van became the HHL clubhouse on wheels. On designated Wednesday nights, as many as eighteen players would crowd into the van, sit on benches and enjoy an official league "feedbag." These post-game meals celebrate any and all occasions—a fortieth or fiftieth birthday, the birth of a child, Christmas, Chinese New Year, St. Patrick's Day, etc. Shadow serves up the annual hamburger feedbag. All the Virgos on the team have a feedbag on the last hockey night in August. Real and his brother Sarge always lay on the annual B.C. salmon feedbag. And one year, when HHL hockey fell on Robbie Burns's birthday, the team enjoyed a homemade haggis. There was some concern that

this tradition might be lost when Shoji replaced the cargo van
with a 1983 GM passenger van that contained several rows of
upholstered seats; it wasn't so much the loss of the old clubhouse that was the problem but, as Paul McGavin put it, "God
forbid you should have this team all facing the same way."

A tradition even older than the feedbag is the one for supplying and serving the team's dressing room beer rations. Early
on, each HHL member brought his own beer and confusion
reigned. Some brought Labatt's bottles. Others brought Molson's cans. There was some imported beer and even the odd
microbrewery product. To bring consistency and a steady flow
of suds to post-game festivities, the league created a "beer-
ocracy" and placed Kent "Baron" Bitz, a clothing wholesaler
by profession, in charge. For some fifteen years now, Baron has
assigned two team members to buy, chill and bring two dozen
bottles of imported and/or unpasteurized beer to the dressing
room to quench the team's collective thirst.

No hockey fraternity as close-knit or off-the-wall as this
one could exist without publishing a permanent, printed
record of its illustrious activities. That's why in the fall of
1977 team photographer, reporter and archivist Al Harvey
launched *The Blue*, the team's news magazine, with the subti-
tle "Voice of the Hamburger Hockey League" and a masthead
that read "published now and then." *The Blue*, at first an
eight-page folded newsletter of photocopied typewriter copy,
has since grown to become a staple-bound, thirty-two page,
glossy-paper magazine with typeset copy, photos and cap-
tions, cartoons and classified ads.

Initially the magazine had no photographs at all; by the
mid-1980s there were colour photos throughout and a back
cover feature called "What sort of man reads *The Blue?*" with
a full-page colour shot of celebrities such as Premier Mike
Harcourt or hockey commentator Howie Meeker. The front-
page story in the very first issue in September, 1977, was
headlined "Dad Dickson Scores Son! Wife Gets Assist." It
quoted the reaction of then HHL player Rob Dickson to the
birth of his son, "first in the League's history...'It was like a
goal mouth pass from Kenny Ford.'" A dozen years later, a
photo feature depicted Burgers and their children whacking

golf balls from the beach of John Ramsden's ocean-front cottage into the Strait of Georgia as part of the team's "Longest Drive" contest. The article concluded by reporting that "the traditional salad and BBQ salmon feedbag followed, and after Skippy (C.J. Cox) presented the awards, the boys were home for an unusually early evening."

As numerous issues of *The Blue* demonstrated over the years, the Hamburger Hockey League gives some of its best performances away from the ice. There is Grump's Halloween "Off The Property" party, at which awards for the best (and worst) pumpkin pie of the year are presented, as well as Q's annual "Q-B-Barb" that features barbecued food and tabletop hockey played no better than their hockey on ice. And no self-respecting Burger dares to miss the annual HHL Banquet.

Originally staged at restaurants in Gastown or at UBC frat houses and billed as "the father and son banquet...with a couple of fathers, no sons," the banquets in recent years have been held at Trader Vic's, the real one, at Vancouver's Bayshore Inn. As well as dinner and drinks, the banquets usually include the presentation of the "Humanitarian Award," the "Cheap Skate Award," the "Feedbag of the Year Award," the "Good Shit Award" and nominations for the HHL Hall of Fame.

The highlight of most banquet evenings has been the guest speaker whose role is to roast members of the Hamburger Hockey League and/or provide a keynote address. The speakers—a different Burger masquerading each year—have included the Goddess of Hockey, a Dr. Strangelove-type character named von Schleissen and in 1982 a mythical goon from the Eastern Hockey League.

"It was the tenth anniversary of the league," remembers Murray Hamilton. Like his friend Al Harvey, Hamilton grew up in the Kerrisdale area of Vancouver and had enjoyed very little childhood hockey. Harvey constantly coaxed Hamilton to join the HHL and only succeeded when Harvey "badgered me into being guest speaker at their annual banquet."

Harvey and Hamilton put their heads together and invented a character based on a fellow they'd known at their local school board. His name was Syd Lash. Lash was six-foot-five, weighed 230 pounds and habitually regaled them with stories of survival in the backwoods. Harvey and Hamilton decided an ex-hockey star named Lash would deliver a speech to the Burgers about violence in hockey. When he arrived at the banquet, Hamilton hadn't shaved in three days. He wore a black leather jacket, black pants and dark sunglasses, and was set to deliver the wildest hockey recitation the Burgers had ever heard.

"You're probably wondering who this fellow sitting with us is," said Harvey, rising after the meal. "I found him through the local speakers' bureau. He's an oldtimer with the Eastern League....Fellow Burgers, I give you one-time hockey great with the Roanoke Rebels...Syd Lash!"

The assembled crowd of about thirty well-fed hockey players greeted the stranger with warm applause. They were ready for a good time and Hamilton wasn't about to let them down.

"Hockey is in my blood," Lash began. He provided a brief sketch of his colourful career in the semi-pro leagues. Then he paused and said, "But today I can't play the game I love. Today, I'm serving a two-year suspension....And it's bullshit I tell you. Bullshit!"

Lash then began pulling newspaper clippings from his pocket documenting what he claimed was a conspiracy against him. As he read the headlines, he became more and more emphatic and emotional. He played on the audience's sympathies and they ate it up.

" 'Lash's ice antics provoke arena riot,' " Lash recited from the headline. "What crap!"

The Burgers began booing Lash's detractors.

Out came another clipping. " 'Dad won't be coming home this Easter because of Syd Lash.' " Jabbing his finger at the crowd, he shouted, "That's a bum rap....Violence is good for the game!"

Each time Lash read a headline and added his rebuttal the hooting and hollering grew louder. Within a few minutes the entire audience was into the spirit of Hamilton's charade.

" 'Don't bring your kid to see this man play hockey,' " scowled Hamilton, reading another headline. "Now I've got a two-year suspension and they want me to do time helping the boy scouts...WHAT IS THIS WORLD COMING TO?"

The crowd's shouting endorsement reached a crescendo.

"Burgers," Lash concluded, "I'm telling you tonight...I've had it with this Eastern League...and if you Burgers will accept me, I'll come and play in your league!"

The crowd leapt to its feet, applauded wildly and began chanting, "Lash. Lash. We want Lash!"

That's how Murray Hamilton made his debut as a member of the Hamburger Hockey League. He was a true Burger. On the ice, he was just as shaky on his skates as the next guy, just as inept when it came to scoring but just as eager for a brand of hockey that was, ironically, the exact opposite of that espoused by Lash, his alter ego—competitive, spirited but mostly fun, because everybody's got to go to work tomorrow morning.

Back at the Kitsilano Community Centre Ice Rink, Real's red team has scored five unanswered goals against Lash's white squad. After the fifth goal, Real takes a breather at the red bench. Someone asks, "Should we maybe let up?"

"No way," snarls Real as he twists an imaginary knife in the air at Lash. "Run up the score, boys."

But Lash, who is notorious for his pep talks at the bench, encourages his troops. "Look, guys," he says, "I want to see some heart out there. Besides, I've got big money on this game."

"Yeah," says a teammate. "All of five bucks..."

Nevertheless, Lash's speech inspires some of his team members. In the next white team rush, Lash's boys knock Real's red squad back on their heels. There's a flurry of shots. One from Train. Another from Krutov at the point. And a third from Skippy that eludes goalie Robert Viens. Lash's white team is finally on the board.

The tempo of the game quickens. Real's team scores two more amid shouts of "Here comes the red tide." But then Skippy goes end to end to pop one for the whites, and moments later so does Lash.

"Where'd you learn to do that, Lash?" taunts Real.

"Keep watching," says Lash. "I'll show you some more."

But there isn't any more scoring for Lash's team. Not

tonight. As Real's players tally goals eight and nine, on the red bench former rock band singer Dennis Peck begins the victory chant. "Na na na na. Na na na na. Hey hey. Good-bye."

Unlike most of the other Burgers, "Pecker" played a lot of hockey as a boy in the B.C. interior. In Cranbrook where he grew up, "you either played hockey or went skiing." He learned to stickhandle on a backyard rink, dreamed of buying that more expensive CCM stick and rooted for the Leafs on *Hockey Night in Canada* until he saw the Beatles on *The Ed Sullivan Show* and decided to become a rock 'n' roll star. In 1980, when he was thirty-four, he got back to hockey with the Burgers and has been a fixture in the HHL ever since.

"It's the personalities I like here," explains Peck, "the characters, the people...I've played with other oldtimers' groups, but here the social side is the key...the cookouts...talking hockey all night long...the friendships."

Even though he's on the losing side tonight, recruiter Mike "The Kid" O'Brien agrees. One of the youngest Burgers, O'Brien doesn't play with any oldtimers' teams other than the HHL because, "Here we play for fun....When I've travelled to Saskatchewan, for example, I'd go there Monday morning, work my ass off through Wednesday; then, instead of leisurely flying back Thursday, I've flown back home late Wednesday in time to get to the rink to play hockey....Some of these friendships I couldn't find anywhere else....The boys care about one another."

Never was that caring more evident than in March, 1991, when Paul McGavin, a.k.a. "Lump," took a puck in the eye during a hockey game at the Richmond Arena. The injury didn't seem serious at first. After it happened, the six-foot-four, 240-pound McGavin quietly showered, dressed and got himself admitted to hospital.

"How did you get here?" asked the doctor in the emergency ward. He realized that McGavin was hemorrhaging severely inside his head. "How can you stand the pain? How can you talk? How can you even move your head?"

Three operations, four months and much pain later, Lump was still in there fighting—fighting a diagnosis that he would never be able to speak again, that he would never be able to walk again and that he would never lead a normal life. He credits his own psychological makeup, his family's devotion and the support of his Burger teammates for his miraculous recovery.

"They were there from day one," says McGavin. "Even though I didn't want to disrupt other people's lives, they came through...offering assistance...I knew if I needed anything at all, they were there for me like family."

Though his teammates couldn't restore the sight to his eye, Lump's Burger chums visited, provided moral support to McGavin's wife and did the next best thing to being at his bedside as he recovered. They recognized the seriousness of his eye injury and immediately made face shields mandatory in the HHL. Lump got a lot of satisfaction from knowing his fate was less likely to befall any of his friends in the league.

It's midnight now. Manuel the maintenance guy has shooed the last of the Hamburger Hockey League players off the ice for the last scrape and flood of the night. Frankly, neither Lash nor any of his teammates needs too much encouragement to retire to the dressing room. His white team has been buried 9–3 by Real's red team. Lash will have to pay Real the five dollars he won in the game two weeks before. Worst of all, the entire humiliating evening is about to be recorded for posterity.

In the centre of the dressing room amid naked players, hockey equipment and two coolers of the Baron's finest beerocracy brew stands Real with a microphone in his hand. He has only peeled off his red sweater, shoulder pads and shinpads. Still in his skates and hockey pants, his socks down around his ankles, Al Harvey has paused to register a brief description of tonight's game into his dictaphone-style tape recorder.

It's the official HHL diary.

"A grudge match between Real and Lash," begins Real. "Real looking to recoup his fiver from a couple of weeks back....Real again picked red with Robert in the nets, also Weez, Pecker, Courtenay, Q, Shadow, Jack Avery, casual Calvin and Bruce. Four on the red bench..."

He stops the tape, takes a swig of beer, looks at Lash and continues his account of the game.

"Lash's whites with Trader in goal were Krutov, Skippy, Gilles, Sluggo, Quack, Santa, Kid and the Train. Five on the white bench. Final score was a satisfying 9–3 pasting for Real's reds, returning a fiver to his wallet."

With the official diary entry complete, Real signals to Lash to fork over the wager, and rubs it in by asking, "Did I see you out there tonight?"

"Listen, Real," Lash counters, "if you hadn't spent so much time flat on your back on the ice, you'd have seen how well I was playing." Lash then pays off the five dollar bet. Real smiles. He's victor for the week.

Sometimes, though, the victor in Hamburger Hockey isn't necessarily the winner of the bet. Sometimes the night's satisfaction comes not from scoring goals but from earning the longest laugh or pulling the best prank. Although Al Harvey's best buddy, goaltender Vic Shoji, has let in nine red team goals tonight, there was one night back in 1988 when Trader beat everybody on the ice. And he wasn't even playing in goal.

It was the year that a regular Wednesday night Hamburger Hockey League game happened to fall on December 7. Feeling the need to avenge several painful losses in the nets and realizing the glorious opportunity presented by HHL night coinciding with Pearl Harbor Day, goaltender Vic Shoji set a diabolical plan in motion. For weeks in advance, Trader worked secretly in the basement building a styrofoam and cardboard replica of a Second World War Japanese fighter plane. The Japanese Zero had wings, tail section, canopy, water bombs and a paint job that included rising suns and an inscription on the fuselage: "Dec. 7, 1988. Pearl Harbor Part II. We're back!" When it was finished Shoji literally wore the aircraft. His head and shoulders protruded from the cockpit with his legs and feet beneath like landing gear.

Trader had also preplanned the theatrics that would accompany his entrance in the fighter plane on that fateful night at Kits Rink. He rented a video of *Tora! Tora! Tora!*, Hollywood's epic 1970 movie about the attack on Pearl Harbor, and copied some of the sound effects and music. He then arranged for Lash to sneak into the Kits Rink office and commandeer the arena P.A. system at an appointed time.

"I had made up this story," explains Shoji, "that I was going to be tied up in a meeting that night and couldn't come out to play goal....But I actually went to the arena earlier, snuck in through the fire exit at the back and set up this tarp at the end of the arena so no one could see beyond the glass....I hid there until Lash put the sound effects on the P.A. "

"At exactly 11:51 on the night of December 7, 1988," reported *The Blue*, "the rink P.A. system crackled, 'This is not a drill! Repeat! This is not a drill!'"

"The game stopped....Suddenly the rink's end gate burst open and a Japanese Zero, lost in a time-warped flight pattern since WWII, ominously advanced on the defenceless Burgers on the ice."

"Nobody knew what was going on," says Shoji. "Guys on the bench looked totally confused. And I skated onto the ice [wearing] my airplane....I had about fifteen water bombs... and I reached down and began throwing them at the guys....

"Meanwhile, Al's girlfriend snuck into the dressing room, put a big garbage can in the middle of the room, set off a string of firecrackers inside the can, and then took everybody's clothes off the hangers and threw everything around the room like there had been a big explosion in there.

"It was wonderful," concludes Shoji. "My sneak attack was a complete success!"

The chaos was so complete in the dressing room that it took some of the players until two in the morning to retrieve clothes that were draped over fluorescent lights and to track down lost wallets, shoes and keys.

"Retrieving one's pants," Al Harvey recorded in the HHL diary, "became a major task....Everything was hopelessly mixed up."

However, then Trader Vic softened the blow by introducing bottles of Japanese sake to help the Burgers celebrate and savour his coup. A feedbag was held in the clubhouse/van as Trader's "night of infamy" spilled into the parking lot of the Kitsilano Rink.

The HHL dressing room clears slowly most Wednesday nights. The Train almost never gets to the showers because he's generally still taking his skates off when the rest have stripped, showered, dressed, packed their hockey bags and made their way to the clubhouse. Nobody wants to leave the social interaction—the verbal shots, the paying off of the bet, the beer-ocracy and the recording of the diary. Even Manuel the ice man is regularly invited into the dressing room after he has cleaned the ice and shut down the Zamboni. And it's not, as some might think, an exclusive, male-only fraternity. Sue Rittinger, an RCAF captain, joins the Burgers at the Kits Rink when she's in town from Edmonton; she's got her own dressing room and after the game blends in with everyone else sipping a beer and rehashing the game.

"Not everybody can become a Burger," says Ted Schultz, one of the originals. "Younger guys, casuals with more talent, sometimes come out to show everybody how good they are. Sometimes it takes months before the penny drops. You can almost see the light go on, 'Okay, I think I've made my point. Now let's start playing hockey that includes other people.'"

"This is a social hockey league," nods Bill Harvey. "If you're not a team player, you're not around for very long."

"It's basically pick-up hockey," agrees Bryan Burke, who first got into hockey playing house league at law school. "Nobody is serious about it. In fact, if you get serious, if you start to use the body, there's a lot of peer pressure not to do that....Hamburger hockey is non-competitive...West Coast non-competitive, if you like."

"For me," says Murray Hamilton, "Hamburger hockey is an amazing escape. It's like a field of dreams....Just a different world for me to walk into and to be connected with hockey and the Canadian game. It's my skate into this other place. We've all got the pressures of daily life, but I leave all that behind when I go into that rink. When I walk through that door I have another identity. I'm this guy called Lash."

When he first heard about the HHL, Paul McGavin thought, "This is what I've been looking for. My hockey skills are terrible. I'll fit right in....And when I first walked into that dressing room, there was Al Harvey and others I remembered from grade school. It was like a homecoming...I don't play Hamburger hockey today," Lump says, because of the after-effects of losing his eye in 1991, "but in time, I'll play again."

Al Harvey's red squad has won the game. He personally has won the five-dollar bet. He's documented both in the HHL diaries. He's enjoyed his share of the Baron's beer. And he's among the last to leave the Kits Rink dressing room because Sir Real cannot get enough of this atmosphere. He stays to the very end as if memorizing the sights, sounds and smells of this hockey mythology he has helped create.

"Hockey is the common thread that brings us all together," emphasizes Al Harvey. "But from that we've developed very strong camaraderie....As I look around the dressing room before and after a game, I can say these are my favourite friends....We're the best of pals...."

An advertisement appeared in the sports pages of the *Ottawa Citizen* during the fall of 1992. It was about the size of a hockey puck.

"Are you tired of sitting on the bench watching your team-mates score?" the ad copy began. "Are you tired of getting cold during a hockey game because you're not getting any ice time? Come to St. Laurent, where you can get your share of ice time." An address and phone number accompanying the advertisement directed those interested to the St. Laurent Hockey Association in the east end of Ottawa.

The response to the ad was remarkable. Registration for the league's seven senior and oldtimers' divisions was so strong that during the 1992–93 season the SLHA had to add two full teams to its oldtimers' schedule. And at that there were still many applicants left on waiting lists to get in.

Why? What made the SLHA so attractive? Was it the facility? Was it the ice times? Was it the level of competition? Perhaps it was all these factors. The arena, at least twenty years old, was slated for a $9 million retrofit. The oldtimers' games were scheduled at reasonable times—Tuesday and Thursday evenings and weekends. But most enticing was the heart of its program. St. Laurent's adults played house-league-style hockey with the emphasis on camaraderie and improving hockey skills and teamwork, and with rules and referees that enforced non-contact play, sportsmanship, exercise and fun, and with equal playing time guaranteed.

In other words, organized hamburger hockey.

"Hockey the way it's supposed to be," says co-ordinator Al Kemila. "It's hockey that allows players with a mix of talent…and a mix of ages to be thrown together.…It's hockey that solves the player's frustration of sitting, waiting to play.…It's hockey run according to the rules…for people who want things to be friendly, and who don't want to be hurt or to hurt anyone else.

"It provides a chance for an older generation deprived of an opportunity to play to belatedly get out and enjoy themselves and be the kids they never got to be."

Kemila speaks from experience. Born in 1939, the eldest of five children on a farm near Niverville, south of Winnipeg, Al never owned a new pair of skates, only hand-me-downs for pond hockey. Because the town administration decided to build a curling rink, not a hockey rink, Al learned to sweep and curl stones but not to skate and shoot pucks. He didn't put on a pair of hockey skates again until he was thirty-three.

By then he was living and working in Ottawa with the National Museums of Canada. His two sons were playing minor league hockey in the St. Laurent area when the community staged a novelty hockey game during the 1972 local winter carnival for adults with limited skills. Kemila bought skates and an adult-sized stick, he borrowed shinpads, gloves, a helmet and a jersey from his sons, and he found himself hooked on hockey.

The year after the novelty game, Kemila and some friends rented ice regularly for shinny. By 1975, they had two full adult teams and had joined the St. Laurent Hockey Association. For the first few years this neighbourhood hockey organization was pretty informal. Weekly games featured the yellow sweaters versus the reds. There were great differences among the adult players—some were as young as seventeen, others in their forties; some were talented, others just learning to skate. But the play was uniform. Everybody got equal ice time and the games followed a strict code of discipline.

The typical SLHA player "first comes out when he's about twenty-five," says Kemila. "He is unco-ordinated, weak, larded over...clearly not an athlete. Mentally he is with it, physically a stumble bum...skating with his knees locked backwards...trying to swing his legs from the hips...throwing his body out of balance...and counter-balancing it by swinging his stick a lot. He is the antithesis of a hockey player....

"But after six or seven years playing in the oldtimers' recreation division, he is one of our best attenders....His teammates accept him as being a valid and useful member of the team. They pass the puck to him. They give him shifts. It never occurs to him or his teammates because of a game situation that he should maybe sit on the bench and let a stronger player get an extra shift near the end of a game. Or if his team has a penalty and is short-handed in a close game situation, he will still go out and take his usual shift....

"He gets a real charge out of being in the dressing room, hearing the B.S. from the rest of the players. He doesn't really try throwing too much of it himself, but just being there is a real thrill for him....The point is, that division and those players understand that this particular guy is what [the association is] aiming at."

The St. Laurent Hockey Association currently operates seven adult recreational and competitive divisions with nearly forty teams and 500 players. It has just added an over-forty division. If the retrofit of the St. Laurent Arena goes ahead, it will one day house ten adult divisions, perhaps some of them mixed. It's a recreation whose time has come. Yet as recently as a generation ago—in Al Kemila's father's time—this game would have been considered science fiction.

"I lost my father to a heart attack in 1968," says Kemila. "He was fifty-two when he died. I am now past his age and enjoying the leisure activity he never had....My two sons see me playing hockey and realize that I can do what they are doing....It's a dream I never knew I could have."

Another group playing its own brand of hamburger hockey has in the process created a flourishing business in Toronto's west end. After years of hearing horror stories about adult players being injured in industrial or loosely governed non-contact hockey, Steve Edgar joined fellow oldtimer Ed Mayhew to form True North Hockey Canada, a sixty-four team recreational hockey league for adult men and women.

True North originally advertised in Toronto area newspapers for "sportsmanlike" adults to join a recreational league in Etobicoke. This campaign attracted only a few players. But in 1985 they used a more direct advertising approach, calling on all "rotten players" to join. They got triple the response. Since then, each year six or eight beginner teams have signed up, taken instruction in an eight-week hockey school, then played eight, stop-time regular season games. The $355/per player fee also includes jerseys, playoffs and a wide array of awards.

As with the St. Laurent group, True North rigidly enforces the rules. Referees and line officials from the Metro Toronto Hockey League officiate the games. The league enforces a penalty cap regulation—after thirty minutes in penalties, a player sits out a game and, after forty minutes, another game. If a player reaches fifty penalty minutes, she or he is expelled from the league. League statistics show that in 1993–94, 95 percent of beginners had twelve minutes or less in penalties.

"Ignorance is bliss," says accountant Naomi Faigaux. She joined True North when she was forty-three, never having worn hockey skates on her feet or held a hockey stick in her hands in her life. At the hockey school she wondered aloud, "'My God, how am I ever going to do that?'"

After four years in the league, Faigaux recognizes that learning the game from scratch takes more time than she may either have or care to give. But mastering hockey is not why she's there. She's there because there's room for her level of play. "Most of [us] understand that hockey is to be played for fun," she says, "and that's why I'm still playing...and, I hope, improving."

That's why adult recreational hockey thrives. That's why it may outlive professional hockey in Canada. There will always be hockey players such as Guy Vanderhaeghe, the members of the Hamburger Hockey League, Al Kemila and Naomi Faigaux. There will always be adult players with limited athletic gifts, adult players who didn't play organized hockey as children, adult players who develop traditions and rules for their group's own needs, and adult players who play hockey to get some exercise and to have fun with friends. Oldtimers' hockey can serve them as well as it serves the competitive tournament team, the charity fund-raisers, the university alumni, and the ex-NHLers.

EIGHT

"The Target"

In May, 1993, goaltender Greg Harrison was half a year away from his fortieth birthday. Although at one time he had fully expected to play in the NHL, Harrison was now coping well with the realization that at best he would be called regularly to play goal for the Toronto Maple Leafs during practices. With the demands of his thriving business—manufacturing custom-made goalie masks—he seemed content to build his enterprise during the day and then be a freelance netminder for old-timers' teams in the evenings and on weekends.

Freelancing is a standard practice among goaltenders who let it be known that they'll hire themselves out to any team needing a goalie for a game or a tournament. The goalie's reward ranges from a playing fee to free ice time and/or free beer after the game to the simple pleasure of knowing your skills are in demand. Greg Harrison liked this sort of arrangement and, since his schedule had become unpre-dictable, he felt it might be the best way to keep his goaltend-ing skills sharp.

On this particular weekend in May, no fewer than four old-timers' teams had invited him to play goal for them in Friday-to-Sunday tournaments. Checking the schedules and locations of the tournaments Harrison figured he could actually play for two different teams in two different tournaments on the same weekend. He agreed to play net for the Weekend Wailers at an oldtimers' tourney in Barrie and for the Sundridge Oldtimers in a tournament near his home in Brampton.

The time between scheduled games, he calculated, left him enough time to travel the 100 kilometres (roughly an hour's drive) and make it onto the ice for each of the two teams all weekend long.

At first everything went according to plan. On Friday evening, Harrison and the Weekend Wailers won their game in Barrie. That meant that the Wailers' next game would be Saturday afternoon at 5:30. At nine o'clock on Saturday morning he joined the Sundridge team in Brampton and won again. Their next game would be Saturday evening at nine allowing him to play his Wailers game from 5:30 to 6:30 and then get back to Brampton in plenty of time for the next Sundridge game.

A few minutes before the beginning of the Wailers' 5:30 game in Barrie, Harrison got a call from his team in Brampton. Their scheduled nine o'clock game had been moved up to eight o'clock. When the Wailers' game ended, Harrison didn't even stop to shake hands with the opposition. He was off the ice, out of his equipment, in and out of the shower and down the road to Brampton in minutes. He stepped on the ice and into the Sundridge net just before eight o'clock.

The madness intensified the next day.

Sunday's schedule called for Harrison to play at 9 a.m. and 1 p.m. in Brampton and at 11 a.m. and 6 p.m. in Barrie. As he had discovered on Saturday, with one hour's playing time and one hour's travelling time, meeting the demands of both teams in both tournaments wasn't impossible, just a little gruelling.

Harrison and his Sundridge teammates won their nine o'clock game Sunday morning, but "at this point," recalls Harrison, "time was too tight for me to take all my gear off. I took off my skates, goal pads and chest protector. Threw those and my mask and gloves in my bag. Took my pants off in the truck. So I'm driving in my Jimmy in my underwear, jock and suspenders.

"I got to Barrie and the Zamboni's on the ice for the eleven o'clock game. I dressed during the two-minute warm-up. Stepped onto the ice with the wrong sweater on because I'd kept shuffling bags back and forth. Played the game without a

The Hamburger Hockey League assembles for a lot of nonsense and a little hockey each Wednesday night at the Kitsilano Rink in Vancouver.

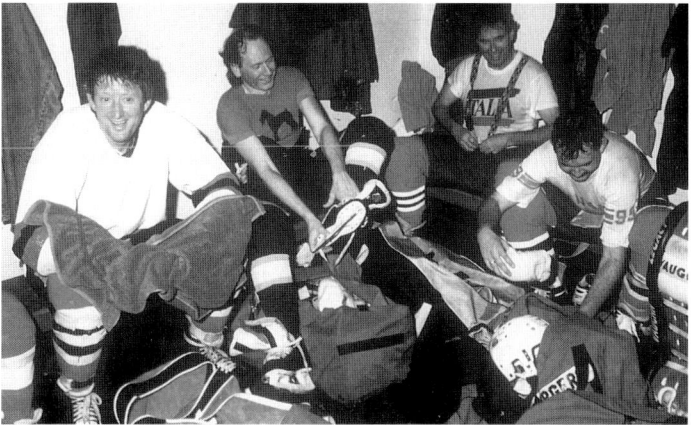

So that no delicious detail of victory or defeat is lost, Sir Real (left) documents the results into the official HHL pocket recorder. Weez is there to verify.

The December 7th that shall live in HHL infamy occurred in 1988.

"Lambs to the slaughter," the North Bay CFCH Statics borrowed air force shirts and took on the Flying Fathers in a "friendly" fund-raiser in 1964. (front row, l to r: Terry McInnis, Clancy MacDonald, Kenny Wells, Don Hummel, Reg Carne, Terry Spearin; back row: John Klimits, Dave Downs, Pete Handley, Jim Hunnisett, Ron Weller, Alan Delaplante, Greg Lawrence, Norris Whitfield, unknown.

En route to an audience with Pope Paul VI, the Flying Fathers pose with their unique gift. (back row, l to r: Fr. Steve McLellan, Fr. Paul Lennon, Fr. Bill Scanlon, Fr. Brian McKee, Fr. Pat Blake, Fr. Bill Lee, Fr. Bill Redell, Rollie Richer; front row, kneeling l to r: Bud O'Connor, Fr. Les Costello, Fr. Art Appleton, Fr. Dave Currie.)

Sister Mary Shooter joins the opposition in Sudbury, but ultimately plays for no one but herself.

Penance the wonder horse upstages the opposition goal-tender at the Arnprior arena in 1974.

Fr. Vaughn Quinn on his hockey pulpit during a game against the Durham Regional Police.

The Fathers perfected the art of pie throwing on such victims as this member of the CKSO media team in Sudbury.

Whatever shots goalie Michael Beacom misses in net, he more than compensates for it with his caricaturist's pen, even in a self-portrait.

"Have Goal Pads, Will Travel" Netminder Greg Harrison discovered that no goalie can be in two places at once.

"I'm in my own real-life beer commercial," says goalie Sean Rossiter, who often plays with the Vancouver Flames.

John Kasperski (far left) substituted in net for the Wolfe Island Old Timers during a Peterborough tournament championship match in 1985 and played the game of his life.

The CNIB told Bill Loretti (left) and Dave Bayford "the blind don't play contact sports." Twenty years later, their creation – the Ice Owls – plays oldtimers regularly.

Eighty percent of the members of the Ice Owls Hockey Club are legally blind.

Blind goalie Lorne McKee blocks a shot by listening for the puck.

Ethel Cey (front right) sits with her eleven sons, three of her daughters and other supporters of Team Cey at the World Family Recreational Hockey Tournament in Chandler, Quebec.

Team Cey – all brothers from a single Saskatchewan farm family – savour their world championship in 1990. (l to r: Gerry (with cup) Joe, Harold, Gary, Roger, Kevin, Bob, Mike and Jamie)

Calling herself "the Margaret Thatcher of oldtimers' hockey," Cecilia Shortt checks out the Snoopy Tournament program with some team reps.

In 1975 when he was 66, the late Dr. Toshihiko Shoji (kneeling centre) imported the oldtimers' hockey concept from Canada and assembled the oldest oldtimers' team on earth in Japan.

They loved oldtimers so much, the New York Apple Core went out and got their own arena. (Bob Santini at far right.)

Clare Green was playing shinny in frozen ditches in west-end Toronto before most of his competitors at the Snoopy tournament were born.

The mascot of the Snoopy Tournament may be a comic strip character, but the Toronto Antiques wear their gold medals as proudly as if they were Stanley Cup rings.

warm-up. We won. Then I whipped off the ice and back down to Brampton for my one o'clock game."

On his return to Brampton, Harrison's well-laid plans disintegrated. The tournament schedule was falling by the wayside. Partly because the tournament involved prize money—$1,200 for the winners—and partly because playoff games inevitably end in ties that have to be broken by sudden-death overtime or shoot-outs, games were being pushed later in the day. Harrison's one o'clock game went into overtime and then into a shoot-out, finishing an hour later than scheduled. The Sundridge Oldtimers won which meant another game—the final—at five o'clock. He called the Molson Park arena in Barrie, hoping that delays there might have pushed back the Wailers' final later than six o'clock.

No dice. The Barrie tournament was right on time and Harrison couldn't be in two places at once. Because he had agreed to play with the Wailers first, he felt obliged to leave his Sundridge teammates and be in Barrie for the Wailers' final. Sundridge was forced to find another pick-up goalie and lost the final 4–0.

Harrison returned to Barrie for his fourth contest of the day. "I wasn't into the game," he admitted, "and we lost 2–0....I've played on a lot of oldtimers' teams since but never again in two tournaments at once, not when I would be risking life and limb getting from one place to the other."

While most oldtimer goalies don't race up and down highways all weekend long to play hockey, almost all are driven by a special passion for the game—a passion to continue to perform, a passion to at least appear cool in the face of each onslaught, a passion to deflect not only the rubber but also the fury of the opposition. Inevitably, whether there's a collision along the boards, a bad call by a referee or a verbal exchange between benches, all the temper of a hockey game is directed at the net and the goaltender defending it. Goalies also possess a passion to be perfect, while forwards can lose the puck and defencemen can fail to stop a play, both can expect teammates to cover for them. The goalkeeper has no such support.

Russian goaltender Vladislav Tretiak suggested that courage sets a goaltender apart from the rest. He compared the goalie's role to a border guard's: "The net is your border and you have to stand bravely for it." Tretiak won three Olympic gold medals and ten World Championships.

Montreal Canadiens' Hall of Fame goalie Ken Dryden, who played his final professional season in 1978–79 at thirty-one, recognized that while "a goal goes up in lights, a permanent record for the goal-scorer and the game, a save is ephemeral, important at the time, occasionally when a game is over, but able to be wiped away, undone, with the next shot." By the end of his final season Dryden had made a sufficient number of significant saves that for the sixth time in his eight seasons with the Canadiens he helped bring the Stanley Cup home.

One might think for an oldtimers' goaltender that the passion for "standing bravely" or making "important" stops would become less of a priority. However, in the heat of a game, no matter how old he is, successfully anticipating the play, co-ordinating the defensive reaction with the offensive action, deflecting the rubber and the aggression, and not making a mistake, are still the epitome of the goalie's game.

Greg Harrison is a perfect example of a goaltender. Growing up in the late 1950s in Scarborough, in the east end of Toronto, Greg bought his first pair of goalie skates for a dollar at a used skate exchange. In his first game as a tyke, his record was four shots on net, four goals against. But he studied Jacques Plante's book *Goaltending*, learned to crouch like Terry Sawchuk and used his legs butterfly style like Glenn Hall. He was coached in high school by a gruff old character named George McGratten who ranted at his goalie protégé so furiously that he carried a vial of nitroglycerine pills to prevent heart attacks. Harrison got five U.S. scholarship offers but decided instead to play for the Yeomen at York University and eventually had a tryout at an NHL training camp with the Washington Capitals in 1974. He didn't make the cut but takes great pride in the fact that the Leafs still regularly request his services at Gardens' practices. Some of his greatest goaltending thrills have come at an age when goalies are considered over the hill.

In 1991, when he was thirty-seven, Harrison was asked to play the part of a goaltender in a scene from *The Cutting Edge,* a Hollywood love story about a young up-and-coming hockey star, played by D.B. Sweeney, who sustains an eye injury and then turns to figure skating where he meets the love interest, Moira Kelly. In the crucial injury scene, filmed at Hamilton's Copps Coliseum, NHL defenceman Chris Chelios plays the bad guy who injures the hero. The producers decided they needed some action sequences so they put Chelios on the ice against Harrison in net.

"I figured, well, he'll just take a couple of easy shots on me for the cameras," recalls Harrison. "But right away he came into the slot around the hash marks and just blasted a slapshot into the top corner, glove side. I wasn't ready for it...but I thought that's no way to start off shooting on a guy for the first time....

"So I said to myself, 'You bugger, if that's the way we're going to play, you're not going to score again!'

"I don't know how many more shots he took. And he'd score by cutting across and going to my stick side. But he never again beat my glove hand with either a wrist shot or a slapshot. It felt great."

Harrison had a photo taken of himself, the co-stars of the movie and Chris Chelios standing together in the net. Chelios autographed the picture: "To Greg...Work on that glove hand. Chris."

Cherubic NHL goalie Lorne "Gump" Worsley was always asked what makes a good goaltender. "It helps to be crazy," Gump would always say. "Not all goalies are crazy, though. Only about 90 percent of them."

Worsley was crazy enough and good enough to play professional hockey for twenty-two years between 1952 and 1974. He goaltended for three NHL franchises, winning rookie of the year honours with the New York Rangers as well as four Stanley Cups and two Vezina Trophies with the Montreal Canadiens. When he retired from the Minnesota North Stars in 1974 he was forty-five years old.

As an oldtimer, Lorne Worsley played only three games, all within a few years of his professional retirement. He played a couple of charity games in Montreal and one in Toronto because, "You feel a genuine obligation to pay back to the game and its fans. They made us popular."

Just before one game Worsley was approached by a video crew. He agreed to wear a wireless microphone and a small transmitter strapped to his side under his goalie gear so that they could catch some of Gump's on-ice chatter for the television coverage. Gump enjoyed the game for its fun and rekindled friendships.

"But then you put some of that old stress on yourself," Worsley said. "You say you're going out there to put on a show...and then pride takes over.

"During the game Frank Mahovlich broke in on me. And I said to myself, 'There's no way he's going to score on me. This may be his building. But he's not going to beat me.' I went down to make the save...and I came down on the steel box [of the microphone transmitter] and broke three ribs. Pride took over and it was as if it was a real game."

During his twenty-two years as a professional goaltender Worsley had never broken a single bone in his body. Moreover, despite not wearing a mask in more than 900 appearances, he suffered only stitches to his face and a shiner from an egg thrown by a fan in New York. Only in an oldtimers' game did he actually break bones. Soon after, Gump gave away his pads to his son and hasn't played a game since.

Cesare Maniago, Gump's partner in the nets with Minnesota, experienced the same kind of renewed motivation playing oldtimers.

After eighteen seasons in the NHL (with Toronto, Montreal, the New York Rangers, Minnesota and Vancouver) Maniago retired in 1978. In 1980, he was invited to play in a fund-raiser at Madison Square Garden where the fledgling Phil Esposito Foundation had arranged a so-called fun match. The game pitted ex-Ranger greats such as Andy Bathgate, Dean Prentice, Red Sullivan, Vic Hadfield, Brad Park and Rod Gilbert against all-stars Jean Béliveau, Bernie Geoffrion, Frank Mahovlich, Gordie Howe and Cesare Maniago.

With the Garden full of frenzied fans preparing for the regular season Ranger game to follow, the oldtimers took to the ice for the first of two twenty-minute periods of non-contact, no-slapshot, not terribly competitive hockey. However, at the end of the first period, when the teams took a breather for the ice to be scraped and flooded, Maniago remembers the all-star dressing room taking on the atmosphere of a real NHL grudge match.

The all-star oldtimers were down to the Ranger oldtimers 1–0. Initially it didn't seem to matter. But after a few minutes of rest, Gordie Howe got up from his seat and began to talk about the game. "We're not playing as hard and as capably as we should be," said Howe, not pointing fingers.

The dressing room grew quiet.

"I don't want to be embarrassed and lose a game to those guys across the hall, do you?"

A room full of the best-known faces in modern hockey history began to shake their heads. Maniago recalls thinking about his own NHL days when management was ruthless and dictated exactly how you were to perform. He remembered that players did what they were told for fear of losing their jobs but played hard for their own self-worth. It was as if that old-fashioned discipline was being resurrected by Howe's speech.

"You know what we're made of," continued Howe. "We've got to have more pride in ourselves, guys. Hold our heads high. Why should we lose and they win?"

Maniago sat in awe realizing why his teammates were consummate professionals, how their intensity made them what they were and why these men were household names. He left the dressing room feeling he had to do his part and not let the team down.

In the second twenty-minute period the all-star team turned up the tempo of the game sufficiently that Maniago had to handle only a few shots. His teammates backchecked ferociously. They moved the puck with the accuracy and authority of men on a mission. They even threw some body-checks against the Rangers. The intensity of the game got too much for Red Sullivan and Bernie Geoffrion; with their hearts racing, they retired from the game.

By the final buzzer, the all-stars had bounced back and won the match 2–1. Emotion united the team. Players who had known some of the greatest thrills and successes in hockey were jumping up and down, shouting, hugging and patting each other on the back. They called it a great comeback. They had proven what they were made of. Although he had never experienced it, Cesare Maniago said the euphoria among those oldtimers was almost like winning the Stanley Cup.

It's generally agreed by those who do not play goal that those who do, whether youngsters or oldtimers, are a breed apart. As Gump Worsley admits, they're crazy. They march to the beat of a different drum. They are driven by some sort of death wish or masochistic tendency to stand there, take the punishment, smile and live to fight another day. If defiance and survival are key to a young goaltender's psyche, they are crucial to an oldtimer in the nets.

"Guys always wonder," says oldtimer goalie Sean Rossiter. "They always think there's something wrong with anybody who's decided to become a netminder. And the truth is that goalies are deadly competitive guys. They're perfectly willing to endure all the inconveniences, let alone the dangers of playing goal....You do get hurt."

The scars are not immediately obvious but Rossiter's forty-eight-year-old face has weathered more than a hundred stitches from goaltending that predates the mask era. His upper body was once temporarily paralyzed when he lunged backwards to smother a loose puck and bounced his head twice on the ice surface. Another time, he took a stickblade in the left eye; his retina was torn, his eyeball filled with blood and he remained flat on his back, blindfolded for a week before a complete diagnosis could be made.

"Still, I remember the story of Terry Sawchuk," continues Rossiter, "taking a shot on his eyeball. It had to be popped out of its socket to be stitched. Sawchuk insisted on having it done only under local anesthetic, and having mirrors rigged up so he could watch the operation....Sawchuk had a level of courage, a pain threshold I just can't even imagine....When I was a kid and when they were pros, goalies weren't coached. Goaltending required independence and intellectual rigour."

Not only because of his own injuries but also because he studied the game as he played it, Sean Rossiter has exhibited these two qualities himself. First playing parish hockey in Ottawa and then house-league hockey on the Prairies, Sean was quick to realize that most players sat on the bench for two-thirds of a game, while the goalie played the game from start to finish and "held victory or defeat in the palm of his hand....Goaltending was where it was all happening." At twelve, in his first game in the nets, Sean got his first taste of victory—a shutout.

However, it was when playing goal for a bantam team in southwestern Ontario during a losing season—ten losses in a row—that Sean really learned to play goal. He learned not to blame his defencemen. He learned to try to make the save no matter what the circumstances. He learned never to give up. He also realized that in a world with only six NHL teams and six NHL goaltenders there weren't going to be any openings. His prospects of being another Sawchuk were nil.

In his thirties he took up adult recreational hockey in the Vancouver area. As he searched for a permanent position with a regular team, Rossiter experienced life as a freelance goaltender. It was equally instructive.

This game was often hacker hockey in empty arenas after midnight, when players paid three dollars each for an hour's ice time, when nobody's reflexes were particularly sharp, when few bothered to backcheck and when "the ones who aren't good enough to play at a civilized hour really want to put that puck in the net. They even want to beat you during the warm-up. It's Pulled Groin City out there [and] the goaltender is nothing but a target!"

In 1979, Rossiter met a rock music promoter who was successful and wealthy. But he had never played hockey and suddenly wanted to. He started a team and named it after his business—Concert Box Office (CBO). For Rossiter the invitation to play with CBO was a dream come true. It meant a regular team, "a team with numbered sweaters, horsing around in the dressing room—my own real-life beer commercial....And we had a kind of second-hand glow from the entertainment industry and many of its more expensive tastes in refreshments. We had the mellowest locker room in all of hockey."

Having played oldtimers for fifteen years, Rossiter understands more about goaltending and being an oldtimers' goaltender. It's not just reading offensive plays, setting himself for
the oncoming breakaway and withstanding the onslaught of
pucks coming at him. It's as much a mind game as one of
endurance. He has realized the psychological value of staying
upright in the net like Ken Dryden or of using his stick to poke
the puck from an incoming forward like Jacques Plante. At age
forty-three he has come to understand the importance of the
goalie stance, that everything depends on bending the body at
the knees, not the waist, that by doing so, a goalie's height in
front of the net is diminished only by the length of his thighs
and that this sometimes prevents back problems later in life.

Perhaps most crucial of all, Rossiter has learned as an oldtimer how to take a goal—whether to react in disgust by
quickly flicking the puck out of the net or smash his stick over
the crossbar or linger sprawled on the ice dramatizing the disappointment or rise in defiance and quickly reset for the next
face-off. Whichever reaction he chooses, Rossiter concludes
"that even if goalies seem to blame others for their misfortunes
(and, of course, any goal against is the culmination of a series
of mistakes that could have been corrected anywhere along the
line), nevertheless, any good goalie will blame himself...."

"You have to believe that if you'd done the other thing,
you'd have made the save...that you went down too early, that
you didn't slide across, that your stick wasn't flat on the
ice....You have to feel it was your fault.

"I appreciate it when a defenceman comes back to me at
that awful moment to say 'Look, I should have had him, blah-
blah-blah.' The defenceman feels he's been stripped naked
and that I'm blaming him. But the truth is that I didn't see
him miss the open guy. I don't see much of that—the bodies,
the sweaters—I'm looking at the puck on the end of somebody's stick."

Strangely, it's this immersion, this total and critical focus
on stickblades and the motion of the puck, that provides as
much satisfaction as grief for a goalie. It's in these moments—
an offensive player bends his stick into a wrist shot, pulls it
back for a snap shot, corrals the puck for a backhand or

throws his body into a deke—that a goalie can feel the greatest exhilaration. As these events unfold in front of him, a goalie's instincts can seem to take control and shift him from being a still body to being impregnable. Goaltenders call it "being in the zone."

"There have been times in my adult career, and this is where it gets really mystical," says Sean Rossiter, "when you're in some zone, where not only can nobody beat you but you know nobody can beat you. You know you're going to stop everything. You're hot. Everything is happening in slow motion in front of you....

"At these times, I feel that there's a big hand behind me blocking the net. Even if I only get a piece of the puck, it's going to go off the outside of the post instead of the inside...that even if there's an open man, the puck will bounce over his stick....That even if the puck deflects, it'll miss the net....I'm on top of it. No accidents will happen. There'll be no fluke goals. And at these times, that's the reward. You're doing it. And life is grand."

As much as a goaltender likes to believe he can prepare for and psych himself into these moments of excellence, generally they just happen. Presumably, the better the goalie, the more often the excellence. But, like flashes of brilliance, entry into the zone can occur when a goalie least expects it.

It was a Sunday afternoon in late February, 1985. Thirty-six teams of oldtimers from across Canada were competing in the COHA's Reunion '85 Tournament in Peterborough, Ontario. Among the visitors were fifteen teams that had competed in John Gouett's and Gerry Aherne's original National Oldtimers' Hockey Tournament in 1975, the tournament generally accepted as the birth of oldtimers' hockey.

One Sunday match featured the Emily Omemee Goodtimers from the town of Omemee just outside Peterborough. As their name suggests, winning wasn't the highest priority on the Goodtimers' agenda. Throughout their ten- or twelve-year history they had probably lost more games than they had won. Their last game at the Reunion tournament was no exception. They'd been thumped. With the tournament winding down,

the Goodtimers had retired to their dressing room to commis-
erate before cracking open a few beers.

Around the room were veteran Goodtimers—Mac Ellis,
Ron Fisher, Teddy Higgins and the team's two goalies, Al
Legacey and John Kasperski who alternated games. "Kas"
Kasperski at six-foot-five-inches and over 200 pounds looked
more like a basketball guard than a hockey goaltender. He
had actually gone to Eastern Michigan University in the
mid-1960s to play basketball while working on his science
degree. But as an adult approaching forty Kasperski was
picking up the game he had never learned as a boy—hockey
for the fun of it.

Kasperski had been in the nets for this latest loss at the
Peterborough tournament. But minutes after the game, it was
history. Kasperski was now enjoying one of his favourite oldtimer moments—that first swig of beer to wash his thirst
away. His gear was half off and splayed across his corner of
the dressing room floor.

Somebody shouted, "Hey, Kas, did ya get sunburn from
the goal light goin' on all night?"

He'd heard the line a thousand times before but it still got a
couple of laughs. It helped put another tournament loss into
perspective.

At the same moment Jim Orr, the Reunion '85 tournament
director, opened the dressing room door, looked around, saw
both the Goodtimers' goalies and asked, "Which one of you
didn't play last game?"

"I didn't," said Al Legacey. "Why?"

"We need a goaltender," said Orr. "Kingston's goalie's
banged up his leg and can't play. Will you take his place?"

Legacey shook his head. "No. I'm finished."

"That's fine," said Orr and turned to Kasperski. "How
'bout you, Kas? Will you help us out?"

Kasperski looked at the equipment lying on the floor and
thought about his losing record and his opened beer. But he
didn't want to let Orr down. "I'll do it. But you let them know
what they're in for. I'm not your ex-pro."

"Don't worry about it, Kas," smiled Orr. "You'll like these
guys."

The Kingston team Kasperski had just agreed to join was the Wolfe Island Old Timers, the hockey club formed in the winter of 1975 when car salesman Sid Fawcett heard about the first Peterborough oldtimers' tournament. As in 1975, the team remained unconcerned about winning but was still serious about having fun. Despite this, the Wolfe Island Old Timers had miraculously made it into the division final at Reunion '85 against a strong team from eastern Ontario. The Cornwall Hubs had won their last ten tournaments in a row and in an earlier game against Wolfe Island had thrashed them 9–1.

"We've had the crap kicked out of us all through this tournament," Fawcett explained to Kasperski.

"Yeah, well, I'm just your local goalie," Kasperski said.

Fawcett replied, "And we're just a bunch of bums you're playing with. Cornwall has killed us before so don't worry about it."

With that, Kasperski suited up again and joined his surrogate teammates on the ice against the heavily favoured Cornwall Hubs. Sensing yet another loss, the Wolfe Island crew asked organizers to shorten the final game from three twenty-minute periods to two and Cornwall agreed. The Reunion Division B final began. Just three minutes into the game Wolfe Island scored.

"And I went into the zone," says Kasperski. "There are times, sometimes in big games, when everything goes right for you. I've probably played 500 games. And I've experienced the zone maybe three times, when everything is perfect. You couldn't get a .22 past me. I'll stop it."

Kasperski felt rejuvenated, confident and entirely focused on the game. Because Kasperski seemed so impenetrable, Fawcett and the team that was sure it couldn't win suddenly couldn't lose. The Wolfe Islanders really began to pour it on. They played well beyond their level of competence. They backchecked tenaciously and took the momentum of the game away from Cornwall entirely. By the end of the first period, the underdogs were leading 2–0.

In the second period Kasperski remembers the players feeling certain they could win. His confidence had rubbed off on the Wolfe Islanders. He remembers his teammates coming back to him before face-offs and saying, "We've had a rivalry with these guys for years. But we're going to win this thing. Hang on!"

"And I did," recalls Kasperski. "I was flopping all over the place, hanging on to the puck whenever I could to give the guys a rest."

Eventually, Cornwall got on the scoreboard but not until the twelve-minute mark of the second period. It was too little too late. With just over a minute left in the game Wolfe Island's Morley Hunt took a pass from John Redmond and Eddie Deans and scored the insurance goal. Against all odds Wolfe Island had won the game 3–1 and the division championship.

"The guys went nuts," says Kasperski. "We had won it all. They gave me Wolfe Island hats and pins and I couldn't buy a beer. About two weeks later, I got a parcel in the mail. They had had a special Wolfe Island sweater made for me with 'Reunion Champions' and my name written on the back.

"The best part was, they gave me a free lifetime pass for the Wolfe Island ferry. And, boy, did I eat that up....I found out, the next time I was in Kingston, that the ferry was free for everybody anyway. They just couldn't resist the final joke."

Another facet to playing hockey in an area bounded by a painted semicircle, two steel upright posts, a crossbar and a mesh cage is the attention one gets whether or not there are spectators. Goaltending—good or bad, NHL calibre or old-timers—tends to be the focus of the action. While a forward can instigate the play toward the net and the defenceman can slow its progress, the outcome is determined in the goal-tender's territory. Depending on the results, the goalie is either applauded or cursed.

The impact of this attention can be total humiliation. As the legendary Glenn Hall once observed, "Having a goal scored against you is like having your pants taken down in front of 15,000 people." The attention can also trigger unique reactions, such as Ken Dryden's patented "thinker" pose, leaning on his goal stick with his arms crossed after a play in front of his net. New York Ranger goalie Gilles Gratton believed he was a reincarnated jungle cat. Former player and Winnipeg Jets general manager John Ferguson remembers Gratton throwing off his lion-faced mask one night and growling and pouncing on an opposition player "like a cat on a mouse."

For goaltenders the attraction to the goal mouth is almost magnetic. That's the way it was for Michael Beacom. Partly because his father's work (making stained-glass windows for churches) took the family to communities all over western Ontario, "Beak" didn't even step into skates, let alone into the net, until high school. But he took to it right away. He loved being on the ice, skating even with the heavy padding and feeling the stick in his hands. He thrived on what he calls "the risk and the challenge" of playing goal.

"I've always believed that the guy in the net is a hockey player first and a goaltender second. Goalies should be able to handle the puck, skate as well, if not better, than most players, and be responsible to make decisions....Goalies can be of great value to their teammates. You're not standing in the crease anymore. You're a hockey player.

"If it was in baseball, you'd be the pitcher. If it was football, you'd be the quarterback. It's something that makes you want to be in pressure situations."

Beacom seems to relish the pressure. He embraces it even in his chosen occupation as a freelance artist. After art school and a stint at 3M Corporation, he went off on his own, illustrating for magazines, creating advertisements, including the widely published Terry Fox poster, and doing caricatures at competitions. At the 1988 Calgary Winter Olympics, he completed 1,430 drawings in nineteen days. More recently he has developed his annual "Pardon My Misconduct" oldtimers' hockey calendar.

Take Beacom's pen away, give him a goal stick and some tough opposition and he's right at home. He's thrived on a competitive environment since playing industrial hockey in the 1970s when not only a trophy and money were at stake but so were bragging rights. In those days industrial hockey on a Saturday afternoon drew twice as many fans to the London Gardens as the Junior A London Knights.

"It was win at all cost," admits Beacom. "You're talking about winning a trophy and maybe $500 to $1,000. But money wasn't the incentive....It was the crowd, the human adrenalin, the pride. You were performing and being watched and criticized and applauded by 5,000 people in the stands.

"I played five years with 3M...and probably the highlight was playing against Ford in the playoffs and going the full seven games. I think it was 1978. The place was filled to capacity. It was tied until we got the deciding goal in the last minute to win 4–3. When the game ended the entire place erupted. A standing ovation. Hats flying. And people coming onto the ice. It was like a Stanley Cup.

"The same thing happened during an oldtimers' tournament in St. Petersburg, Florida. I was playing with Jack McIntyre's London Oldtimers. We ended up playing in the final against Finland. We beat them 4–3 in overtime...and at the end of the game it was bedlam. We were mobbed. We lost our sweaters and our sticks....It doesn't matter whether it's industrial hockey or the F division of a Canadian Oldtimers' [Hockey Association] tournament, you still have that same feeling, attitude and thrill. It's human nature."

Since turning thirty-five in 1979, Michael Beacom has devoted his time and energy to two pursuits—his illustration business and oldtimers' hockey. At thirty-four he was scouted by the Dorchester Diggers oldtimers' club and has been a regular on such other teams as the London Old Indians, the London Road Apples, the Dorchester Mavericks, the Southwestern Industrials, the St. Thomas Whalers, the Port Stanley Cardiacs and numerous other teams from the original Southwestern Ontario Oldtimers' Hockey League. Like Greg Harrison, Beacom's motto is "Have Goal Pads Will Travel." The phone often rings at home in the evenings and the caller will say, "Mike, our regular's got a bad knee. We need a target."

"Say when," Beacom will answer. "I'll be there."

On the other hand, some former professional goalies are loathe to strap on the goaltending gear as oldtimers. No matter how attractive the adoration of a crowd or your teammates, no matter how thrilling the thought of saves and shutouts, no matter how satisfying a goaltending victory, the lustre of the game between the posts is gone.

By 1983, Gordie Laxton had spent eight seasons in the NHL. He had been a first-round draft pick, thirteenth overall, of the expansion Pittsburgh Penguins in 1975. Despite a promising debut that year, beating Washington 4–2 at the Capital Centre and winning his first three official starts, Laxton ultimately played goal in only sixteen or seventeen games and sat on the bench for about 150 others.

"But in 1983 I was done," shrugs Laxton. "My contract was up. I was twenty-eight years old. I was considered an old man in a young man's game....I stopped playing and never put the pads on again. In fact, I sold them to a kid who needed equipment. I gave him a good deal and just gave it up."

For Gord Laxton life as a goaltender had not been a picnic. When he quit he was not giving up an awful lot of fun. His role as a backup goalie to Gary Inness and Michel Plasse in Pittsburgh meant that the opportunity to play came only from an injury or a lopsided score. The rest of the time it meant plying his trade in the minors, travelling mostly by bus or train, taking his lumps at minor league rates, hoping for another "crack at the bigs" and worrying about the prospects for any career outside hockey if he didn't make it. No matter how Laxton viewed it, goaltending was little more than a job. In fact, when he thought about it, from his childhood days as a goalie in Montreal to his final days in the Pittsburgh farm system all he remembered about playing goal was lugging his gear around on his back, stabbing his fingers while sewing up his gloves and tiring of patching and repatching his pads.

A few years after he retired, Laxton's co-workers in Grand Rapids, Michigan, invited him to play goal in a game of pickup hockey. They knew he'd been an NHL goalie and thought he'd enjoy strapping on the pads again. He eventually agreed to play but as a defenceman, not as a goalie.

"Playing goal was something I did for so long," says Laxton. "I enjoyed it. But it was a job....I'm on the other side of the fence now. I don't have to worry about 15,000 people booing and the red light coming on behind me. When I wake up in the morning, I think, 'There's five billion people in the world who don't give a damn about what I did the night before.'"

Ex-Chicago Blackhawk Murray Bannerman was just as reluctant to return to the net as an oldtimer but for different reasons. It wasn't so much the physical intensity of the position as the psychological pressure. Bannerman remembered the joy of playing goal as a kid in Winnipeg when he just lived for his Saturday morning house-league games. But along the way Murray lost his innocence and, for him, so did the game.

He turned pro with Vancouver in 1977–78 and in 1980 was traded to Chicago where he played until 1984–85 when he retired. Four years after he left the NHL, Bannerman was approached by the Blackhawks Alumni Association to play a charity game against the Hollywood All-Stars.

"Believe me, I didn't want to play," admits Bannerman. "I enjoy being involved with our alumni. I enjoy everything else that goes with it, like contributing to charities for kids, getting to see the guys and the camaraderie....But as far as going out onto the ice again, it's the downside of all the good things you feel about the alumni association.

"It's a whole different world for a goaltender....As a professional goalie, two things motivate you—fear of getting hurt and fear of failure. So no matter [what kind of game], those fears are going to be there, whether it's for serious or for fun."

When teams in recreational and oldtimers' leagues around Chicago invite him to play goal, Bannerman always declines. They insist it will be easy for him because he was a pro. They assure him their games are friendly. They tell him the experience will be as nostalgic for him as it is for them.

The fact is, it can't be that way for Bannerman. As a professional he was reasonably certain that teammates in practice and opponents in games knew where the puck was going when they shot it. Recreational players don't. Bannerman fears he could be injured in these games. Similarly, no matter how friendly and non-competitive the players claim the game will be, there will always be an over-exuberant rec player out to prove he can beat any former pro. And as for rekindling the fun of the game?

"I'm not that crazy," says Bannerman. "I'll go out and skate for fun. But I don't consider playing goal anywhere as fun. Being back in the dressing room, that's easy to do. I've been putting on goaltending equipment since I was five years old.

"The hard part is not being able to do the things I used to do. As a goalie it's hard to come back and play in a game when you don't practise, to be in condition and to have the kind of reactions you need as a goaltender. The only way to be good at stopping the puck is to stop it. There's no substitute. When you're out of the game a while, the things you used to take for granted and were no problem before, are now a chore....

"You can't go back."

When Ken Dryden chose to depart from the pros at the end of the 1978–79 season, he ended a professional goaltending career with many more highlights than either Bannerman's or Laxton's. But like Laxton, Dryden decided that in leaving the NHL he must also leave the goal crease. Like Bannerman, Dryden knew that if he continued to play goal after retirement his game would deteriorate. The lack of sufficient practice and professional opposition would reduce his level of skill and any satisfaction he might get from playing goal as an oldtimer.

However, Dryden still had an appetite for hockey. In 1979, he and his family left Montreal for Ottawa so that he could become a full-time lawyer. He found coursemates who played pick-up hockey on Sunday nights. But he would not play goal, in part because "every goalie...has witnessed a lifetime of defencemen's and forwards' blunders and you figure, given a chance, you would be far better than they ever were. And this was my chance.

"I still played on my goalie skates," says Dryden. "I had tried forwards' skates and found them awful....I was so inept and so clumsy in them that I thought it was two completely different ways of skating and something I wouldn't really be able to adapt to. I liked my goalie skates so I just kept skating in them."

Not long after he began playing with the Ottawa recreational team, Dryden took a stick in the eye and was laid up with bandages and a patch for a week. In another game as a novice defenceman, Dryden was rammed into the boards from behind and took eight stitches above his eye and four below. Later, during a charity match against the Flying Fathers to raise money for injured cyclist Jocelyn Lovell, Dryden was paired with ex-NHL defenceman Jack Bionda. During their first shift on the ice, Bionda and Dryden were scored on twice.

While he had escaped the humiliation of playing in goal as an out-of-practice oldtimer, Hall of Famer Ken Dryden had discovered "how the other half lives....I decided if I was going to play the rest of whatever time I'm going to play, I'm going to play it without these goalie skates."

It took some time to adapt to regular skates—being pitched forward on shorter rocker blades, learning the balance technique for making sharper turns and skating without bulky goal pads strapped to his legs. Even after ten years of playing out of the net Dryden admits, "I still skate like I've got my goalie skates and goalie pads on. I'll never get to the point of throwing away everything that conditions me that way."

Goaltending equipment, or at least the effect of wearing it for eight NHL seasons, may have been a mixed blessing for Ken Dryden the recreational defenceman but, for the player in the net, it is survival itself. Whether a young pro or a seasoned oldtimer, the layers upon layers of leather, cotton wadding, foam stuffing, straps, bits and pieces of shatter-proof plastic and strips of surgical and hockey tape bound around digits, limbs and aging equipment are sometimes the only way a goalie can get up the courage to go out on the ice and face a barrage of rubber.

The pads, protectors, plastic, foam and even the face masks—they are what many goaltenders refer to as their "tools of ignorance." Many of them are the inventions of goaltenders themselves. Former Leaf goalie Mike Palmateer added an appendage to his catching glove—a piece of leather webbing that connects the cuff to the tip of the thumbpiece—that goalies refer to as "the cheater." To compensate for the open space above his goalpads between his legs, commonly referred to as the "five-hole," Blackhawks goaltender Tony Esposito asked his wife to sew a triangular elastic panel used in maternity clothing into the crotch of his pants. The whole trend began in 1930 when a Howie Morenz wrist shot broke goalie Clint Benedict's nose; Benedict spent a few dollars to build a leather mask that covered the bridge of his nose, his cheekbones and his forehead. Benedict abandoned the protector soon after and it took another thirty years before Jacques Plante re-introduced the goaltender's face mask for good.

Far from being a tool of ignorance, face masks are important to goaltenders for many reasons. At the least they are a psychological lift. At best they are a place behind which goalies can hide their shame, anger or fear.

Someone once asked Jacques Plante, "Doesn't wearing a mask show you're scared?"

"If you jumped out of a plane without a parachute," replied Plante, "would that make you brave?"

At his Brampton, Ontario, shop, oldtimers' goalie Greg Harrison fashions custom-made, state-of-the-art face masks for a living. In thirty-five to fifty hours, for a minimum of a thousand dollars, Harrison takes an original face mould, pours a positive clay bust of his client, fashions a stainless steel wire cage and a fibreglass mask shell—cut, sanded, sealed and painted to the goalie's specifications. Harrison has learned the art of mask-making by trial and error in the shop and on the ice.

"When I was seven I wore a Louch mask," remembers Harrison. "It was like a clear Plexiglas welder's mask....It had a big red chin piece, a strap system and a bolt digging in either side of your head....I felt like Frankenstein.

"The first mask I made, I took a papier-mâché bowler hat, the kind they make around Halloween, and I cut off the brim, made slits for my eyes and my nose. My mom made me the straps. It looked like Charlie Hodge's face mask. But it was stolen."

Harrison later tried Cooper masks but they blocked his vision. In Junior B he experimented with the bar-style masks but he wasn't satisfied, either as a goalie or a mask-maker. Then in 1977 with the encouragement of NHL goalie Dave Dryden, he began experimenting with the cage-and-mask combination—a design that fits the contours of the goalie's face and protects the eyes without obscuring vision. After Dryden, Harrison's client list grew to include Belfour, Cheveldae, Hayward, Beaupre, Ranford and Potvin. Each goalie swears by Harrison's design and marvels at his artful painting. In 1981, the McMichael Collection, the Ontario art gallery that specializes in the works of the Group of Seven, featured the mask artistry of Greg Harrison. But the greatest compliment of all came from a goalie who had never worn one of his creations.

At a Hall of Fame induction dinner in the mid-1980s, Harrison took the opportunity to approach one of his idols— three-time Vezina Trophy winner Glenn Hall.

"Mr. Hall," said Harrison, "I've been wanting to meet you for a long time."

"What's your name?" asked the soft-spoken Hall.

"Greg Harrison."

"Geez," Hall exclaimed. "Somebody was just telling me about you the other day. I only wish I'd met you fifteen years ago. Then I wouldn't have all these train tracks all over my face."

NINE

A League of Their Own

Nobody could ever get lost inside the Mid-Scarborough Arena in Toronto's east end. The layout of the two ice pads is typical of arenas built in the 1970s. One side of the rink has the bleachers with the dressing rooms beneath. The other side holds the benches and the penalty box. One end houses the entry door for the Zamboni while the other contains the lobby and glassed-in viewing area.

If there were any doubt in a player's or spectator's mind over which way leads to the rink, huge, brightly coloured graphics on the cinder-block walls point out Dressing Rooms 1, 2, 3 and 4, and arrows direct everybody's attention to the ice surface beyond.

By 7:15 on a winter Saturday evening, most of the old-timers playing in this fund-raising game are on the ice warming up. A few stragglers are still making their way along the rubber mats to the ice surface. Among them is thirty-six-year-old Geof Collis. He and a couple of his teammates pull on gloves and adjust their helmets as they walk. At the entrance to the ice, Collis walks past the gate and appears momentarily disoriented.

"Over here," shouts another player directing him to the ice.

"Lost again, eh, Geof?" teases a teammate.

"Hey, don't forget," Collis shoots back, "I'm impaired."

Players at the gate and others within earshot laugh out loud. Geof Collis is dead right. He is impaired—visually. He has some peripheral vision and a spot of sight in the centre of

205

his eyes. He sees the world as if a doughnut were placed in front of his field of vision. But vision is an inaccurate term. Geof Collis has been legally blind for nine years.

Eighty percent of his teammates are legally blind as well; only two members of his squad can see. The other eight skaters have no more than 10 percent vision. But lack of sight has never stopped either Collis or his teammates. This team has played regular games on Sunday mornings for fifteen years. It's competed in tournaments across Canada. It has even played exhibition matches against NHL oldtimers and against sighted teams in Helsinki, Leningrad and Kiev.

These are the Ice Owls. They've been playing competitive hockey since 1972. Tonight, their opposition is the Scarborough Civics, an oldtimers' team made up of City of Scarborough employees. All of the Civics are fully sighted. They've been playing the Ice Owls for nearly ten years. But they'll still have their hands full.

"They're good," says Kevin Mercer, a recreation supervisor and defenceman for the Civics. "Just because they're blind doesn't mean they can't play hockey."

Geof Collis is a perfect example. He had much of his sight at birth in England. As a boy, the only sports Geof knew were soccer and rounders. The family moved to Canada in 1967 when Geof was ten but he didn't take to hockey until ten years after that. Soon he was addicted. He would work all day as a butcher's apprentice and go to the rink five and six nights a week, playing sometimes until two and three o'clock in the morning.

Hockey was his game. In his first seven years of hockey he played everything from full contact open hockey and industrial league to tournament competition. No matter where he was—at work in the butcher shop or at home trying to get to sleep—he replayed rushes up the ice, stickhandling moves and goals scored. At twenty-seven, he was an exceptional player.

That year, when he went for a routine eye examination, he failed the field of vision test.

"I'm going to have to take away your licence," the doctor told him. "You don't have enough vision to drive. You're blind."

The news was a terrible blow. Until then, Collis believed that his 10 percent field of vision was common. When he realized that not everybody had these dark spots in front of their eyes, he hid his impairment from people on the job and at the arena. His self-esteem, his enthusiasm and, worst of all, his confidence on the ice suddenly deteriorated. He started over-analyzing the hockey skills he had taken for granted. He became severely depressed and almost gave up what up until then had given him great pleasure. That's when he heard about the Ice Owls.

"A bunch of blind guys playing hockey?" scoffed Collis. "I didn't think much of it. Then I decided to give it a try. Well, I was an instant celebrity. These guys thought I had played Junior A hockey or something because I tore the place up. It was quite a head show and I loved it."

The Ice Owls Hockey Club was born as a result of someone else's frustration with the game although Dave Bayford is not visually impaired. Around 1970, Bayford was spending much of his leisure time coaching bantam level hockey in the Scarborough East Minor Hockey League. Rewarding at first, his work with minor leaguers soon became a chore because of meddling parents. Some wanted more ice time for their sons. Some insisted Dave teach the kids the hitting game. Others came into the dressing room to criticize his coaching style. It all came to a head during playoffs in the spring of 1972.

"It was the finals," remembers Bayford. "One of my buddies, Bill Loretti, was coaching the one finalist team. I coached the other. The game got so intense with violence and fights that [Bill and I] ended up in the penalty box actually fist-fighting each other.

"Well, after the game, we both said, 'We don't need this.' It was ruining our friendship. Ruining everything. All because of politics and the win, win, win attitude. That was our last game."

Later that night, Bayford and Loretti met at a bar. They patched things up and commiserated over a few beers about the state of hockey. They wondered where they could go to escape the politics of teaching and coaching minor league hockey. One of them raised the subject of disabled athletes such as the blind.

"That's what we have to do," declared Bayford. "We've got to teach blind people to play hockey!"

"You're nuts," said Loretti.

"No, I'm not. That'd be a hell of a challenge."

"Well, for one thing, how are they going to see the puck?"

"I don't know," Bayford admitted. "We'll have to come up with a puck that makes noise so they can hear it."

Even the Canadian National Institute for the Blind was sceptical. One CNIB representative told Loretti and Bayford that the blind didn't play contact sports and worried that hockey wasn't a safe sport for the visually impaired. The two ex-minor hockey coaches assured the CNIB that all players would be fully equipped and protected. A mailing went out that summer. That fall, thirty people showed up to hear Bayford's wild idea and about a dozen signed up for the first practice at Mitchell Field rink in the north end of Toronto in December, 1972.

"It was basically an outdoor rink in an open field. I can remember it being fifteen below zero," recalls Larry Nelson. Then just twenty-five, Nelson was operating a smoke shop at a downtown Toronto office building. He had lost his sight following an accident when he was three years old and had only 7 percent vision. "When some of us stepped on the ice, we didn't think we'd even be able to stand up on the blades, let alone play hockey."

Practising hockey skills wasn't even on the agenda that first Sunday night. Pucks and sticks were left off the ice. Bayford and Loretti's priority was to get these novice players used to the size of the rink. The first drill consisted of lining up all the players at one goal line and telling them to count the number of strides they took before they hit the boards at the other end. That first dash down the rink was mayhem—arms and legs tangling, bodies hurtling and tumbling, and finally the thudding as everybody hit the boards.

"I remember crashing into the boards," says Nelson. "But then we actually counted our strides. That's how we would know where the ice ended and where the side boards were. If a totally blind person hears sound coming back at him, he knows there must be a solid wall there. After a while, going up and down and from side to side as hard as you can, you know where the boards are. You feel where they are....It's like being in an alley....Sounds help us judge the distances."

"I can see better at night than in the daytime," explained Jim Kigaituk. A visually impaired Inuit from the Northwest Territories, Kigaituk came up with the team name.

"The owl, like most of us, is at its best in the dark."

The benefit game between the Ice Owls and the Scarborough Civics is immediately a noisy affair. The usual hockey cacophony fills the Mid-Scarborough Arena—shouts of encouragement, skate blades scraping across the ice, sticks cracking against each other at face-offs. Above it all rises the distinctive sound of the puck.

The Ice Owls' official puck is the result of a long process of trial and error. The problem with a regular puck is that when it stops on the ice, none of the blind players can find it. So Bayford and Loretti experimented. First they tried a tin can for a puck, then a tin can with marbles or ball bearings inside, a wooden puck and one with a chain attached to it.

The best of the prototypes was a puck developed by the Canadian Maple Leaf Chapter of the Telephone Pioneers of America, a group of telephone workers who develop devices to assist the disabled. The Pioneers took an empty plastic computer tape case, seven inches in diameter and two-and-a-half-inches thick, glued a rubber ring around it and rigged an electronic buzzer inside. It worked until snow and ice gummed up the buzzer speaker or the regular wear and tear of a hockey game shattered the plastic case.

Ultimately, the most successful puck design was the simplest. The Ice Owls went to a toy manufacturer for a hard plastic wheel from a push-toy. They drilled a hole through to the hollow centre of the wheel and inserted several steel piano tuning pins provided by their first goaltender, piano tuner Lorne McKee. The combination of the hard plastic wheel clattering across the ice and the tuning pins rattling inside gave the Ice Owls a relatively lightweight, durable puck they could hear above any arena din.

"The puck's about twice as large as a regular puck. It

bounces pretty well. And you can get it into the air," says Eddie Parenteau, a defenceman with no more than 5 percent vision. "It sure beats the tin can we used to play with."

Born visually impaired in Saskatchewan, in 1966 Parenteau was sent at the age of six to the Ontario School for the Blind in Brantford for his education. Children there played shinny on small sheets of ice with a forty-eight-ounce juice can for a puck. The players stumbled and tumbled through their hockey games. Nothing stopped them except when a train rumbled by the school. Then nobody could hear where the tin can was. The kids called the trains "blind man's fog."

"The hockey was pretty barbaric and scary though," recalls Parenteau. "It was okay when the juice can was new; it made a lot of noise bouncing along the ice. But after a while somebody would smash his skate on [the can] or crush it in half. And there'd be jagged edges all over it. It could really fly. And you had guys with no vision at all taking head-level slapshots with this jagged tin can. We had no equipment back then and some guys got some nasty cuts from it."

Aside from adjusting to a more civilized puck, when he joined the Ice Owls in 1981 Eddie Parenteau had to adapt to playing indoors. Each rink has a different sized ice surface. Parenteau, like the rest of the Ice Owls, skates lengths and widths to build a mental picture of the rink's dimensions. He also tunes his ears to the acoustics of each arena to distinguish the clatter of the puck from the din of the arena.

An Ice Owls game is like listening to a play-by-play but without the idle chatter, verbal jousting or words of encouragement. The Ice Owls talk to each other to initiate plays, find open players to pass to or co-ordinate their defence. Depending on the location of an oncoming rush, Eddie Parenteau calls to his totally blind defencemate Bud Lambert and current goalie Mario Ros.

"Left side," Parenteau shouts.

Ros and Lambert acknowledge the instruction.

Then Parenteau quarterbacks the defensive reaction. His chief tactics are to get in the forward's way and force him away from or behind the net, or occasionally to throw himself in the way of a shot. If he happens to find a forward standing in front of the net, Parenteau never hesitates to use his stick and his body to distract the offensive player.

"I'm a banger," says Parenteau, "and I'll occasionally get called an S.O.B. because I get in guys' faces. But that's my style and it's all part of the game."

As defencemen Parenteau and Lambert call to each other, Ice Owls' goalie Mario Ros moves from side to side depending on his defencemen's directions. He'll sweep his goal stick back and forth as the action comes in front of the net. When he hears his defencemen shout, "Shot," he'll drop to the ice with his legs outstretched across the crease, butterfly style, or stack his pads to one side or the other to block the shot.

Mario Ros started off life neither blind nor a goaltender. He grew up in an Italian neighbourhood in Toronto's west end where he played baseball, football and road hockey. But because he experienced early eye troubles—cataracts, glaucoma and later a detached retina—his parents wouldn't allow him to play ice hockey. Mario endured thirteen eye surgeries until at the age of twenty-one he lost his sight completely.

Through the CNIB Mario began using a cane, reading Braille and working with a seeing-eye dog. In 1978, he met Bill Loretti and joined the Ice Owls as a defenceman, "using my other senses to see the game....You can tell how close to the boards you are by the sound of the blades reflecting off them. But you can also tell if you're close to somebody; the heat radiates from them. It's a type of radar."

The only handicap rule that assists the netminder is the height restriction rule. Adhesive tape wrapped around the goal posts three feet off the ice indicates the height beyond which any raised shot is illegal. All other aspects of the game are the same as the sighted version.

"As a goalie, I listen not only to the sounds on the ice, but to my defencemen. Eddie tells me when they're at the blueline or closer. Bud is totally blind but can tell me where the puck is....I keep my left hand, my glove hand, touching the left post. I use the butt of my goalie stick to touch the right post. That gives me my bearings....I only come out of the net to the edge of the crease; otherwise I lose track of where I am.

"I'm just like any other goalie....My equipment is the

same. I use my stick for low shots and keep as low to the ground as possible....The exciting part is being able to stop a shot, putting your knee on it, stopping it between your elbow and your ribs, catching it in the air....Just finding it is great."

Mario Ros may not have seen many of the pucks coming his way but in the nine years he has played goal for the Ice Owls he has witnessed a lifetime of thrills. There have been the annual tournaments of the Canadian Blind Hockey Association with teams from Montreal, Ottawa, Edmonton, Calgary, St. John's and Quebec City. They played the Flying Fathers. They played against the Scarborough Civics at Maple Leaf Gardens and met Mike Palmateer who presented Ros with a set of goalie pads. But perhaps his greatest thrill was a fourteen-day hockey tour of Finland and the Soviet Union in 1988.

"In Kiev," remembers Ros, "they didn't know what to make of us. They asked us to show them how a visually-impaired team could do it. So we played."

The Ice Owls' game at the Kiev Sports Centre in Ukraine called upon every aspect of the team's sixteen years of physical, sensory and emotional training. There was the language barrier, the unfamiliar customs, the food and water quality. But the toughest obstacle of all was the international-sized ice surface. It was massive. During their only practice—at six o'clock in the morning—Dave Bayford and his father Archie ran the same orientation drill Dave had used on his novice players at Mitchell Field back in 1972.

"You're not going to bloody believe this," Dave Bayford told his players, "but it's so goddamned big here you're going to get tired just going from one side to the other." Instead of thirteen strides from side boards to side boards, there were thirty. Then Bayford took Ros behind his net.

"You could play an entire game back here," said Ros.

The Ice Owls were an instant hit. Not only did they hand out sticks of gum, pins, ballpoint pens and hats, they played remarkably well in unfamiliar surroundings against a sighted Russian squad. The 500 Ukrainian fans on hand, who included students from a local school for the blind, waved a huge Canadian flag; they cheered wildly each time the Ice Owls scored and booed each Russian goal.

After the game, the Ice Owls retired to their huge dressing room. There was a knock at the door. In came the opposing coach with congratulations and a six-year-old girl in tow. The coach explained that the child had watched the game and wanted to meet the Ice Owls' goalie. She approached Mario Ros, greeted him and kissed him on the cheek.

Though he couldn't see her, tears rolled down Ros's cheeks.

Outside, the roadway leading from the arena was lined with children and adults, some waving Canadian flags and all shouting praises for the Ice Owls. As the bus pulled away, Bayford and his team members opened the windows, leaned out and waved goodbye for the last time.

"They can keep their Stanley Cup," says Archie Bayford. "That was quite a moment."

In the Ice Owls' dressing room at the Mid-Scarborough Arena, emotions are mixed. The Scarborough Civics have beaten them 6–2 but the fund-raising event has netted a few dollars for the Owls' bank account. The money will go toward ice time and equipment for next season.

It's a bittersweet night for Geof Collis in particular. Despite his severely restricted vision, he scored a couple of pretty goals. However, earlier in the day he put in his last shift as a grocery store meat-cutter. Until recently, he kept his impairment a secret but when he admitted he was having a problem he and his employer agreed that operating cutting utensils was too dangerous. Now he's thinking about taking a computer course at the CNIB. But all the internal turmoil evaporates, if only temporarily, on the ice.

"I get a rush every time I play with these guys," says Collis. "When you go out and play a good game, maybe score the winning goal, it's like being Wayne Gretzky."

For Larry Nelson, one of the oldest members of the team, there's added pleasure. His son Lawrence often joins the Ice Owls as one of their fully sighted forwards. "That way," says Nelson, "he can show up his father just like other sons."

"The biggest thing is the freedom," says Mario Ros. The

first time his parents, Lidia and Renaldo, watched their blind son play goal with the Ice Owls, they cried. "Playing hockey makes me feel great. I'm proving to myself that I can do something everybody else can."

"It's a godsend to some of us," says Eddie Parenteau. "It's something we can do like fully sighted people....It's normalcy."

Many elements of their game set certain players and teams apart, even among oldtimers. For teams such as the Ice Owls, it's the way they play the game or that they play the game at all. For those who have played for the Maple Leafs or the Canadiens, it's the intensity of competition between these two clubs.

The Toronto-Montreal rivalry began in the 1940s when the Leafs' goalie Turk Broda, forward Syl Apps and coach Hap Day regularly faced the Habs' Bill Durnan, Rocket Richard and Dick Irvin. This classic intercity tussle for hockey supremacy continued into the 1950s when Toe Blake coached the Canadiens, including Jacques Plante, Henri Richard and Doug Harvey, past Punch Imlach and the Leafs for two of their five Stanley Cups of the decade. In the 1960s Punch, with Johnny Bower, Frank Mahovlich and Tim Horton, returned the favour for one of the Leafs' four Cups of the decade.

In the years of the original six, Toronto met Montreal at least fourteen times during each regular season, often with back-to-back games at Maple Leaf Gardens on a Wednesday night and, after an overnight train ride to Montreal, at the Forum on the Thursday night. To add to the intensity of competition, the Canadiens' and Leafs' management absolutely forbade fraternizing. The Leafs' Billy Harris remembers making his way through the Montreal sleeper car on one of those overnight train rides. "You looked straight ahead and there was no socializing, not there and not during the pregame warm-up."

That fierce and celebrated rivalry ended in the final minute in Game Six of the 1967 Stanley Cup final at Maple Leaf Gardens. Toronto was leading the series three games to two and the game 2–1. The Habs had pulled Gump Worsley for a sixth attacker and a last-ditch effort to even the game and the series.

Jean Béliveau and Allan Stanley faced off in the Toronto end. Stanley won the draw and tied up Béliveau. Red Kelly got control of the puck and dumped it up along the boards to Bob Pulford who lifted a pass across ice to a charging George Armstrong. The Leaf captain trapped the puck as he cleared centre ice and snapped it into the empty Montreal net. It was 19:13 of the third period. The Leafs had just clinched their eleventh Stanley Cup by defeating their arch rivals from Quebec.

That summer, as the Leafs' fourth Stanley Cup of the decade went on display in the Hockey Hall of Fame, the NHL put the finishing touches on an expanded league.

Instead of anticipating fourteen clashes with their long-time rivals, Canadiens and Leafs fans could expect to see new faces and new teams from Philadelphia, Pittsburgh, St. Louis, Minnesota, Oakland and Los Angeles. Instead of cheering Dickie Moore, Doug Harvey and Jean-Guy Talbot in their traditional red, white and blue jerseys, they saw them in the blue sweaters of St. Louis, coached by Habs' alumnus Scotty Bowman. Leafs fans would also have to get used to seeing the goaltending hero of the '67 Cup win, Terry Sawchuk, in an L.A. uniform with ex-Leaf Red Kelly coaching behind the Kings' bench.

The Leafs-Canadiens rivalry seemed dead and gone—until the 1990s brought Montreal and Toronto alumni back to revive their historic rivalry.

It's a Sunday afternoon in April.

Much has changed at Maple Leaf Gardens since those madly competitive days of the six-team NHL. During the Harold Ballard regime, Punch, Stanley, Pully, the Chief and all the others from the 1960s Leaf dynasty weren't welcome at the Gardens. Foster Hewitt's broadcast gondola was torn down. The portrait of Queen Elizabeth II was removed. In the seats, the blues had become reds and the reds golds.

"Welcome, ladies and gentlemen," announces CBC-TV broadcaster Ron MacLean over the public address. "Welcome to the third annual Toronto-Montreal Alumni game for the King Clancy Cup."

His voice booms from the Gardens' rafters where eleven Stanley Cup banners and two retired sweater numbers—Ace Bailey's No. 6 and Bill Barilko's No. 5—still hang. While it's not filled to its capacity of over 16,000, the Gardens today holds nearly 11,000 paying customers. They've arrived on a Sunday afternoon to watch the third round of a renewed Habs-Leafs rivalry between oldtimers from the teams' golden years.

The Gardens' lights dim. Spotlights begin sweeping across the ice surface to the strains of Aaron Copland's "Fanfare for the Common Man." The crowd begins whistling and applauding. The music fades and one by one their heroes are introduced.

"First from the 1980s," announces MacLean on the PA, "a veteran of seventeen seasons with the Habs. Eight-time all-star. Two-time Norris Trophy winner. With his name inscribed six times on the Stanley Cup....The 'rookie' of the Montreal Alumni team...Larry Robinson!"

Despite the partisan crowd at the Gardens, the applause grows as Robinson skates to the Montreal blueline. MacLean introduces Pierre Larouche, Mario Tremblay and Rejean Houle from the 1970s, Jacques Laperriere, Jacques Lemaire and Yvan Cournoyer, today's Montreal Alumni coach, from the 1960s, and finally Jean-Guy Talbot and Henri Richard from the 1950s.

"For the Toronto Maple Leafs' Alumni Association," continues MacLean as the applause swells to welcome the hometown Leafs, "a veteran of the 1980s, dangerous Dan Daoust!" Daoust skates to the blueline to begin the parade of ex-Leafs onto the ice. From the 1970s there are Jim Dorey, Mike Palmateer and Dave "Tiger" Williams. From the 1960s come Mike Walton, Norm Ullman, Ron Ellis, Bob Nevin and Andy Bathgate. And receiving the greatest applause, from the 1950s, are Eddie Shack and Red Kelly, the coaches of the Leafs Alumni today, Carl Brewer, Billy Harris and the Big M, Frank Mahovlich.

"You didn't have to get up for games against Montreal," recalls Mahovlich. "They were a dominant force and we were always in awe of their passing and their power play....Their theory was: if you had the puck, the other team couldn't score."

With the lights now fully on, the Big M and the Pocket Rocket approach centre ice for the ceremonial face-off from the widows of former goaltending greats Turk Broda and Bill Durnan. Before the puck is dropped, Mahovlich leans forward and kisses Beth Broda. Not to be outdone, after the face-off Richard kisses Nancy Durnan. Rivals all the way.

They face off for real. They line up—Nevin, Harris and Mahovlich against Houle, Robinson and Richard. On his first shift, Henri Richard, now fifty-seven, sprints up the right wing past the Leaf defence, goes around the net and passes in front. Palmateer stops the shot but by the time the Leafs have mounted a return rush Richard is back to ride Mahovlich out of the play, giving him a playful hug as he finishes his check.

"I played against a lot of these guys in junior," says Richard, referring to the old days of the interlocking Quebec and Ontario Junior A schedule. "But we were never allowed to meet them. Last night over a few beers, we talked about the old days. It was a lot more fun."

After Richard's dazzling rush, the Montreal oldtimers seem inspired. Murray Wilson beats Palmateer. But three minutes later the Leafs' Jim McKenny tips a Pat Boutette screened shot from the point past Steve Penney to even the score. Then Bill Derlago and Brian Conacher combine to put the Leafs ahead 2–1 at the end of the first period.

Up in the greys (which have not changed colour since the six-team days) spectators move to the concession stands. They munch on hot dogs, gulp down soft drinks and exchange views about how their Leaf heroes are holding up.

"It's hockey the way I remember it," says former Toronto Marlie goaltender Al Randal. "They may be older and slower but they still have the finesse."

"And Palmateer's right on the ball," adds John Kaunds, who played goal in field hockey in India before emigrating to Canada in the 1970s. "There's no such thing as oldtimers' field hockey."

"Just the old age brought me out here today, the nostalgia," says a fan from Ajax, Ontario. "It's the first time I've seen the

Leafs and Canadiens renewing that old rivalry. Brings back a lot of memories."

Forty-five seconds into the second period Montreal ties up the game on a Jacques Lemaire snapshot from the face-off circle. Less than thirty seconds later, the Leafs reply as Bill Derlago gets his second of three goals this afternoon, completing a pass from Brian Conacher and Brad Smith. Suddenly, in a mostly offensive game, the signature styles of all these former NHL greats begin to emerge—the crisp Ron Ellis pass, the Peter Mahovlich six-foot-four-inch reach, Carl Brewer's agile footwork on the point, Steve Shutt's playmaking and, at age 60, Andy Bathgate's hefty wrist shot.

"It's not like the old days," admits Bathgate. "One day I was practising penalty killing. I came around the net at one end of the arena and with kind of a slingshot action fired the puck up the rink. I got such a good whip out of my stick that the puck cleared the glass at the other end and shattered the clock on the wall."

That unique whipping action, created by his curved stick blade, prompted one of the most important innovations in modern hockey. As a kid in Winnipeg, Bathgate played a lot of shinny. In the springtime when the ponds got slushy and wet, Bathgate's stick, made of a single piece of wood, would warp and the blade would bend. Instead of throwing the stick away, he used the curve to give his shots greater velocity and unpredictability.

As a professional with New York, he would drive his equipment managers crazy by rejecting sticks that couldn't be bent into a curve. When he found sticks with the proper wood grain, he would soak them in hot water and bend them in the door jambs of the washroom doors. Bathgate would have three sticks ready before each game—one for each period. Once in the late 1950s, when the Chicago Blackhawks were visiting New York, Stan Mikita asked Rangers' trainer Frank Pace if he could borrow one of Bathgate's sticks. Strangely enough Pace agreed. Early in the game, Mikita slapped a shot from the blueline. The speed and trajectory of the puck fooled the Ranger goalie and it dropped into the net. Chicago beat New York that day 7–3.

"What happened to my stick?" Bathgate asked Pace after the game.

"Stan Mikita borrowed one," said Pace.

"Great," said Bathgate. "He just got five points today with that son of a bitch." Both Bathgate and Mikita later asked stick manufacturers to experiment with fibreglass to create permanently bent stick blades and the "banana blade" was born. Forty years later, Bathgate's innovation has changed the game. Nearly every hockey player—professional and amateur, minor leaguer and oldtimer—uses the curved blade he invented.

In spite of all the history inside the Gardens this April afternoon, it's the skating and the old rivalry the fans have come to see. "Competition with the Leafs is always at a very high level," says Rejean Houle, the president of the Canadiens' Alumni Association.

"I've been on five Stanley Cup winners with Montreal. I'm proud of them. But we haven't won a Cup here in Toronto. Nineteen sixty-seven was the last time we played against them in the Stanley Cup final. They beat us." Houle was a junior then but he has never forgotten. Every time the Leafs' and Habs' alumni meet, Houle treats the game as another chance to avenge the loss of the 1967 Cup.

Just before the second period ends Houle gets his chance. Richard launches another of his high-speed rushes from the Habs' defensive zone, spots Houle making a dash behind the Leaf defence and puts him in alone against Palmateer. In the near collision at the net, the puck bounces off Houle's glove and in behind the Leaf goaltender. The goal is disallowed.

"This is wide-open hockey," smiles Houle. "You've got more space. And if you can turn on the jets, it's just as exciting as the old days. But while the mind is always racing, it's the legs that can't keep up."

It looks as if the Leafs' legs are holding out better than the Canadiens'. At the end of the second period, Toronto leads Montreal 4–3.

During the final intermission, several of the teams' top guns keep the fans away from the Gardens' concession stands by conducting a shoot-out. Pierre Mondou is first up; he beats the Leaf goalie on the stick side. Next is Tiger Williams who makes the big deke and also beats the Canadiens' net-minder to the stick side. Following his goal, Tiger does his famous victory skate down the ice riding his hockey stick hobbyhorse style.

But the real crowdpleaser is Frank Mahovlich. With a nod from the referee, the Big M launches into his trademark big strides. They still look powerful and effortless. He circles the Leaf net to gain momentum so that by the time he picks up the puck at centre he's only three or four strides away from the Canadiens' net. Now at top speed, Mahovlich wrists the puck past Penney high on the stick side. The crowd explodes with delight as the Big M rounds the net, his stick thrust in the air, en route to the bench for congratulations from his Leaf teammates.

As the third period begins, it's clear there's more at stake here than victory in a friendly Sunday afternoon game at the Gardens. This is the third and rubber match game between these two teams of formerly mortal enemies. There's no more good-natured chatter between the two benches. Winning is the objective. The game grows more intense. As it does, the hometown crowd begins to chant "Go, Leafs, Go!"

"I think everybody just picked up the tempo," says Peter Mahovlich. The Big M's younger brother became a Canadien following a trade with Detroit in 1969 after which Peter shared in four Montreal Stanley Cup wins. "It's a fact of life with these two teams. The skating gets a little quicker, the passes a little crisper, and the shifts a little shorter, because the competitive instincts come to the surface."

Despite the adrenalin-fed enthusiasm on both sides and the end-to-end rushes that now dominate the play, the third period is all Montreal. Eight minutes into the final period, Pierre Larouche scores on a breakaway. Thirty seconds later he scores again on a two-on-one. Then Peter Mahovlich sneaks into the slot in front of the Leafs' net and sets up Yvon Lambert for the final goal, giving the Canadiens a 6–4 win over Toronto.

Once the Canadiens' oldtimers have congratulated each other in a mob scene in front of goalie Steve Penney, they line up to congratulate their arch rivals. Henri Richard lingers for a moment's chat with Billy Harris and Carl Brewer. Peter and Frank Mahovlich embrace each other in a friendly bear hug. The partisan crowd forgets the Toronto loss and gives its old-time idols a standing ovation.

To conclude the formalities, Henri Richard proudly accepts the King Clancy Cup and the bragging rights that go with it.

"It all starts off being fun," says Larry Robinson. "But no matter how old we are, we're still competitive. Winning isn't the only thing but there was a lot of pride coming through in that third period. You better believe it."

In the hospitality lounge across from the Leafs' dressing room a little while later, Molson's public relations rep Norm Webb extends a hand to former Leaf star Dave Williams. "Thanks for coming down for the game, Tiger," he says.

"No problem," says Williams. "Had a good time...except I hate losing to those bastards."

The Habs–Leafs rivalry suffered a setback after the 1967 Stanley Cup final. Thanks to league expansion and divisional realignment since then, the two franchises will probably not meet in a Stanley Cup final ever again. But as long as the Leafs' and Canadiens' Alumni Association teams continue to square off each year at the Forum or the Gardens for the Clancy Cup, the traditional rivalry between these two original-six cities will remain very much alive.

Legendary rivalries in hockey are not restricted to NHL cities. At one end of the hockey arena in Wilkie, Saskatchewan, there's a familiar-looking face painted on the cinder blocks. It's Yosemite Sam—the diminutive cartoon character from the Wild West with his oversized cowboy hat, an even larger moustache and pistols drawn. Sam is the logo for the hometown Wilkie Outlaws of the Wild Goose Senior Hockey League of west-central Saskatchewan. Around the arena hang other smaller banners identifying the Outlaws' competition from towns throughout the district—Eston, Kindersley, Unity, Macklin and others.

"Hockey's a religion here in Wilkie," confirms farmer Joe Cey who played with the Outlaws for ten seasons. "One time the Outlaws were playing in the provincial semi-finals and we lost to the Kerrobert Tigers. My cousin and another guy were so upset they took a dummy of Yosemite Sam to the top of the town water tower, lit him on fire and dropped him over the edge. That's how serious we are about our hockey."

If hockey is a religion in Wilkie, Saskatchewan, then the Cey family members—eleven sons and seven daughters—are its greatest disciples, beginning with Joe's father, Bill Cey. He was attracted to hockey as a boy in the 1930s. Each November the local recreation committee hauled water to the one-room schoolyard and built a rink. From shinny Bill moved to school hockey and after the war to senior hockey when there were no contracts, no pay cheques and plenty of bruises and stitches. These were the days of intense rivalries between prairie towns, when tempers ran high on the ice and off and when winning was everything.

"A really good rivalry between towns had no compassion," says Bill Cey. "It's a small war. You've got to beat that town and that's it."

The 1959 season was Wilkie's most successful. The Outlaws hadn't been beaten all year. In the first round of the Saskatchewan Amateur Hockey Association playoffs, Wilkie handily knocked off the Kindersley Klippers. They next met the Debden Rockets in a two-game, total-goals series. In the first game, with the help of ex-Chicago Blackhawk Fred Saskamoose, Debden overwhelmed the Outlaws 11–5.

Wilkie had to score six goals and keep Debden scoreless in game two just to tie and force overtime. To the delight of a capacity hometown crowd, Wilkie scored seven goals and held the Rockets to just one goal, forcing a ten-minute overtime period to decide the series.

"Ten bucks to the guy who scores the winning goal," said Outlaws' manager Ray McGillivray in the dressing room trying to spur his team on.

A discussion followed about the relative merits of having forwards and defencemen all trying to score that crucial goal. Cooler heads prevailed. It was decided the reward would be forty-eight beers because the winner wouldn't and couldn't drink it all himself. That way, everybody would share the reward.

On his first shift of overtime, defenceman Bill Cey followed forward Rudy Weber into the Rockets' end. Weber dug the puck out of the corner and threw it toward the slot in front of the net. All in one motion, Cey pinched in from the point, picked up the pass and fired the puck into the net. The crowd nearly tore the roof off the old Second Avenue arena in the commotion that followed.

"It was the highlight of my career," says Cey as the Outlaws went on to win the Northern Senior Championship. After that winning season, Bill Cey retired from playing but not from hockey. He coached and managed the Outlaws and eventually became a hockey promoter as president of the Wild Goose Hockey League.

The excitement and competitive spirit of hockey was never far from the centre of life on the Cey farm. "When winter chores were finished," remembers the eldest son, Gerry, "there was never any question. It wasn't like, 'What're we going to do?' It was, 'How quick can we get our skates on?'" Lester, the third son, recalls rubber boots used as goal posts on the frozen dugout at the farm and floor hockey played in the hayloft. Jamie, the Ceys' fourth youngest son, describes the procedure: "when Mom and Dad left the house, within ten minutes, out came the rulers and erasers and five or six of us would be into a hockey game on the kitchen floor."

One by one, eleven Cey sons left the kitchen for the hockey arena and left the family farm to make their own lives.

Gerry, born in 1952, played forward for the Humboldt Broncos of the Saskatchewan Junior Hockey League before settling down to farm two sections west of Wilkie.

Kenny rose to Junior B before he too got into mixed farming near Scott, Saskatchewan.

Lester won the Centennial Cup Championship with the Prince Albert Raiders of the SJHL and then began a career with SaskTel.

Kevin, the fourth son, played senior hockey for three different Saskatchewan towns but settled in Unity to work for the Saskatchewan Wheat Pool.

Before he took a job with the United Grain Growers in Naicam, Bob played senior hockey in Wilkie.

The middle son, Harold, played for two different senior teams in the Wild Goose Hockey League; he farms near Wilkie.

Roger, the seventh son, played on three championship teams in the Wild Goose Hockey League; he farms near Phippen.

Jamie played all his senior hockey with the Wilkie Outlaws and then found work with a Wilkie-based transport company.

Joe, the ninth son, played junior hockey in Battleford and in ten seasons with the Wilkie Outlaws helped win eight provincial and two league championships. Joe farms the original family farm.

Sons number ten and eleven, Mike and Gary, have gone off to the University of Saskatchewan for agriculture degrees and have played campus hockey along the way.

Bill Cey had set a precedent. Throughout their hockey careers, whether stellar or not, none of Bill Cey's sons lost his father's passion to play inter-town prairie hockey, and all but one, at one time or another, wore the green and white jersey of the Wilkie Outlaws. It was a family tradition. A passion.

For a couple of seasons however that passionate brand of inter-town hockey nearly pulled the tight-knit Cey clan apart. In the 1979–80 season, Bill Cey was vice-president of the Wild Goose Hockey League and responsible for its long-term welfare. A new franchise—the Unity Miners—was about to enter the league. It would be allowed to import and pay two players from outside the town. Harold Cey was living and working in Unity and had signed up with the Miners. So Bill met with sons Gerry and Lester, who lived in Wilkie, and encouraged them to consider joining the Miners.

If they did, the league would feature three Cey brothers with the Wilkie Outlaws and three with the Unity Miners, a rivalry that league organizers up until then could only dream about.

"You've got to be kidding," said Lester.

"We're Wilkie boys through and through," added Gerry.

"I know that," said their father. "But things are tough on the farm. You could each make a hundred dollars a game....It'd be an opportunity to get a payback for some of the years you've invested in hockey. Besides there are still three [Ceys] playing in Wilkie. It'll give balance to the league and create tremendous interest and friction. It'd be good for the game."

It was certainly good for the gate. Whenever Unity and Wilkie met that season and the next, it was standing room only at the local arenas. Fans came to the games with signs supporting their favourite Ceys or with slogans such as "We'll have the last Cey." At cash registers, over gas pumps and all along coffee counters in both towns of 1,500 people, a Miners-Outlaws game really meant Gerry, Lester and Harold Cey versus their three younger brothers, Roger, Jamie and Joe. As Bill Cey had predicted, a rivalry was born.

But while the battle between Ceys was great for Wild Goose hockey, it was not especially positive for the Cey family. Lester lived and worked in Wilkie; some of his neighbours couldn't accept his decision to play for Unity and called him a traitor. The attacks were only verbal but they certainly made life in town uncomfortable for those two seasons. The stress even got to the boys' mother; Ethel Cey attended the games at first but eventually refused to watch. "I couldn't side with one and not with the other."

Lester enjoyed playing a tenacious brand of hockey even against his younger brothers. But he hated the idea of body-checking them; he called possibly coming to blows with his brothers "a dry-mouth experience." On the other hand, Jamie, Roger and Joe welcomed the challenge of facing their older, more experienced brothers and relished every game against the Miners. They weren't about to be shown up. In the heat of the contest, Jamie vowed that he "would never back off from them in the corners...but fight them tooth and nail."

The rivalry heated up all season. When the Outlaws played in Unity, busloads of fans followed and vice versa. Nobody was disappointed. The Ceys versus Ceys always lived up to its billing. Then, late that season, during an inevitable playoff showdown between Unity and Wilkie, a Miners' defenceman took Outlaws' winger Roger Cey heavily into the boards. Roger hit his head, fell and lay motionless on the ice.

In an instant, five Cey brothers were at Roger's side. All the cockiness, all the bravado and trumped-up rivalry between them evaporated.

"I was right over top of him," remembers Gerry. "He's wearing a Wilkie uniform. I'm wearing a Unity uniform. But what mattered was that we were brothers."

As Roger came to and it was clear he had no serious neck or back injuries, Gerry turned to his younger brother Joe (of the Outlaws) and asked, "If he doesn't make it, can I have his hockey gloves?"

It broke the tension. Roger would be okay although Joe recalls thinking, "If it had been anybody else but my brother saying that I would have driven him one."

The battle between the Unity Ceys and the Wilkie Ceys lasted a couple of seasons launching a healthy rivalry between the Miners and the Outlaws. It rejuvenated senior hockey in a couple of west-central Saskatchewan towns. But the Cey brothers soon gave up the artificial family turf war and were reunited at home in Wilkie. The Outlaws, featuring various combinations of Cey brothers, went on to pound the opposition relentlessly. Between 1980 and 1992, the team was crowned Provincial B champion ten times.

But for all their hockey experience, not until the World Family Recreational Hockey Tournament did all the Cey brothers get the chance to play together.

Late in the winter of 1990, during a regular day at the Saskatchewan Wheat Pool, Kevin Cey picked up a copy of the Saskatoon *StarPhoenix*. Among other stories, he read the latest on Mark Messier and the Edmonton Oilers; sans Gretzky they were en route to their fifth Stanley Cup in seven years.

"But then this other hockey write-up caught my eye," remembers Kevin. "It was about the Larocque family from Gaspé that had gone to a family hockey tournament, an annual competition in Chandler, Quebec, for hockey players all in the same family...and I got to thinking...."

The *StarPhoenix* article went on to say that the Larocque family with ten sons playing had earned a place in the *Guinness Book of World Records* as the hockey team with the most brothers playing together.

Not surprisingly, the newspaper piece caught the attention

of several of Kevin's brothers. Joe had spotted it and phoned Lester and Harold. Before long the brothers had called a meeting to discuss whether there was enough interest to form a Cey family team, raise some money and travel to Quebec that coming Christmas to participate in "Tournoi Mondial de Hockey Familial."

"There was excitement in the air at that meeting," says Harold Cey. "We thought there's a real opportunity here...to put our community on the map...to play as a team...as a family....It sent a chill down my spine just thinking about it."

Kenny Cey hadn't played hockey in over a year. After a couple of seasons with the Wilkie Outlaws in the early 1970s, he had played a little recreational hockey with the X Outlaws in the 1980s. But unlike his older brother, Gerry, and so many of his younger siblings, Kenny had never been on a championship team. He wondered if this might give him that chance.

Roger wasn't crazy about the idea at first because the tournament would be recreational hockey. To Roger, that meant heads-up, be-creative-with-your-stick, play-with-finesse, old-timers'-style hockey, not take-the-man-out, grab-the-puck-and-be-physical hockey, the brand he'd played all his life. Roger was his father's son.

Jamie was in for the biggest shock at that first meeting. He had finished playing senior hockey the year before and also had no intention of playing rec hockey. Jamie, Joe and Roger had been very successful as forwards for the Outlaws, playing dump and chase and check hockey.

"But I arrived late," says Jamie, "and it was pre-determined that I was the biggest and would have the best chance of having most of the pucks hit me. I guess I had stopped the most erasers in our kitchen hockey days. Anyway, my brothers had already decided that I was going to be the Team Cey goalie."

Calling Jamie a goalie was one thing. Making him competent was something else. First, he is left-handed and left-handed goalie gloves were not readily available in Wilkie. After a little scrounging in February and March of 1990, they found some used gloves in a nearby town. Next he got used goalie pads although Jamie is five-foot-eleven and the goal pads were for a netminder who was six-foot-five. To complete the preliminaries, he borrowed a goaltending booklet from a seven-year-old neighbour.

Led by their father, Bill, the Cey brothers began practising two and three times a week, partly to get used to playing together but also to draw attention to their objective—winning the family tournament in Chandler, Quebec.

But the tourney was only nine months away. The biggest problem at this stage wasn't stopping pucks—it was finding the cash to get the team to Chandler. Roughly $1,200 per person was needed for travel and accommodation. All the brothers were as naive about fund-raising as Jamie was about blocking shots. Joe figured all they had to do was find the addresses of thirty large corporations, write letters requesting sponsorship and wait for the cheques to roll in, but all their requests for corporate sponsorship were turned down.

After their initial disappointment, the Ceys hit upon a new strategy. The Chandler tournament was billed as a world tournament. They were going there representing not only eleven sons and the rest of their family but as ambassadors of their community. Why not finance the enterprise on that basis? Why not take on the world in Quebec on behalf of their friends, their neighbours and the merchants of their hometown? Why not bring home the Chandler Cup for Team Cey and the people of Wilkie, Saskatchewan?

"We decided to make up a booklet telling our story and featuring the advertising of our sponsors," explains Joe. "Each brother committed himself to selling ads to cover the $1,200 needed to get him to the tournament. We even sold ad space on the uniforms we would need....We went to everybody we knew in this part of Saskatchewan."

The formula worked. Because so many of the Cey brothers were farming in the area, Kevin sold ads to half a dozen local farm machinery dealers. Harold had never sold anything in his life and expected a local law firm would laugh him out of their office but they loved the idea and bought a full-page ad. Roger sold a full page to a feed company owner who "wasn't even a hockey fan!" Lester landed three sponsors in one day. Jamie's boss at a Wilkie trucking company promised he'd buy half a page if the local hotel bought the other half; Jamie sold them both. And because they didn't want to miss out on a good thing, a local metal fabricator approached Kenny and he sold that company half a page.

"I remember I was a couple of sponsors short," recalls Joe. "I was sitting with the office manager of the Co-Op mall in North Battleford talking to him about our trip. He was from a big family like ours and right there he wrote out a cheque for $600."

By the time harvesting was complete, all the pieces of the Ceys' grand plan were in place. The sponsors had all paid up. Airline tickets were bought. Hotel arrangements were confirmed. Some of the brothers had even brushed up on their French. Just before the trip, Team Cey fulfilled a promise to their sponsors. The brothers rented a Winnebago and did a circuit of exhibition games in small towns around the region—Naicam, Kelvington, Edam, Dodsland, Macklin, North Battleford and Unity. The pretournament tour wound up back in Wilkie with a game against the Outlaws. That November night, hundreds of people from around the district filled the Wilkie arena to speed their hometown heroes on their way. A CBC field crew from the television show *On the Road* was there as well to begin a documentary about Team Cey. Producer Malcolm Hamilton planned to follow the team all the way to Chandler and the World Family Recreational Hockey Tournament championship.

"Most of the brothers had learned how to win at hockey," says Joe. "It's why the Wilkie Outlaws had been so successful, because enough of us knew what it took to win. Our goal was to win this tournament at Chandler, not to finish second or third."

Two days after Christmas, in near blizzard conditions, Team Cey (eleven Cey brothers and Gerry's son Jeff as the team trainer) and their fan support (three wives, three sisters and their mother, Ethel Cey) rolled out of Wilkie bound for Saskatoon and a flight to Montreal. Bill Cey had agreed to stay behind; somebody had to take care of things back on the farm. Lester had mixed feelings about going away; because his wife Pam had lost both her parents at that time of year, he didn't like leaving home at Christmas. Kevin, Harold and

Roger had never been on a jet before. In fact, most of the Cey family had not left west-central Saskatchewan before let alone travelled across the country for a hockey tournament.

Three thousand kilometres, two plane rides, a four-hour bus trip and a day later, Team Cey was at the eastern tip of Gaspé in Quebec, preparing for the tournament. Aside from travel weariness and the last minute purchase of neck protectors, which they had suddenly discovered were mandatory, the Ceys in their brand-new green and white jerseys hit the ice eager and ready for their first opponents—the Hudon family from Varennes, Quebec. In the stands, their cheering wives, sisters, mom and a cousin who'd arrived from the Maritimes were decked out in the team's away sweaters. The CBC television crew began to roll the first of its hours and hours of tape.

Team Cey won their first game 9–1.

The next day Jamie Cey, the rookie goaltender, recorded his first ever shutout as the Ceys defeated the Lords from St. Juste du Lac, Quebec, 9–0.

Sunday, December 30, 1990, came early as Team Cey met the Sutton family from Chandler in the morning semi-final. The Ceys again rolled over their opposition, 9–2, setting the stage for the showdown everybody expected—the final that afternoon between the Ceys and the defending champion Plourdes from Pidgeon Hill, New Brunswick.

Unlike their first three games, the final would not be a cakewalk. Several of the Cey brothers had watched the Plourdes play. They were seven brothers and two sisters but in close games they would shorten their bench and go with their best five players. If the Plourdes had an Achilles' heel, it was that the Ceys outnumbered them and might simply outlast them. But in a game that consisted of three ten-minute stop-time periods, the stoppages would give the Plourdes time to catch their breath. Otherwise, the teams were well matched.

The Cey dressing room before the final was the usual mixture of nerves and confidence, of clowning and calm, of forced nonchalance and flashes of intensity.

Although Gerry, the eldest, functioned as the family leader, all the brothers considered Lester their inspiration; he lifted the team with words of encouragement in the dressing room and on the bench. Some needed the bolstering more than others. Jamie realized his limited goaltending experience was a liability. Kenny, who generally avoided pressure-filled situations, needed encouragement as well as a dose of wild strawberry extract to calm his stomach before the game. Harold, the team comic, had his diabetes to worry about so the brothers made sure there was always plenty of pop and juice on hand.

"Let's try to keep it close in the first period," Harold said. "Stay within four goals of these guys, okay?"

Joe was the power behind the team. While he could be wound up tighter than a spring, Joe exuded confidence. He always looked unbeatable, focused; for the other ten Ceys on the team, Joe was a presence they could all draw on. By both example and attitude, Joe was team leader. Until Sunday, Joe had had a lot on his mind from co-ordinating travel and lodging for the family to accommodate the television crew. Now it was time to do what they had come here to do.

In the stands the Team Cey supporters were outwardly confident, but, "we had a lot of butterflies," Ethel Cey admitted before the game.

After the opening face-off, the Plourdes came on very strong. Their system was designed for eight skaters. Their defencemen never became part of the offence and their forwards rarely backchecked. To conserve energy, their rushes were calculated; they would build a play slowly out of their end, wait for an opening and then explode toward the net. The Ceys had two units of five who played for roughly equal times. Each unit played an all-out press most of the time.

For the first two thirds of the game, the Plourdes' system worked. The Ceys' did not. After two periods the Plourdes led Team Cey 3–1.

Back in the dressing room, the Cey brothers tried to analyze their predicament. Individually they had often faced comeback situations. It was not impossible to mount a charge this late in the game but Joe and Lester began to show some frustration.

"We gotta get mad at them out there," one said.

"We gotta get some goals happening," added the other.

Kevin was feeling doubtful things would ever go their way. He had pulled his groin and quietly told Gerry. Gerry tried to steady his brothers. He got them talking about their play and ways to fix what they were doing wrong.

"They're plugging up the middle," somebody said.

"Yeah, it's like a wall out there," another confirmed.

On the other side of the dressing room, Joe withdrew into himself. He covered his head with a towel and leaned forward with his face in his hands in an effort to focus on what had to be done. Mike, his younger brother, hadn't played with Joe that much and thought that Joe had given up, that they were going to lose.

"So how are we gonna beat them?" somebody asked.

"I don't know," admitted Lester, "but I know one thing. Nobody's quitting." That was the right response. The Ceys left the dressing room renewed. Loud cheering from their family and friends among the Chandler spectators buoyed their spirits as they returned to the ice. The third period began.

Then disaster struck. Back on defence, Harold mishandled the puck; the resulting breakaway gave the Plourdes an unexpected third period goal and a stranglehold on the game. They now led 4–1 with less than half a period to go.

"It was slipping away," Gerry thought.

"I thought we'd just sold the farm," Kenny figured.

His stomach rolled with the realization that he had never been in as stressful a game before with so much at stake. It was almost too much to take.

Then, a sign of life. Joe and Kevin broke into the Plourdes' end. Joe raced the defenceman toward the corner for the puck while Kevin went headlong for the net. Joe got to the puck first, slapped it in front and Kevin backhanded it over the Plourdes' goalie.

It was now 4–2 for the Plourdes with four minutes left in the game. The momentum was shifting.

During the next sequence of plays the teams faced off in the Team Cey end and the Plourdes won the draw. The puck came back to the point. The Plourdes' defenceman quickly snapped the puck toward the top corner on Jamie's glove side.

Jamie caught it and stopped the play, surprising even himself with the save.

The Plourdes realized their opponents had found some life and play intensified. Bumping got rougher along the boards and in the corners. The referee, sensing this, began to call penalties. The Plourdes and Ceys were going to play four-on-four hockey for much of the rest of the game.

Lester, Joe and Gerry had a quick huddle at the bench. Kevin's groin was hurting badly. He was pretty well finished. They talked to Kenny who had hit the wall emotionally; he bowed out. In an instant Team Cey decided how they would play the final minutes of the game. They would shorten the bench and use their talents to greatest advantage.

"Joe," said Gerry, "don't come off the ice anymore."

Joe didn't bat an eye. He understood.

"Harry," continued Gerry. "You and Roger'll alternate on defence. Joe, Lester and I will go up front."

That meant that Bob, Mike and Gary would sit out the rest of the game too. They understood and nodded in agreement.

The strategy paid off. On the very next play, Gerry raced a Plourdes' defenceman for the puck into the Plourdes' end. From behind, Gerry could hear Lester shouting, "Hurry! Go hard!" Gerry got there first and dug the puck out. Instinctively he threw it into the slot. Joe got hold of Gerry's pass and put the puck up into the top corner of the net.

The Plourdes now led by just one.

On the next face-off in the Plourdes' end, the puck came back to Harold on defence.

"It was like the old days in the Wild Goose League," says Harold. "I saw Joe going for the front of the net and fired it along the ice to him. I knew he would be there and he deflected it up over the goalie into the net."

In a matter of two minutes, the game the Ceys feared had slipped away forever was tied 4–4. Less than two minutes were left in regulation time. Both teams knew that if one side got a goal quickly it would crush any hope the other had of coming back.

"Let's not let this thing go into overtime, guys," Gerry told Joe and Lester as they lined up at centre ice.

The teams were back to full strength. Play went back and forth, it seemed forever, with no real scoring chances. Both sides were waiting for a break. Then, as the Ceys got the puck into the Plourdes' end, Joe got into a tussle with a Plourdes' defenceman behind the net.

In the instant in which the Plourdes' goalie turned his head and moved his body to the side where Joe was standing, Joe managed to kick the puck along the ice to Lester who was just behind the net at the opposite post.

Lester got his stick on the puck, went from his forehand to his backhand and stuffed the puck into the open corner of the net.

As soon as the puck crossed the line and the goal light went on, Lester began leaping up and down like Mike Foligno. His brothers nearly crushed him in the group bear hug that followed. Even Kevin vaulted over the boards and joined the scrum of Ceys congratulating each other.

"Guys," Gerry sighed to his brothers, "let's just stay right here...forever." It was too powerful a moment to let pass. Gerry wanted to savour the feeling as long as he could.

Forty seconds were left on the clock. Nothing on earth could tear the victory from their grasp now. If Joe had been heroic in scoring and assisting the comeback goals, he was a tiger in the last half-minute. In their last desperate attempt to break out, the Plourdes fired the puck up the ice. Joe was on the blueline and swung his stick like a baseball bat. He smacked the puck out of the air and into the stands, just as the game-ending buzzer went.

Team Cey had won the championship 5–4 with a story-book ending.

Centre ice was chaos. This time all the Ceys converged—brothers, sisters, wives, trainer, and one mother. There was an orgy of hugging, kissing and tears. It continued as the Cey brothers were presented with the Chandler Cup so that they could do a circuit on the ice. In the bleachers, TV producer Malcolm Hamilton was delirious with delight. For a time, all his weeks of planning and shooting looked to be slipping away. Instead he had "a real Cinderella story."

Back in the dressing room, Harold gulped down juice. Don

McRae, the Ceys' cousin from New Brunswick, cried tears of joy. Kenny was sick. The rest drank beer, stripped off their jerseys and let the win sink in.

"Hey, guys," Gerry suddenly blurted out. "You know how the winners of a big baseball game go sit out in centre field and celebrate....Let's go do it here."

A couple of glances back and forth and the brothers were on their feet again, heading back to the ice. They sat in a circle, just as Gerry described. The stands around the arena were empty. Many of the overhead lights were already dimming. But Team Cey savoured the last moments of a classic recreational hockey championship.

"Suck this up," said Gerry. "Enjoy it."

"La premiere étoile," shouted Mike, imitating the Montreal Forum announcer giving the three star selections. "The Cey family 'ockey team." He added, "Does it get any better than this?"

Not for Kenny. It was his thirty-seventh birthday and this was the first championship team he'd ever played on.

The last of the champagne was sipped from the Chandler Cup as it was passed around the circle. Several of the brothers said a prayer. They complimented their tournament rivals, the Plourde family. Some remembered aloud the sponsors who'd gotten them there. And they praised their mother and father who had raised them all and had given them direction and opportunity in life.

"Winning by coming back with those heroics in the last four minutes," said Gerry. "I have no trouble saying it was the best championship I have ever won."

"I don't know that I've ever experienced a better feeling in sport in my life," added Lester.

Concluded Jamie, "It was the most emotional point of our lives together as brothers."

TEN

Playing for Peanuts

As the Air Canada airbus breaks through the clouds on its descent into San Francisco, all eyes turn to the windows to search for the familiar landmarks of this northern California tourist hotspot. They recognize Alcatraz, Golden Gate Bridge, Candlestick Park and the downtown area called Fisherman's Wharf. But none of these is their destination.

Inside the airport terminal, several hundred tourists, travellers and the members of three oldtimers' hockey clubs gather at the baggage carousel. Players from the Central Ontario Over-65s, the Toronto 50s and the Toronto Antiques collect their suitcases and hockey gear.

"Antiques?" says one woman. She's meeting one of the non-hockey passengers and notices the name printed across a duffel bag moving along the carousel. "What an awful way to pack antiques!"

"No, ma'am," pipes up one of the hockey players. "It's hockey equipment."

"In July?" she says.

"Well, you've got me there."

These Canadians are among about a thousand oldtimers, some with their wives, friends and children, who are converging on Santa Rosa, about an hour's drive north of San Francisco. It's mid-July and time for the annual Snoopy's Senior World Hockey Tournament organized by Peanuts cartoonist Charles Schulz.

Each year, in addition to the thousands of oldtimers'

house-league games, once-a-week senior recreational games, shinny matches and pick-up sessions across the country, between October and May the calendar is full of weekend tourneys. Some are local. Many are national, COHA-sanctioned tournaments such as the Hub City in Saskatoon, the Pacific Cup in Victoria, the Prairie Cup in Edmonton, the McMurtry Cup in Toronto and the Monctonian. For those looking offshore, there are annual tour-and-play packages to Florida, Arizona, Nevada, Hawaii and Europe.

"But this Santa Rosa tournament is the granddaddy of them all," says Bob "Taxi" McEachren of the Toronto Antiques. At forty-five he's been the team manager for about five years. He didn't skate, much less play hockey, until he was twenty-five. In twenty years, he's made up for a lot of lost time. Between his shifts driving a taxi, McEachren played whenever and wherever he could, winter and summer. He couldn't wait to turn thirty-five so he could play oldtimers or forty so he could join the Antiques and go to Santa Rosa.

"The year I turned forty and joined the team," says McEachren, "[Don] 'Unc' Hughes, the original manager of the Antiques, died of stomach cancer....It was the month before we were going to California." So Taxi helped organize the annual trek in Unc's stead and he's been doing it ever since. "I'm not a part-timer. If I'm going to play hockey, I'm completely involved."

He's prompt too. On the day the Senior World Hockey Tournament application arrives in the mail at his home, Taxi fills out the forms, buys a U.S. money order to cover the entry deposit and couriers it back to Santa Rosa within twenty-four hours. Competition to get into this tournament is stiff; of the 188 teams that have applied this year, only fifty-six have been invited. The Antiques are back for their fourteenth visit in pursuit of their seventh divisional Snoopy championship.

Their routine is familiar. Pick up the car and van rentals at the Frisco airport. Drive north on Highway 101 to the City of Santa Rosa. Check into Los Robles Lodge. Then, for some, it's off to the pool, the sauna, the outdoor hot tub and the California sunshine. For Taxi and team captain Guy Sabourin, it's up the road to the Redwood Empire Ice Arena.

Outside, with its steep roof, overhanging eaves, redwood stain and gingerbread trim, the arena looks more like a Swiss chalet than a hockey rink. Even inside, the arena, built in 1969 by Charles Schulz for his figure-skating daughter and hockey-crazed sons, doesn't suggest a hockey shrine. There's more gingerbread, huge hand-painted murals of alpine settings, Christmas tree lights, comfortable seating for several hundred and an unlit sign that can indicate different modes of pleasure skating: "All Skate," "Couples Only," "Men Only," "Ladies Only" and "Clear Ice."

In the front lobby of the rink that Peanuts built, however, evidence that an oldtimers' hockey tournament is about to begin is plentiful. Hockey bags and sticks are piled everywhere, especially next to the café entrance. Players of every shape, size and oldtimers' age bracket (from forty to seventy-plus) are renewing acquaintances and exchanging hockey lore. Among them are long-time rivals Bill Triolo, who coaches the Toronto 50s, and John Young, who this year is playing for the Edmonton Vintage Oldtimers in the sixty-and-over division.

"It must've been one of the earliest tournaments," says John Young. "It was the Third World War!"

"What, you Edmonton Firefighters against us Toronto Italians?" asks Bill Triolo. "I remember."

"I'd promised a goal each for a friend's two kids," continues Young. "We went through nearly three periods. We were down a goal and I hadn't scored. A minute and a half to go and I finally got the tying goal. Then the game winner....I retrieved both pucks for the two kids. But I never promised anything like that again."

They laugh and it's Triolo's turn. "They tell me I still hold the record for the most goals in a single game," says Triolo, remembering the first Snoopy tournament in 1975.

"There were only sixteen teams then," adds Young.

"Doesn't matter," exclaims Triolo. "Toronto Italians had to score seventeen goals to take the championship. I scored seven goals. And we beat Santa Rosa 17–0 and won the gold."

In a corner of the lobby beyond the trophy case that contains championship cups, plaques, pucks, photos and other

Snoopy tournament memorabilia is the officials' booth. In front of a large board with a handwritten game schedule is a smiling, middle-aged woman directing officials, registering teams and refs, arranging for back-up goalies and handing out press kits with military exactness. Cecilia Shortt has been co-ordinating the event since it began.

"The tournament actually started in Burbank as part of the Senior Olympics in 1974," says Shortt, a former school teacher from Michigan. "It was one of thirty-five sports.... The next year they asked Sparky [Charles Schulz] if he would handle the ice sports here at the arena....Well, hockey stayed here. We dropped the affiliation with the Senior Olympics in 1978. And Sparky made trophies with the Snoopy character to award to the winning teams.

"But, oh, yes, I'm involved from booking the teams to discussing rule changes to scheduling and promotion....I've been dubbed the Margaret Thatcher of oldtimers' hockey."

The iron lady of Santa Rosa still has a soft spot for the real oldtimers of the tournament. Despite the beehive of activity at her officials' booth, Cecilia notices that Al and Norm Johnson have arrived to pick up the kits for the Ottawa Olde Tymers. They'll be playing in the new over-seventy division against Charles Schulz's Santa Rosa Diamond Icers. She immediately stops what she's doing to dispense hugs and kisses to these two long-time tournament regulars. They offer condolences in return—Cecilia's husband, Murray, the original coach of the Diamond Icers, died earlier in the spring. Moments later, Cecilia runs to answer the pay phone that's ringing in the corner of the lobby.

"Wrong number," she says. "But who knows? It might've been important."

Everything in this city of 100,000 has the look of a place gone hockey mad. Hotels post the names of visiting teams on their illuminated signs and in lobby display cases. Restaurants and cafés offer all-you-can-eat breakfast rates to tournament players. Factory outlet malls invite the visitors to special late night shopping. Every other vehicle on the road is full of visiting hockey players and their equipment piled high in back seats.

The local *Press Democrat* features pictures and stories of visiting teams from Japan, Austria, Switzerland, across the United States and Canada and prints the schedule for local spectators. Eighty-four games will be played over six days beginning each morning at six o'clock and continuing until nearly three o'clock the next morning.

The Toronto Antiques' first game is on the second day of the tournament—Tuesday night at six o'clock—against the New York Apple Core.

The Redwood Empire Arena dressing rooms, unlike everything else in this spare-no-expense rink, are spartan—wooden benches, some lockers, limited lighting and even less ventilation. But it doesn't matter. For most oldtimers this environment is like home. Anticipation fills the Antiques' dressing room. Those who are back from last year want to erase the memory of losing the gold medal to a local Santa Rosa team.

"The refs won't call body contact along the boards, guys," says Phil Nicholas. He's been coming to the Snoopy tournament as a player for years; this time he's the Antiques' coach dispensing last-minute instructions. "They'll only whistle down a high stick. No penalty."

"Ice is soft," adds Taxi, "so play the boards."

Out in the arena behind the team benches, the Antiques set up for the traditional pre-tournament photograph. Their faces reflect a mixture of tension and ease.

"Don't forget, guys," goalie Tony Fallis says, "we've got to initiate the rookies."

Bob LeBrun, one of the rookies, has heard stories of new additions to the team having all their body hair shaved off. Still, he laughs. So do Guy Sabourin and Joe Dinino. They're veterans. They don't have to worry.

Meanwhile, Joe Blazik, Ron Matsuyama, Benny Murata and Taxi look intently at the camera. They're not smiling at all. They were here last year for the loss to Santa Rosa. They've never seen this New York team before and wonder how strong they and the rest of their opposition in the forty-plus division are.

Across the hall the New York Apple Core Oldtimers are suiting up.

"We've never been very aggressive," says Apple Core centre Bob Santini. "Not like most Canadian players. They grew up with the game. We've never had that formal training. We tend to be a little more tentative."

Born in 1932 in the Bronx, Bob Santini played street hockey on four-wheeled box roller skates and shinny on frozen ponds but he didn't play organized ice hockey until he began helping out at his sons' hockey practices in the mid-1960s. Only after he'd been coaching for nearly fifteen years did Santini and a number of friends decide to play hockey themselves.

"We practised in an arena out on Long Island," says teammate Bill Guido. He grew up in New York City loving the Rangers and watching their games from fifty-cent back row seats at Madison Square Garden. When he joined Santini, Guido was nearly fifty and hadn't played hockey in half a dozen years. "In the early 1980s, the arena owners—the City of Long Beach—said it was too costly for them to run the arena. So they shut it down."

"I submitted a proposal to the city," continues Santini. "and eighteen guys [from the New York Apple Core Old-timers' hockey club] invested $5,000 each and we took over the arena...in 1987."

"Until then," says Guido, "we could never afford to go out and rent ice for a weekend tournament. Now we can have our own tournament whenever we like....Not too many teams have their own arena."

The Apple Core–Antiques game is only a few shifts old when the New York squad scores on a relatively harmless shot along the ice. Minutes later they score another on a deflection. They may have come to the game later in life than most of the Antiques and they may have a less aggressive attitude than Canadians, but the New York Apple Core are winning.

The next centre ice face-off sees a transformed Toronto Antiques team line up. All the smiles are gone. It's no longer fun and games and team photographs. It's time to get down to business. At the drop of the puck, the duo of Joe Blazik and Joe Dinino dart up the ice and score on a crisp little give-and-go.

"Wake-up call," somebody says on the Antiques' bench.

"At tournaments you've got to know when to turn it up a

notch," says Dinino. He's just fifty and has almost that many years of hockey experience behind him, many of them with his friend, forty-six-year-old Joe Blazik. Both received their formative hockey training in the west end of Toronto with the Columbus Boys Club, had a crack at junior and played together in the Canadian-Italian Hockey League. The Italian league hockey was competitive and notorious for "lots of stick work, elbows and bangin' in the corners."

"I never give anybody cheap shots, though," says Dinino, referring to the no-slapshot, no-contact oldtimers' hockey he now plays. "But if it's a tournament, I go out to win."

Dinino sets a new tempo for the game. He scores four more times and even gets a penalty shot late in the game. The Antiques' other two lines come to life. Taxi's line gets five goals and Dave Bince's line three.

Final score: Antiques 13–Apple Core 2.

Jokes and banter disguises the relief in the Antiques' dressing room.

"Never saw you play a better game, Taxi," says Butch Crump, patting Taxi on the back. Then he lets the compliment slip into obvious exaggeration. "The guy looks like a superstar!"

"I thought the drama went out of the game when Joe missed the penalty shot," teases Dave Bince.

"Yeah, but thirteen goals," adds Bob LeBrun, "that's unlucky, isn't it?"

They still have some unfinished business to attend to. One by one the Antiques and Apple Core oldtimers emerge from their dressing rooms. They leave the cool of the indoor arena and head for the warm evening air of the parking lot. It's time for the traditional Snoopy's Tournament post-game tailgate party. Along the rows of cars, vans and buses, players gather, pile up their equipment bags and sticks and dip into beer that's been on ice all afternoon. Winners and losers toast each other. The Antiques and Apple Core players begin to mingle and trade caps, T-shirts, pins, business cards and stories. The tale of the Apple Core leasing an arena so they could play hockey amuses the Antiques. But the centre of attention is Apple Core manager Bob "Pops" Burgess.

"I learned to skate when I came over [to Canada] from Scotland," explains Pops in an odd combination of Brooklynese and a Scottish burr. "That was in 1921."

At eighty-six, Pops is a Pentecostal minister with a lifetime of stories. He regales everybody with tales of becoming a chaplain in the Canadian army during the Second World War, meeting legendary Maple Leaf Ace Bailey, playing armed services hockey with New York Ranger Edgar Laprade, moving to the United States and helping to launch and coach the New York Apple Core oldtimers at their Long Island rink in the 1980s.

"Oldtimers is great hockey. Cleans out the cobwebs," says Pops, "but I do think forty is rather a young age to be called an oldtimer."

The parking lot is slow to clear. For some players, keeping the tailgate party going as long as possible is as much a ritual of this tournament as rehashing the plays of the game. However, for a number of the Antiques and other spectators, the 7:30 game that follows the Antiques–Apple Core match is just as important. It features the annual match-up between Charles Schulz's Santa Rosa Diamond Icers and the Japanese Mandai Memorials who are now competing in the new seventy-plus division.

Charles Schulz's hockey history is relatively easy to trace to its childhood roots in Minnesota in the 1930s.

"We used to sneak onto the St. Paul Academy rink and play under the light of the moon," Schulz recalls. "Nobody had pads. We used *National Geographic*s for shin pads." When there was nobody else around to play shinny with him, Schulz's mother would agree to play goal while he practised his shot. In 1974 he launched Snoopy's Senior World Hockey Tournament at his own expense. Neither relentless press deadlines for his Peanuts cartoon nor quadruple heart bypass surgery a few years ago has prevented him from playing hockey regularly with the Diamond Icers.

The story of his Japanese opposition is a little more complicated.

In 1933, while Japanese colonial armies occupied northern China, a twenty-four-year-old Japanese medical student named Toshihiko Shoji was training at the Manchurian Medical College. That autumn, as creeks and ponds froze, Shoji gathered a handful of his colleagues together. He described a winter game he had first seen during the 1920s, when an ice hockey team—the Battleford Millers—had visited Japan from western Canada to play exhibition games.

"We heated willow branches and bent them like field hockey sticks," explained Dr. Shoji, "And we used a small tennis ball for a puck....We used the rules explained in a hockey history book by [the] Spalding [company]."

The Mandai hockey club was born. In the winter of 1936, all thirteen members of the team made the twelve-day trek across Asia, the Soviet Union and eastern Europe to compete in the Winter Olympics at Garmisch-Partenkirchen, Germany. "Hitler and his generals took pictures of us," but they were knocked out of competition in the preliminary round. They continued to play each winter until the war was over.

That's where the story of Mandai hockey might have ended were it not for the creation of oldtimers' hockey in Canada in the mid-1970s. Fortunately, many of the Manchurian Medical College doctors survived the war and went on to medical careers in Japan. In 1975, Dr. Shoji heard about the oldtimers' concept and formed the Mandai Memorial Ice Hockey Club with Japanese doctors in their fifties and sixties.

Until they got their skating legs back, Dr. Shoji and his teammates chose their opposition carefully. At first, they played inexperienced Japanese women's teams. Then in 1978 they headed to North America, partly for the excitement of travelling and also in search of just the right calibre of competition; they chose to play the Port Coquitlam Ambassadors. "Of course," said Shoji, "we lost." But in 1981 the Memorials agreed to join the Senior World Hockey Tournament in the sixty-plus division.

"I think we have won only two or three games ever in this tournament," admitted Dr. Shoji, "but coming to Santa Rosa each year is a medicine for each of us....Looking forward to coming is [our] motivation to keep in good health, to practise and to think young."

This Tuesday night game is a typical, close-checking game between these two longtime tournament rivals. To the spectators, the play of these septuagenarians looks somewhat plodding and slow. But for the participants it's passionate and all-out. The Santa Rosa Diamond Icers are wearing their rust-coloured uniforms. The Mandai Memorials are outfitted in white uniforms with blue and gold trim. As well as a number, each Mandai jersey displays the birth date of its owner. The only date younger than 1930 is that of forty-two-year-old Mandai goalie, Masamitsu Suzuki; the tournament allows goalies as young as forty in all divisions.

"Schulz's breakaway was still very difficult to stop," admits Suzuki who remembers seeing the tall winger "with the yellow helmet, green socks and green gloves" storming in on him. It was late in the game with the score tied 1–1. But Suzuki managed to grab the puck.

A minute and a half into overtime, however, the Diamond Icers claim the win with a clean shot from in front of the net that beats Suzuki. As the players line up to shake hands, the SRO crowd rises to give both teams a standing ovation. Schulz and Shoji take a moment to congratulate each other. Then Schulz skates to the stands to acknowledge some family and friends.

"Well, the tournament is secure for another year," kids a tournament official in the stands.

"I just hope I'm still skating and playing at that age," says Antiques' winger Ron Matsuyama. He continues to applaud and shake his head in disbelief.

Six days of tournament play in Santa Rosa attracts a diverse group of hockey enthusiasts. Certainly the presence of a dozen Japanese doctors who learned to play the game in Manchuria sixty years ago turns heads. Then there are the Grosse Pointe Old Devils from Michigan. Although few spectators realize it, this oldtimers' team that began playing for fun in 1988 is now racing against time. The Old Devils have set up a trust fund to raise money for the family of a teammate who is terminally ill. And there's Clare Green, a seventy-three-year-old lawyer from Keswick, Ontario, who has been playing hockey weekly with the Keswick firefighters for fifteen years—and they're all thirty-five years his junior.

Remarkable too are the Swissair oldtimers. Most began playing recreational hockey in the late-1960s when some Air Canada pilots challenged them to a game. The two airline teams have played almost every year since then in either Montreal or Zurich for the Davis Cup, a cup donated by Air Canada pilot Clint Davis.

To fill out their roster for the Snoopy tournament, the Swissair team has invited some freelancers. One of them is a pharmacist from Batavia, Illinois. As an oldtimers' hockey player Bob Fondriest has crammed more hockey into the past few years of his life than in the previous forty.

"I never played organized hockey as a kid, even living in Chicago," says Fondriest. "It was strictly pick-up hockey...on frozen tennis courts or at the local track and field. I even tried to get a high school hockey team started. Got petitions. Talked to parents. But the insurance was too expensive. So, no go."

Then, a few years ago, he got into a "dads' league" and from there moved to playing oldtimers on several different teams in a number of different leagues three and four times a week, all year round. In 1988, he paid $1,000 to attend a fantasy hockey camp in Montreal. For four days, Fondriest met and played with and against Bobby Hull, Stan Mikita and Gordie Howe, NHL players he had idolized as a kid growing up in Chicago.

"Now I'm here with the Swissair team," says Fondriest. "And I'm wired. Hardly able to sleep. Up at 5:30 in the morning for an afternoon game. Butterflies in my stomach....But when it's all over, it's the camaraderie and the beer. The beer never tastes so good as it does when you've just unlaced your skates and you're dripping with sweat."

Facing Fondriest and his Swissair teammates in the forty-plus A Division is another hockey fanatic. Unlike his cartoonist father, Monte Schulz didn't really take to hockey until he was a teenager. But by then he had the Redwood Empire Ice Arena where he could play whenever he wished. He taught himself power skating techniques—doing crossovers, skating backwards as quickly as forwards, etc. He played some hockey at college and then got really hooked on "this addictive distraction" while playing adult hockey.

"In four years of open competitive hockey," says Schulz, "I was driving from my home in Santa Barbara to Los Angeles to play on three different teams through the winter and I put 85,000 miles on my car." The first year he was eligible for the Snoopy tournament—1992—Monte Schulz called members of the Senior L.A. Kings, some skaters in Santa Rosa and even European players he knew to renew old friendships and to enter the tourney as the United Nations Oldtimers.

"Hockey is not about the people you play against," says Schulz. "It's about the people you play with."

For some of the Central Ontario Over-65s, playing hockey together goes back nearly half a century. Following the Second World War, ice hockey was reintroduced to the U.K. At that time, young Canadian hockey players such as Ken Doig, Bob MacIntyre, Ed Mitchell and Randy Ellis were import candidates for the Scottish Ice Hockey League. They all met overseas while earning £12 a week and playing for teams such as the Dundee Tigers, the Ayr Raiders, the Dunfermline Vikings and the Glasgow Bruins. During that same period, Orval "Red" Gravelle came through Scotland as a member of the Canadian Olympic hockey team en route to a gold medal at the 1948 Games in St. Moritz, Switzerland. In the 1970s they were reunited as members of the Central Ontario Oldtimers.

"What really got us into oldtimers," says Bob MacIntyre, "was the opportunity to travel....We've played in some great tournaments over the years in Holland, Spain, Hawaii, Victoria. We even went back to Scotland...in 1980. We had ten guys who had all played in Scotland. We were all in our fifties and we played a team of kids. The papers really played it up. The BBC was in with cameras. In the final, they were beating us 2–1. With about thirty seconds to go Randy [Ellis] scores to tie. We go into overtime and we score to beat them. They were weeping in the stands."

As soon as they heard about Charles Schulz's tournament, the Central Ontario Oldtimers applied. They've been coming to Santa Rosa since 1979 and have at least eight Snoopy championships to show for it. Each of these men has had plenty of hockey glory. Each has a working career behind him. Some have gone through health and family crises; Randy Ellis's wife, Helen, died this year. But still they gather their ancient hockey gear and their aging bodies and head off to tournaments like this one year after year.

"Here we are and we're still together," says Ellis. "We know each other so well. Our wives, our families all know each other well. There's great friendship here. I think the philosophy over the years has been: the good things, the bad things and the little queer things about us. They don't matter. We don't change. Our hockey doesn't change. But we really care for each other."

The Burbank Old Skates take that philosophy literally. They've been playing together since the Senior Olympics in 1974. Most are in their seventies and each has one ailment or another from heart conditions to cancer. During their Tuesday night scrimmages at the Pickwick Arena in Burbank, California, they rigidly enforce the Carl Adams horn rule; every two minutes the horn that Adams designed blows and the lines change. So far, they've lost three to heart attacks and their goalie John Dobbs has had two heart bypass operations but he's still in the nets.

"Two years ago I was diagnosed with blood and bone cancer," said sixty-nine-year-old dentist Harley Thayer. "One day I will have osteoporosis....kidney problems and anemia. But right now I play hockey. It stimulates me and I feel good."

"After a tournament last year, I had a medical," adds retired aviation inspector Nick Nickerson who is seventy-five. "They found colon cancer...and gave me a colostomy....I was out in seven days and back playing hockey in six weeks.

"I meet Doc [Thayer] each week at the hospital for chemotherapy....Chemo on Tuesday mornings and hockey Tuesday nights....They made arrangements so our treatments wouldn't interfere with this tournament.

"I can't believe I'll go out peacefully," he concludes. "When I go, I want them to dig a hole at centre ice and bury me there!"

One of the oldtimers here in Santa Rosa has an explanation for all the homage being paid to hockey, tournaments and team play. Several years ago he delivered twenty-seven lectures on the subject to students at the University of Guelph. He spent a summer reading everything he could find on the sociology, psychology and philosophy of play. But Eric Nesterenko also has some personal experience on which to draw—a twenty-year NHL career, one Stanley Cup, coaching the Trail Smoke Eaters to the Memorial Cup, and several years playing oldtimers with the Chicago Blackhawks Alumni.

Nesterenko believes that some of the love affair with old-timers' hockey comes from a rekindling of a childhood experience, from the sweetness and purity of the game and from the sense of freedom of movement men experienced as boys playing hockey on the pond or the backyard rink. That image of play is free of responsibility and full of fun.

This summer, at sixty, Nesterenko has joined the Boston Moby Dicks, a fifty-plus division team.

"Every time I play," says Nesterenko, "the patterns of the game re-emerge. We know what we're trying to do and why. We move. We move the puck....With older players we have great respect for each other. Even though the game may get a bit intense...it's not life or death like it used to be.

"It's a wonderful game, truly beautiful. Very simple. Very elegant. Very powerful. And all of us respond to that, particularly with our peers where there is this respect not only for the players but for the game."

Saturday afternoon, the last day of the tournament. The two-story Los Robles Lodge looks like a slum scene from a Hollywood backlot. The pads, socks, pants, skates and jerseys of all fourteen Toronto Antiques are strewn across lounge chairs, makeshift clotheslines and balcony railings to dry in the sun. They and their gear are also basking in success. They've breezed through this tournament defeating all their opposition and are in the final tonight at 6:40.

"What time is it?" asks Antiques' defenceman Guy Sabourin.

"A few minutes later than the last time you asked," answers his wife Alice. She often kids Guy about his obsession with time. One year when she arrived a few minutes late for one of

Guy's games, he skated by her, tugged up his jersey sleeve as if looking at his watch and said, "You're late!"

At one end of the sun deck by the pool, some members of the team are playing euchre. Others finish off rolls of film by taking candid shots of those waiting. But in front of goalie Tony Fallis's motel room it's trivia.

"Who hit the most homers and RBIs after Babe Ruth?" Fallis asks the two or three Antiques nearby.

Nobody answers.

"Give up? Cecil Fielder," says Fallis.

Competition is important to Tony Fallis. Whether it was learning to poke check forwards like his hero Johnny Bower or taking on the challenge of being back-up goaltender for the Toronto Maple Leafs' farm team in Newmarket when he was thirty-eight and beyond his prime, Fallis won't back down. He has changed little as an oldtimer goaltender. He's had six operations on knee ligaments. This is his third trip to Santa Rosa with the Antiques and, "while we won in '88 and '89, we didn't come 3,000 miles this time to lose."

Inside Taxi's room a game of open poker for a quarter a hand is taking place. Ron Matsuyama and Butch Crump are cleaning up but most of those playing haven't got their minds on cards at all. They're preoccupied with the championship game ahead.

"Hockey is a simple game," says Benny Murata. He's from a family of eight brothers and sisters who spent winter evenings and weekends playing shinny on a backyard rink in Niagara-on-the-Lake. He started playing oldtimers with the Antiques in 1988. "You can skate a hundred miles an hour or you can let the puck do the work....Smart oldtimer players use their heads, not their legs."

Murata's easygoing manner carries over to the arena in the hour before the game. While others fidget with equipment bags and tape, Ben sits quietly flexing his legs yoga style.

Chris Nicholls, his defence partner, is equally quiet. He's putting a protective glove over a hand burn from a recent car accident.

Tony Fallis who has been cracking jokes all along and quizzing everyone about trivia has now withdrawn. The

Antiques' goaltender lays out all his padding first, including the helmet he wore as stand-by for the Newmarket Saints; he considers it lucky. He methodically suits up.

Ron Matsuyama puts in his contact lenses. Several players strap on knee braces. Liniment is rubbed on knees and elbows. There's little chatter now. Just the tearing sound of plastic tape being stretched tautly around shin pads and skate ankles. The dressing room grows hotter and more humid.

"Ah, there's nothing like putting your foot into a frozen skate to get you going," quips Gord Strickland, thinking of the realities of oldtimers' hockey back home in Canada.

"No other game in the world like a gold medal game," says Sabourin. "Let's go, boys!"

"Be physical," adds Taxi just before he removes his dentures and leads his Antiques out of the dressing room.

They're ready for their opposition in this forty-plus final — the Vancougars from British Columbia. But there's a delay. This is the eighty-fourth and final game of the Snoopy tournament, and the wear and tear on the ice has left it pocked and gashed everywhere. Because the July heat has built up inside the Redwood Empire Arena, the Zamboni water from the pre-game flood won't freeze.

Officials hold up the game. The pacing and waiting continue.

"Hey, I know this guy," says Brian McFalone recognizing the referee. "I had a run in with him years ago. This ref owns me."

"No, Brian," pipes up Dave Bince. "Your ex-wife owns you."

The close friendship between McFalone and Bince goes back through years of teaching school together in Toronto in the 1960s and following sports together; later when McFalone moved to California they talked to each other by recording comments and sending reels of tape through the mail. "Ninety percent of the correspondence was sports." They've played hockey nearly all of their lives—from minor up to senior and intermediate and on to oldtimers. But not until this year's Snoopy tournament have these close friends, now both in their fifties, actually played hockey together.

"Dave knows how to put the biscuit in the basket," says McFalone. "So he carries the puck and I look for the openings."

"And I love sliding the puck into those open spots," continues Bince, "because a guy like Brian will deflect it into the net or pass it back to you for a shot."

Over the course of this tournament, the Bince-McFalone union on the ice has been productive and once the championship final begins it's the same combination that first puts the Antiques on the board. Next the Dinino-Blazik duo scores. Then a deflection by Matsuyama. Fourth a low wrist shot by Strickland. And to cap off a 5–0 championship win, McFalone takes one of those lead passes from Bince, goes in on the Vancougars' goalie and beats him.

At the buzzer, the Toronto Antiques mob Tony Fallis in the net. It's only later that Fallis describes a discussion he had with the referee before the game began.

"When the ref checked the goal light behind my net at the start of the game," says Fallis, "he told me it wasn't working, that the light was burned out.

"I told him, 'Ref, you won't need this light for at least two periods.' I was in the zone. There was a wall there behind me tonight and there was no way they were going to score."

After the Antiques and Vancougars shake hands, after tournament co-ordinator Cecilia Shortt presents the Snoopy trophy to Taxi and after tournament photographer Bob Koch takes the official division championship team picture, the Antiques retreat to their dressing room for the unofficial celebration.

Out come several bottles of champagne that Taxi had stashed away earlier in the day. Amid cheers, popping corks and congratulations all round, the hockey gear comes off for the last time at the Santa Rosa tournament. The July temperature mixes with the body heat of a final game's exertion to steam up the dressing room. Then—one last team effort—the entire group poses for the dressing room cameras wearing nothing but smiles and their gold medals. It's the crowning moment to a fulfilling week, parodying the controversial Adidas ad that featured the Kick of York soccer club posing in the buff.

"*Sports Illustrated* probably won't publish *this* shot either," says Dave Bince.

"It's a damn good thing," laughs Brian McFalone.

At the last tailgate party of the tournament, cars and vans discharge their remaining beer and soft drinks. The last of the Antiques' victory champagne is doled out in Snoopy tournament mugs. Several more toasts are made to linemates, defence partners, goals scored and shots saved. Again, pins and hats are exchanged. As usual, Guy Sabourin is the most avid barterer, offering to trade T-shirts with the Blue Jays' and Maple Leafs' logos for the most sought-after pins.

"You watch," laughs Taxi, "he'll be trading his gold medal any minute."

For McEachren it's been another successful annual outing. As team manager he's kept things on an even keel throughout the six days. The team chemistry has worked. Everybody's had a good time. The Antiques have been rewarded with a division title. He praises Cecilia Shortt and the Snoopy organizers for mixing just the right amount of fun and competitiveness in the tournament.

That's been a topic of hot discussion all week—the future of oldtimers, both in tournaments and elsewhere. Benny Stein, a member of the Edmonton Vintage Oldtimers, has strong feelings about the competitiveness; he's worried that, "sometimes the less-skilled players ride the bench in certain games to improve a team's chance of winning. The adrenalin of competition is one thing; of course you go out there to win. But it shouldn't be at the expense of others who are just as eager to play."

"Playing the game is paramount," says one of Stein's heroes, Eric Nesterenko. He has spoken out against the roughness and win-at-all-cost mentality that sometimes creeps into the oldtimers' game. "Hockey is still a recreational game. And if it's done without violence and where players have respect for each other [and] enjoy the camaraderie and have a drink together after the game...that's what it's all about."

Of course, one of the toughest questions facing all adult recreational players whether they play a weekly game of shinny at the local arena or reappear annually at the Senior World Hockey Tournament in Santa Rosa is: Will they be back next year? Will they remain as keen to play as Charles Schulz or the Mandai Memorials in the seventy-plus division? Hockey tactics and skills, like riding a bike, are never forgotten but how long will the desire be there? How long will the Antiques and the thousands of others who play this game keep it up?

"As long as we can," says Antiques' coach Phil Nicholas. "You're dead too long."

At about 10:30 the overhead lights in the parking lot of the Redwood Empire Ice Arena are turned off. The arena itself is empty. Only the stragglers at the tailgate party remain. Some local kids who've been emulating the oldtimers by playing ball hockey around them in the parking lot drift away into the darkness. The last of the Snoopy oldtimers pack up their empties and gear and head back to their hotels. Some are already driving down the highway to San Francisco for their flights home.

The tournament is over for another year.

Joining his now subdued teammates in one car, Ron Matsuyama, among the youngest Antiques, has his Snoopy medal in hand. "This is the only game in the world," he says, "where it gets better as you get older."

Bibliography

Amernic, Jerry. "Flying Fathers." *En Route*. January 1983.

"Angels in Disguise Descend on 4 Wing." *Schwarzwälder* (Baden-Soellingen, West Germany). 22 January, 1970.

Beardsley, Doug. "The Sheer Joy of Shinny," in D. Gowdey, comp. *Riding on the Roar of the Crowd*. Toronto: Macmillan Canada, 1989.

Bender, Eric. "The Huff 'n Puffs Score Health and Happiness." *London Free Press*. 25 March, 1993.

Brewitt, Ross. *Last Minute of Play*. Toronto: Stoddart, 1993.

Diamond, Dan and Lew Stubbs. *Hockey: Twenty Years*. Toronto: Doubleday, 1987.

Drennan, Rick. "Oldtimers Hockey Refires Love Affairs." *Toronto Star*, 26 December, 1992.

Dryden, Ken. *The Game*. Toronto: Macmillan Canada, 1983.

Dryden, Ken, and Roy MacGregor. *Home Game*. Toronto: McClelland & Stewart, 1989.

Fergusson, Charles Bruce. "Early Hockey at Halifax." *Nova Scotia Journal of Education*, June, 1965.

Fischler, Stan and Shirley Walton Fischler. *Fischlers' Hockey Encyclopedia*. Toronto: Fitzhenry & Whiteside, 1975.

Fischler, Stan, and Shirley Walton Fischler. *The Hockey Encyclopedia*. Macmillan, New York, 1983.

"Flying Fathers Score in Rome." *Canadian Register*. 14 February, 1970.

Gorman, Jack. *Père Murray and the Hounds*. Sidney, B.C.: Gray's Publishing, 1977.

Grainger, Larry. "You're Never Too Old." *Financial Post Magazine*, March 1980.

Haliburton, Thomas Chandler. *The Attaché*, 2nd and last ser., vol. 2, London, 1844, p. 112.

"Handicap Does Not Stop the Ice Owls." *Scarborough Mirror*. 31 March, 1976

Handley, Pete. "World Famous Flying Fathers Got Their Start in North Bay." *Nugget* (North Bay), 13 November, 1993.

Hanson, Byron, ed. *Seventy Years of Outlaw Terror*. North Battleford, Sask.: Turner-Warwick Publications, 1986.

Harris, Billy. *The Glory Years*. Scarborough, Ont.: Prentice-Hall, 1989.

Hewitt, Foster. *Hockey Night in Canada*. Toronto: Ryerson Press, 1961.

Howe, Colleen and Gordie Howe. *After the Applause*. Toronto: McClelland & Stewart, 1990.

Iaboni, John. "Leafs-Canadiens Reunited Once More." *Molson Legends' Night in Canada Program*. Toronto: Core Media Inc., 4 April, 1993.

"Ice Owls and Civics to Face Off." *Toronto Star*. March 1984.

Ingersoll, Bruce. "The Boys of Winter: Old-Timers' Hockey is Pluck and a Puck." *Wall Street Journal*. 3 February, 1986.

Jenish, D'Arcy. *The Stanley Cup*. Toronto: McClelland & Stewart, 1992.

Lamb, Jamie. "Wanted: Vaccine for Middle-Aged Male Hockey Nuts." *Sun* (Vancouver). 12 December, 1992.

McFarlane, Brian. *Stanley Cup Fever*. Toronto: Stoddart, 1992.

McFarlane, Brian. *Proud Past, Bright Future*. Toronto: Stoddart, 1994.

McGrath, Charles. "Rink Rat." *New Yorker*. 4 October, 1993.

McKinley, Michael. *Hockey Hall of Fame Legends*. Toronto: Viking Press, 1993.

Morris, R. Roy. "President's Message." *Dominion Ladies' Hockey Tournament Program.* Canadettes Hockey Club, Brampton, Ont., 1969-70.

Morrison, Keith. *MBA Hockey Newsletter* (Vancouver). 15 September, 1978.

Murphy, Michael. *Golf in the Kingdom.* New York: Viking Press, 1972.

Nielsen, Jens. "Wilkie's Hockey Dynasty." *StarPhoenix* (Saskatoon). 20 April, 1985.

O'Brien, Andy. "Our Fathers Who Art in Hockey." *Weekend Magazine.* 3 November, 1973.

"Oldtimers Ice Hockey." Bank of British Columbia's Pioneer News, October/ November 1987.

Ormsby, Mary. "Hockey's Worst at Their Very Best." *Toronto Star.* 11 November, 1994.

Rider, Fran. "Women's Hockey Goes Big Time." *Ice Times.* Willowdale, Ont.: Hockey Development Centre for Ontario. November 1992.

Rossiter, Sean. "Back in the Crease." *Vancouver Magazine.* October 1980.

Russell, Burton, and Stan Cameron. *Nova Scotia Sports Personalities.* Kentville, N.S.: David Allbon & Co. Ltd., 1975.

Smith, Michael A. *Life After Hockey.* St. Paul, Minn.: Codner Books, 1987.

Tatham, Dave. "Wolfe Island Pulls Stunning Upset at Reunion '85 Tourney." *Canadian Oldtimers' Hockey News.* March 1985.

Tefs, Wayne. "In a Man's World, the Puck Stops Here." *Globe and Mail*, 1992.

Tretiak, Vladislav. *Tretiak, The Legend.* Edmonton: Plains Publishing Inc., 1987.

Urie, Mr. Justice John J., and Larry Regan. *Final Report on the Canadian Hockey Review.* Government of Canada, Ottawa, May 1979.

Vaughan, Garth. *The Puck Starts Here.* Halifax: Four East, 1995.

Zeman, Brenda and Joe Zeman. *Hockey Heritage, 88 Years of Puck-Chasing in Saskatchewan.* Regina: The Saskatchewan Sports Hall of Fame, 1983.

Newspapers & Other Sources

Arrowsmith Star (Vancouver Island)

Blue (Hamburger Hockey League magazine, Vancouver)

Canadian Oldtimers' Hockey Association Journal (Ottawa)

Canadian Oldtimers' Hockey News (Peterborough)

Canadian Register

Chronicle-Herald (Halifax)

En Route

Examiner (Peterborough)

Financial Post Magazine

Gazette (Montreal)

Globe and Mail (Toronto)

Hants Journal (Windsor, N.S.)

Herald-Gazette (Bracebridge)

Hockey News

Ice Owls Hockey Club Newsletter (Scarborough)

Kitchener-Waterloo Record

Leader-Post (Regina)

London Free Press

Macklin Mirror

Maclean's

Moosonee Freighter

New Yorker

Nugget (North Bay)

Ottawa Citizen

Press Democrat (Santa Rosa, California)

Province (Vancouver)

Scarborough Mirror

Schwarzwälder (Baden-Soellingen, West Germany)

StarPhoenix (Saskatoon)

Sudbury Star

Sun (Vancouver)

Toronto Star

Uxbridge Times-Journal

Uxbridge Tribune

Vancouver Flames Hockey Club Newsletter

Vancouver Magazine

Wall Street Journal

Weekend Magazine

Index